‘There is, to my mind, no one who writes quite like Rory MacLean. If I were forced to reach for a comparison, I would pause over Bruce Chatwin as a possibility, but then probably stretch far, further back: to John Mandeville, to St Brendan and to Marco Polo. These men made their “wonder-voyages” and returned bearing tales that were not to be submitted to the usual tests of verifiability and falsifiability, but in which the actual and the miraculous rubbed shoulders. [...] They sought, in their inventiveness, to pattern reality into a greater clarity.’

Robert Macfarlane

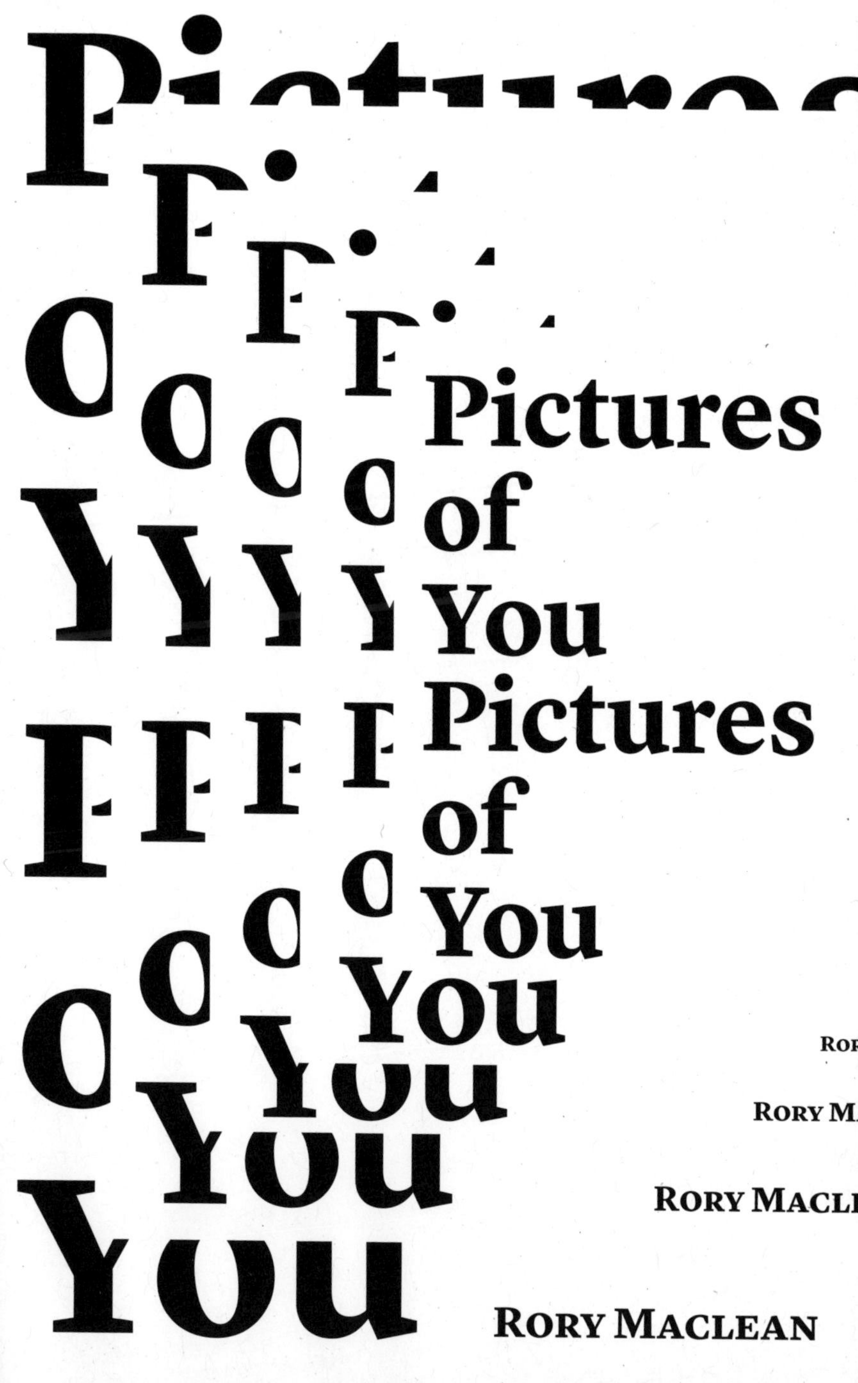
Pictures
of
You
Pictures
of
You
You
Rory Maclean

Pictures of You: Ten Journeys in Time

Rory MacLean

Bone Idle

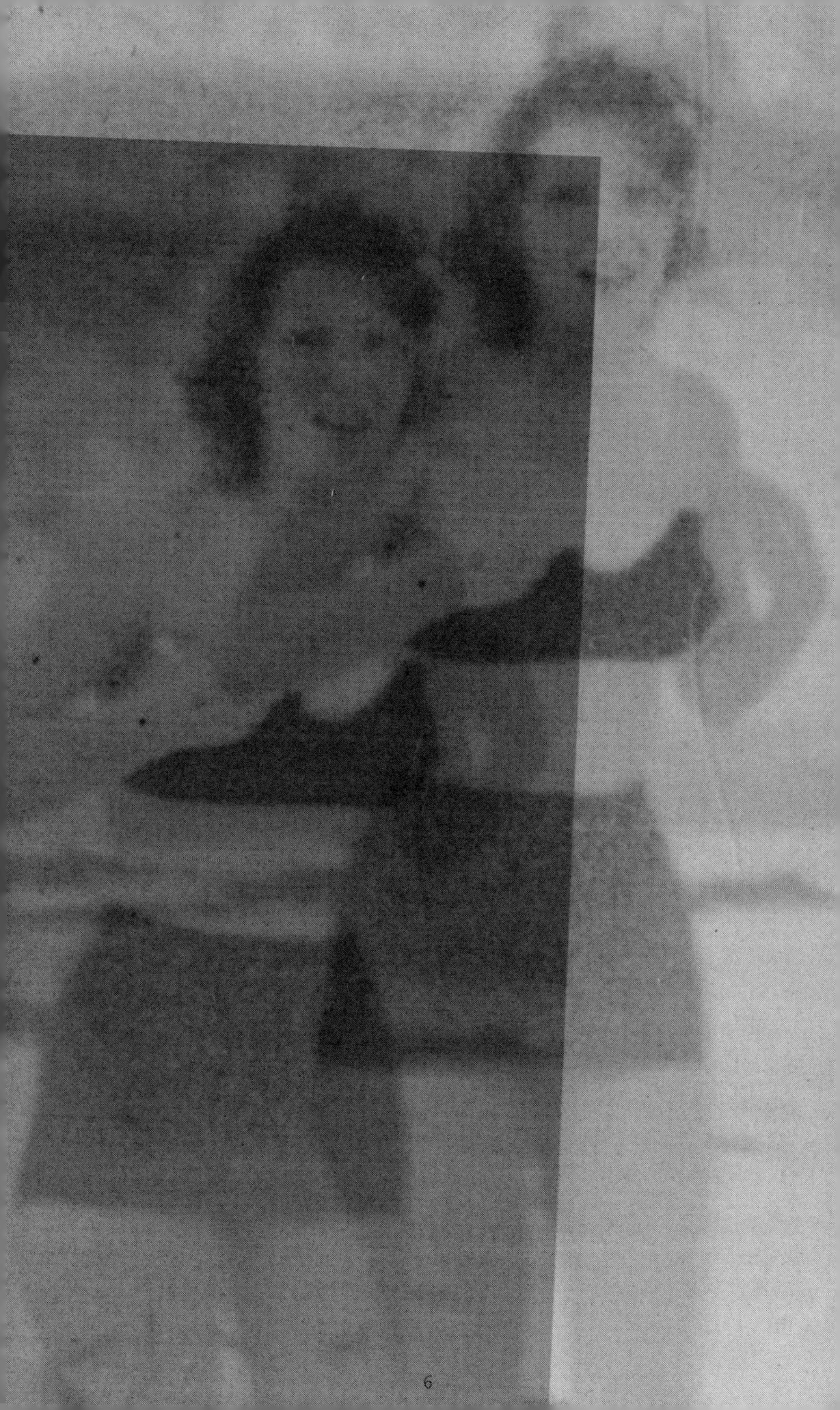

Introduction

I knew the street of old. I had passed along it a hundred times but never noticed the entrance. The gate was easy to overlook: high, wrought iron and set back from the pavement between two lofty Victorian townhouses. Nothing drew the eye to it or the narrow brick passageway that yawned away behind it into the shadows. That first Saturday morning I lingered there at the gate for a moment, feeling its metal pickets warm in my hands, gazing towards the end. On an adjacent wall hung a rusted, century-old Hungarian drinking fountain. Above the basin were the words *Ülj le velem, énekelj nekem, inni tőlem.* Sit with me, sing to me, drink from me. Strange, I thought, in west London.

I knew the code and typed it into the keypad. The lock clicked open. I stepped through the portal and the sounds of the city - a gear-grinding number 9 bus, tennis matches in Holland Park, a tantrum of wailing toddlers at a nearby playground - fell away with the light. I heard my footsteps echo off the walls. The passageway seemed never to have seen the sun. Neither a blade of grass nor gathering moss grew on its scrubbed flagstones. At its end my destination was hidden from the street. The squat and plain building had no street number, no other entrance. I held the key in my hand. At a large white door, heavy with age and humidity, I turned it in the lock and felt the tumblers drop into place.

I stepped out of the dark and into a high, bright sanctuary. Sunlight fell in slanting streaks. On dozens of shelves and desktops rose teetering piles of old photographs and dusty metal tins of transparencies and film. Tall wooden racks were crammed with thousands of numbered manila folders, stacked at wild angles like something the earth had thrust up, a geological slice of civilisation. I moved between them as if through tunnels into history, within a labyrinth of corridors and pathways shaped from floor to ceiling by more columns of photographs. I ventured downstairs and stared in wonder at a basement that was crowded with pictures. I wandered through the image galleries. I brushed my hand across the bulging albums. I paused and picked up a print at random, turned it in my fingers, felt the paper's weight, smelt the distant hint of chemicals, ink and transience. Once the building had been a London family home. Now it was a secret place unhitched from the stream of time: silent, poignant and deserted, yet peopled by the past.

My agent had been sent the key along with an invitation that I could not refuse. I was to have the run of the archive, to do there what I wanted for as many weekends as I cared to do it.

The offer was timely, given another torrent of household bills and overdue debts. It spelt out no specific commission or conditions, apart from the insistence that the archive's curator not be named. Online all I'd been able to discover about him was that he was a very private person, not short of a few bob, who over the last 25 years had collected photographs. *Four million* photographs. I'd learned that the amateur snapshots, press prints, throwaways and daguerreotypes had been plucked from all over, from Berlin flea markets and Beijing recycling plants, snatched from defunct Soviet institutions and bankrupt British publications, bought on eBay and at small-town auction houses. My mysterious patron had created one of the world's most moving image treasures, and told virtually no one about it.

On that first morning I half-expected to find him waiting for me, a silhouette against a window at the top of the stairs saying, 'It's your time. Enjoy it. But use it right.' Yet even in his absence I sensed an urgency in the undertaking, as if I must not waste a minute of this strange, dream job.

I hung my jacket on the back of a chair and began to open files, to peer into albums and shuffle through boxes of loose negatives. Serendipity guided me at first, letting me travel across the eras and ages. I picked up a photograph of a Toronto birthday party at the start of the Great War and saw uniformed men in bushy moustaches raise their glasses to swift victory. Their faces radiated confidence and hope. God

Save the King echoed off the walls of the old University Avenue Armouries. I ventured into the next room and found myself kettled in a shattered Stalingrad cellar with a dozen broken Wehrmacht soldiers. In faded Agfacolor prints the men huddled in the bitter cold, picking at their lice, crushing them between fingernails as Russian guns closed in for the kill. Next in black-and-white I rode alongside an unknown Vietcong tank driver at the fall of Saigon and then lingered over the boorish scrapbook of an anonymous KGB operative-come-pornographer in West Berlin.

Time and again, while holding a child's giddy snapshot or intimate lover's portrait, I was moved beyond words - and then to words - by these glimpses of past lives. I understood quickly that the archive was no unknown thing, no terra incognita. In fact it was quite the opposite. Each album, every snapshot, every precious file was the record of a life, perhaps the only surviving evidence that the individual had ever existed. I realised that the vast collection was a kind of lexicon of lives - a compendium of countless actions, thoughts and emotions that I had been given the chance to discover.

As a travel writer I have always seen myself less a geographer of place, more of the human heart. The wonders - and horrors - I seek are in the lives of ordinary men and women living in extraordinary times, people who are marked and separated by borders and ideologies, courage and cowardliness, war, death and time. I travel to find their stories, to collect narratives, and to bring them home. For as essential as the trips are, my real travelling has always been done at my desk, in the intense distillation of the journey. To my mind it is only by experiencing the world from another person's point of view that we can begin to understand that person or society. Borders and time are bridged most powerfully through characters and stories, by evoking empathy.

At the archive, through the photographs, I began to uncover lives, and ways of living, that called out to be witnessed, valued, remembered. I started to set aside those images that most touched me, that aroused my curiosity, that made me laugh or sigh. I decided to take one photograph, or group of photographs, from each decade of the 20th century. I would research each one until no more hard facts could be distilled and then, from these, tell the subject's possible true story, in their own voice. I wanted to let them live again.

Once memory alone kept alive the stories of those who'd come before us, apart from those living on in the pages of history books or through a portrait painter's oils. Then with the first shutter's snap, *forever* had ceased to be the preserve of the elite. Time past could be held in anyone's hand. Every fleeting life seemed to be caught by the camera, frozen in laughing youth and family albums, shot at summer picnics or battlefronts, locked in sombre 2 x 2 passport photos and exuberant end-of-year school panoramics. The 20th century became the century of the photograph; describing it, shaping it and defining it. But photography didn't only take history - and collective memory - out of the hands of the rich and powerful and give it to the individual. It also became a universal record, encoding in silver halide emulsion some of the moments that counted in the lives of almost every human being, forever.

I held a print in my hand and looked at the remnant of paste on its back. I knew it would be of Auschwitz, or Hiroshima, or Nature's final battle with Man. Or the dying hopes of a doomed aviator. Or the first killing of the Cold War. Or a black sorceress driven to murder. On that first weekend in the archive I tried to add up the instants. I took the standard shutter speed of 1/60th of a second and multiplied it by the average number of photographs that might have been taken of an individual over the course of a lifetime before the digital age. Thirty-three seconds, I calculated. Three score and ten years distilled into less than three dozen heartbeats.

I set a portrait on the desk. It was of a young woman emerging from the waves with the wind in her hair. I didn't know her name, or that of the photographer who met her on the beach. She was someone most of us have never heard of and whose story can now only be divined. I imagined that she had red hair, that her eyes were green. She is adjusting the straps of her top. She is calling to the photographer, 'Wait, wait, not yet.' She's trying not to laugh, failing to hide her smile, wanting the picture to be perfect. And it was perfect. For that moment. For that lost, living moment.

Four million photographs.

33 seconds.

Gone.

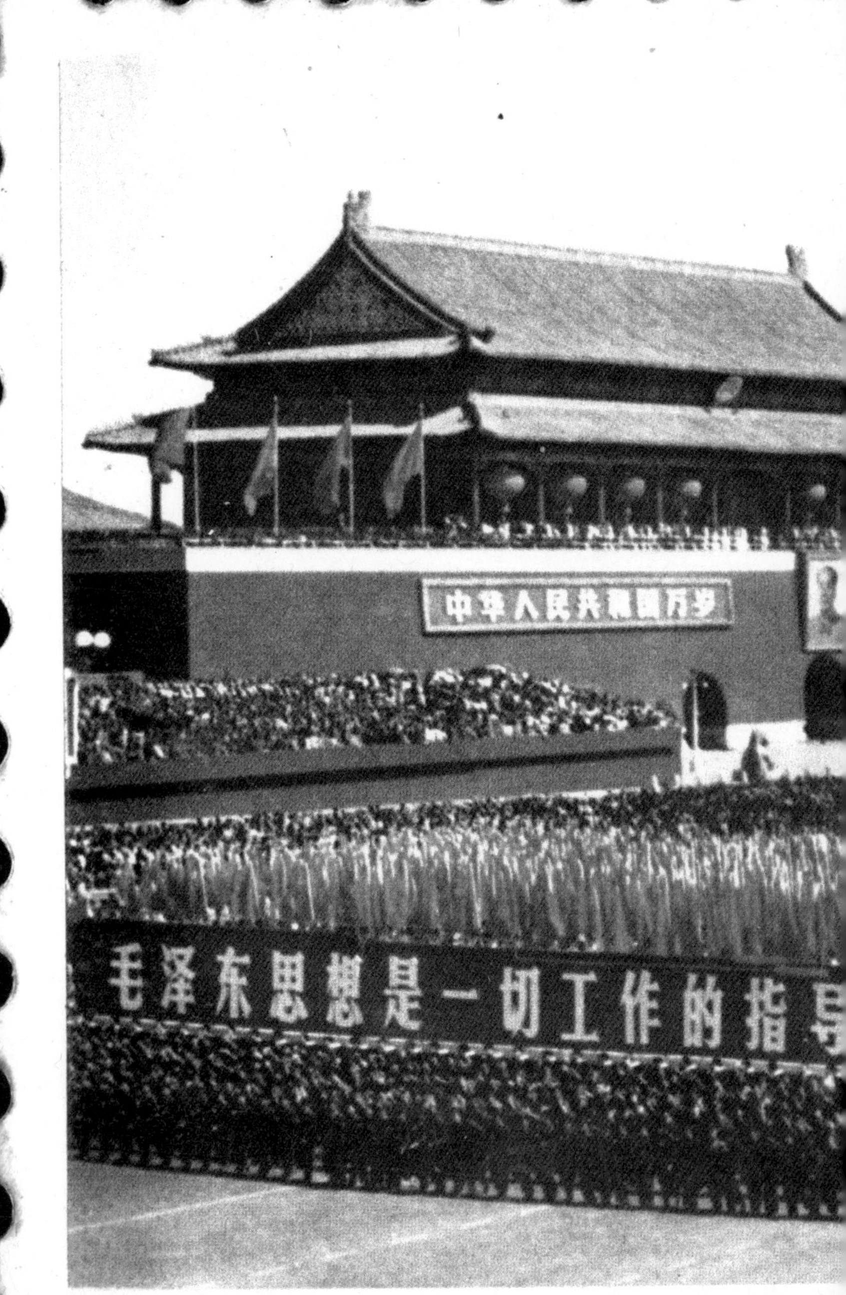
中华人民共和国万岁
毛泽东思想是一切工作的指

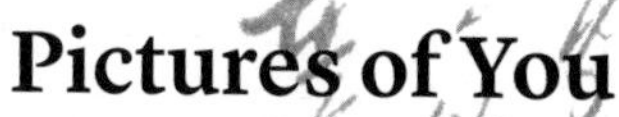

Pictures of You

Xiushan, China 16.02.1999

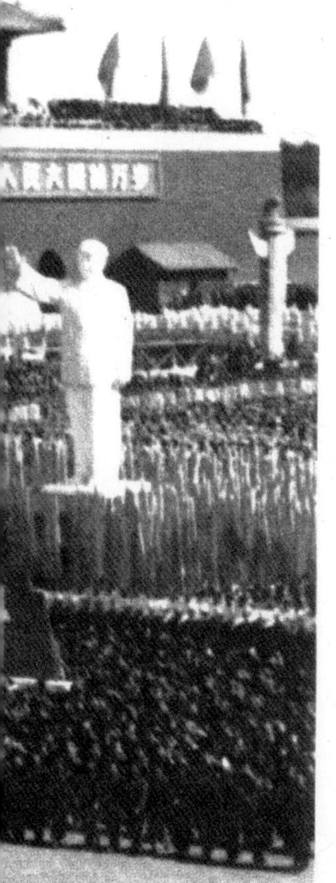

影集

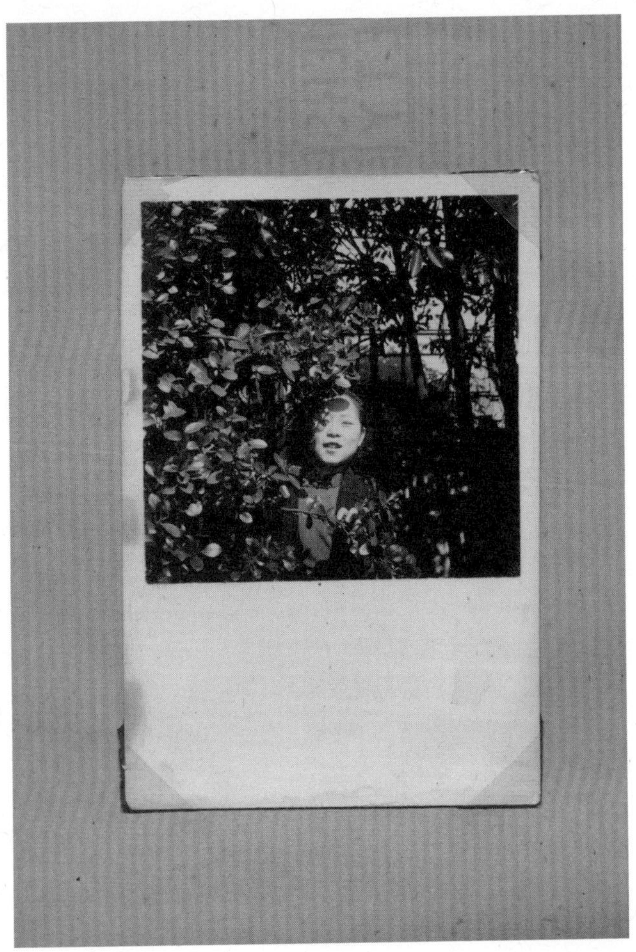

At the end I never thought I'd be alone. I'd never imagined that I would be in pain, that my voice would be too weak to talk, that there would be no one left to share the stories, the memories, the old lies. I'd hoped that there would be a friend or brother here beside me on the eve of the new millennium, sharing tea and silence in my room, touching my hand as we looked back over our century. I'd heard it said that old people always have their memories to keep. But I don't know if my memories are happy, or even mine.

I sit at the east window looking out to sea, at the waves lapping against the rocks. Spirals of wiry hair hang over my forehead as if to block the light. There are cars and a parking lot now, and beyond the fence a concrete wing of new dormitories. Once, long ago, the land fell away from this old house to form a natural theatre. At dusk sampans crossed the open bay from Putuoshan and Dongji. Red-sailed punts brought families ashore with pineapples to trade. Islanders and boatmen gathered on the green banks, laying out their picnics on the emerald grass. Then as the sun slipped down into the sea, a screen went up in the open air and the projector was switched on.

On those salty summer evenings my sisters and I ran arm-in-arm down winding stairways silvered with fallen fish scales, or so I remember. Our eyes were shining, our faces full of eagerness, our hair worn up in a cloud bun. In our excitement we gabbled along the cobblestone lanes. Around us fishermen mended their nets by lamplight. Village cats cocked their ears beneath the racks of drying, dead-eyed tigerheads. Behind them wok and flame hissed and snapped, while in front of us – in that green-banked theatre of dreams – shimmered movies called *Sing-Song Girl Red Peony* and *It Happened One Night*. In the light of the silver screen I sat entranced. I wanted to live the life of a dancer, to be a revolutionary, to build a highway to defend China from the Japanese. I longed to be a film star like Butterfly Wu, to have a courageous heart, to live a story.

But I was a plain girl, one of the nameless ranks, perfectly ordinary, quiet and forgettable. No one noticed me, not at my father's New Year parties, not even when my mother brushed my lips with honey to make offerings to the Kitchen God. My face was too long and narrow – like a young fox, said my father. He told me, 'Silence becomes the dutiful daughter,' and I kept my eyes lowered, as much in shame at my mediocrity as from any sense of duty. I was always overlooked, always at a loss for words. These memories do not make me happy or comfort me in my old age. My island home Xiushan

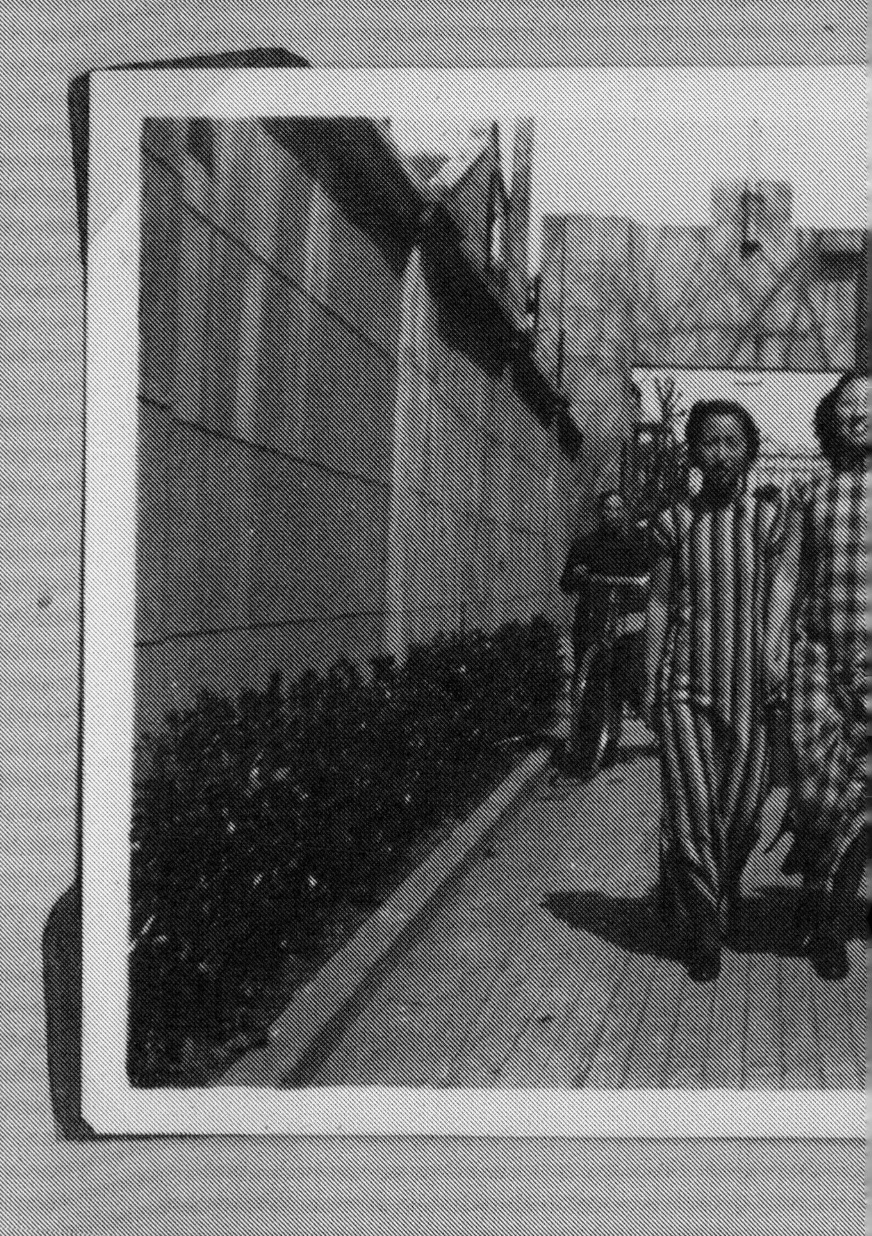

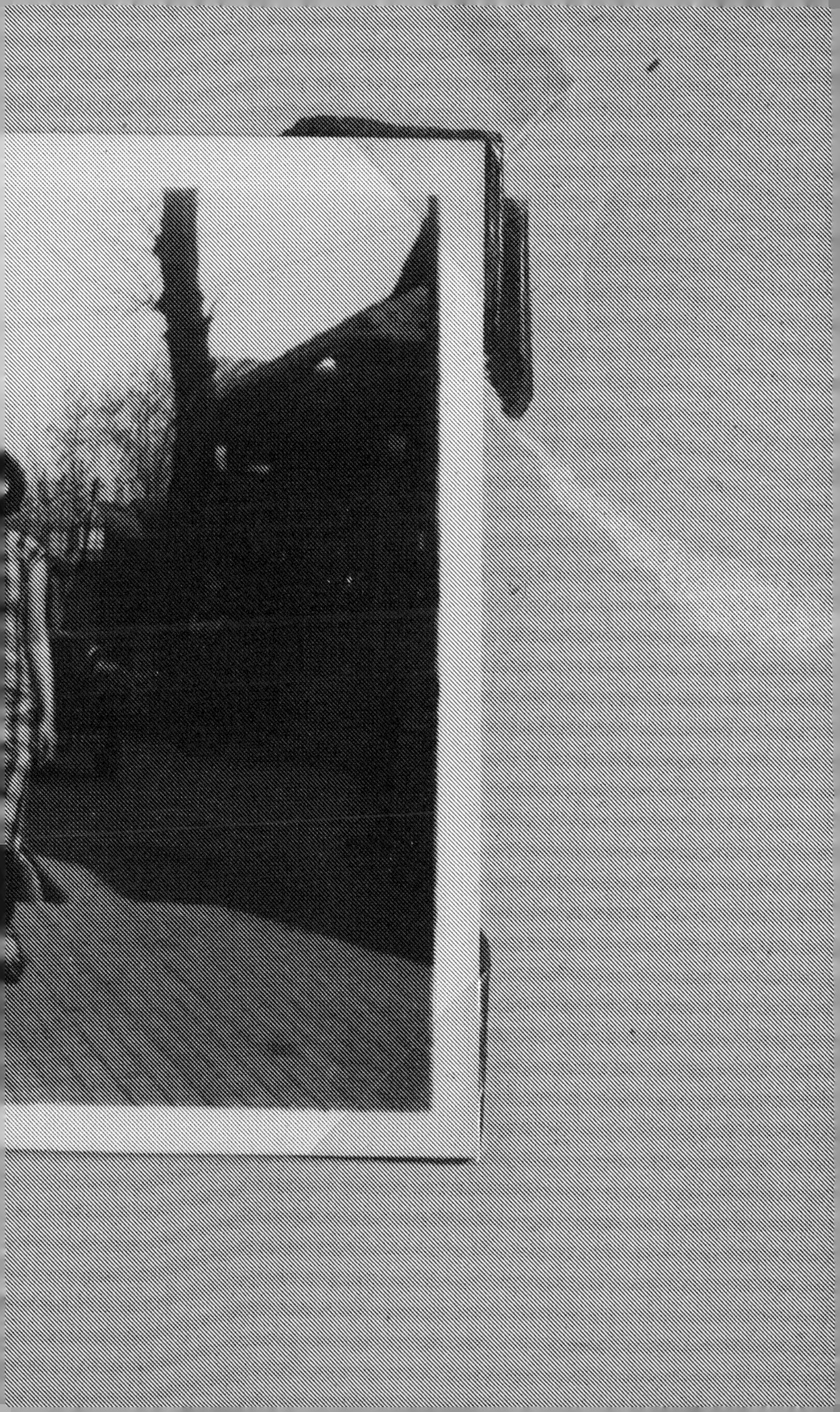

– and the whole Zhoushan archipelago – is the first place the sun rises in China, before Shanghai, before Beijing, yet to me it began to feel like the dead end of the world. I was thirteen when I convinced myself that if I was to be happy, I had to leave the island and become someone else.

I wonder if Akio thought of me, his timid little Ningbo concubine, at his end. When the clanging Japanese warships stirred and frothed our bay's peaceful waters and China seemed lost to the invaders, he had chosen me from a school photograph. I don't know why. As I said, no one had ever noticed me before. His orderly came to the door and told my father that I had been selected 'to study' with the occupation forces. My father objected, but the soldier said that there was no choice. I took my school bag with me.

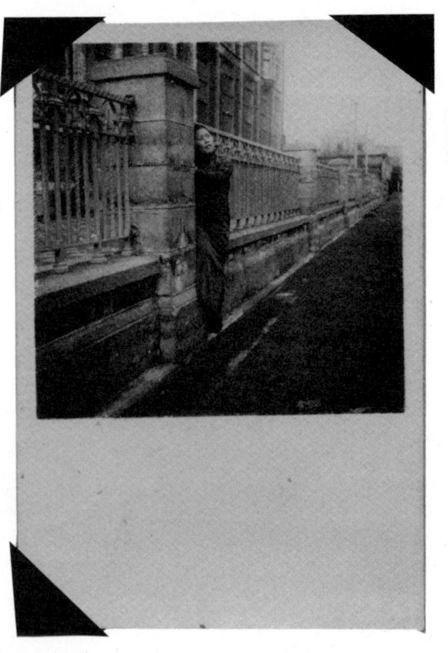

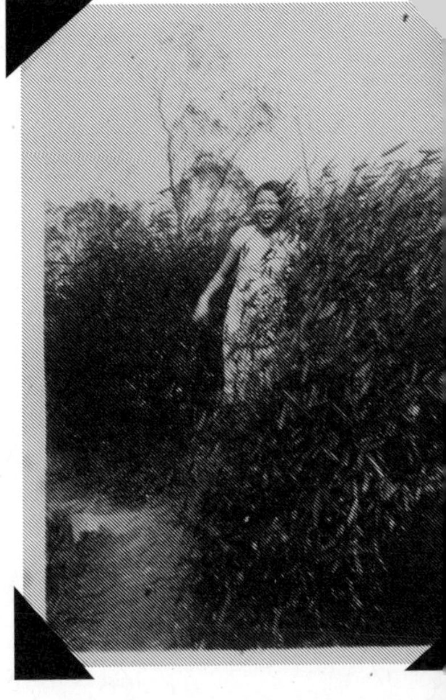

When Akio ordered me into his bed I bowed my head and told him under my breath that I'd come to study. I was very innocent then.

All through the War of Resistance I never once ate acorn meal or sorghum, thanks to Akio, and he saved me from work in a cannery or coalmine. He arranged for me to follow him when he was transferred to Nanjing. I didn't refuse him. I never refused him. But he didn't take me back with him to Nagasaki. To be happy, do the people I remember also have to remember me?

After the war I changed my name and history, and began again. I erased Xiushan and Akio from my past. In Beijing I made a clean start, and my memories from that time might have been happy, had I not been told to forget them. Again I was recruited via a photograph and put to work for their purpose. I served as an attendant on his special train. If one was liked, if one was young, softly spoken – and politically reliable – then in the evening one was invited 'to make him his tea'. In the Forbidden City I had a certain status. I had my own room and a vanity table. To serve his pleasure I applied powder and colour to my face, and vermilion lip balm with a hint of clove. All the girls loved the weekly dance in the Spring Lotus Chamber. I did not disappoint him, our Great Helmsman, until after a year he lost interest in me, as he did with all his pretty dolls. When he was done, his bodyguards told me never to speak of what had happened. So I forgot, and forget.

The baby was also cleansed from my memory. In the birthing chamber the midwife held it face down in a box of clean ashes for less than a minute. It never uttered a cry.

In old age and pain, how can I be happy if all those I knew are dead? I never wanted to return to Xiushan, but in Beijing we had learned to expose class enemies. I understood why the Four Olds had to be destroyed – old ideas, old culture, old customs and old habits. Fate and the Party sent me to Xiushan to help smash the ox devils and snake demons. In China we say, 'Where there is a will to condemn, there is evidence.'

My father, being an engineer, was condemned as a capitalist-roader and paraded through the lanes wearing a dunce's cap. On the placard around his neck his name had been crossed out to show his disgrace. Every few steps he was forced to kowtow to the crowd and bang his forehead on the stone pavement loud enough for all to hear. When he knelt before me, his hair was half-shaved into a 'yin yang head'. Silver fish scales glittered on his broken skin. But he did not lift his eyes, would not recognise me. He knew that for me to survive, he had to die. Later at the barracks I heard that the other Red Guards had split open his skull so that the blood burst out like a singing fountain.

When our old family house was taken, I stole away the photograph album, although by right it should have been burned with the other books and poisonous weeds. Destroy first, and construction will look after itself. I don't know what made me take the risk. I knew that I was meant to leave the past behind. Yet I carefully wrapped the album in oilcloths and buried it in the green banks where we had once watched movies and I had dreamed of becoming someone.

At the Shanghai rallies I wore no make-up, nothing to set me apart from the crowd: hair cut short, grey jacket and trousers, Little Red Book. Ten million strong we pledged to thoroughly smash the remnants of the reactionary bourgeoisie. We lifted up the Chairman's words as universal, absolute truth. We spoke with a single tongue.

I met Bo on a train. He worked at the Central Publicity Department in Shanghai. His courting was cautious, as was both customary and judicious. On a pilgrimage to Hunan – the Great Helmsman's birthplace – he shared with me his enthusiasm for classical poetry, and together, in secret, we composed poems to each other using the same rhyme sequence, as the ancients had done.

I hardly spoke above a whisper. He loved language, he told me. His family background was red, he said, and I fashioned mine to mirror it.

Bo had a gift for storytelling, and travellers gathered like moths around his pool of light on the long night journey. He spun tales of struggle and heroism. I loved his stories and let myself be seduced by them, and him.

In the sunshine behind the works canteen we held hands. Bo imagined me not as Butterfly Wu, but the rouge-faced hero of more suitable narratives like *The White-Haired Girl* and *Taking Tiger Mountain by Strategy*. He wove me into tales of brave struggles against Japanese invaders. In his stories it was me who risked my life to speak out against bloodsucking capitalists. Once when we were walking together and heard *Red Detachment of Women* on the street megaphone, he launched into an account of me as Wu Qionghua, whose wicked landlord had killed her father and taken her as his slave. In Bo's version I struck down the parasites and took command of a female detachment of the Red Army.

Through Bo's stories I began to believe I had a voice. He also gave me the words for that voice to speak, as well as a job. Under his tutelage in the Publicity Department I rose quickly in seniority, helping to monitor the editorials reproduced from the *People's Daily*. I amplified Chairman Mao's instructions on the omnipotence of revolutionary war, repeating his dictate that every comrade was 'to love the people and listen attentively to the voice of the masses'. Comrades were to identify themselves with the masses, never to stand above them, to immerse themselves among them.

That is what we were told to say.

My memories from those days might have been happy if Bo hadn't spoiled them, if he hadn't told me about his father. Who would have thought that he – my own effusive storyteller – could have kept the secret so quiet, that he could have buried it so deeply, that he would confess to me? I was the person he most trusted in the world, he said. Next morning I had to speak out, to tell the Commissar that

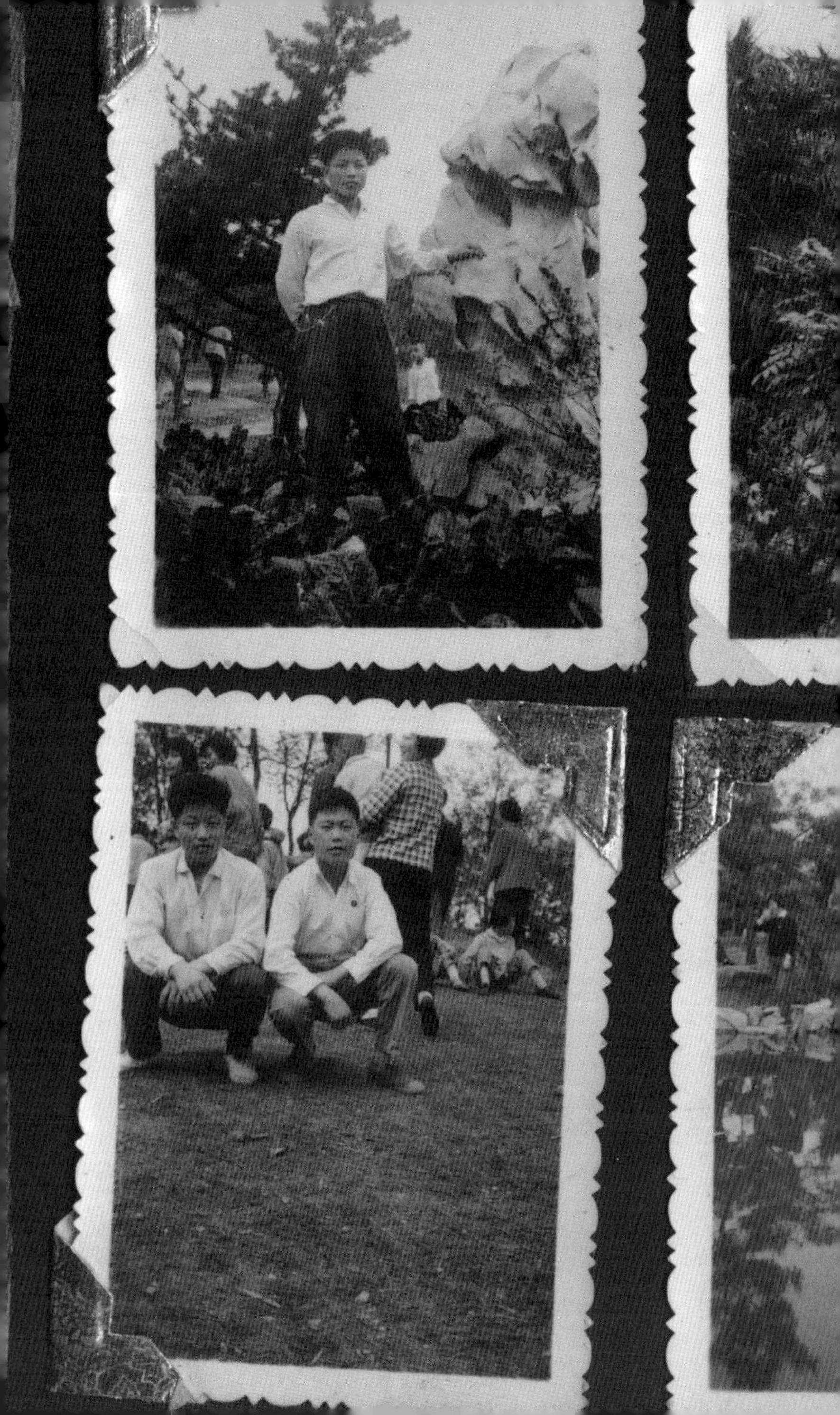

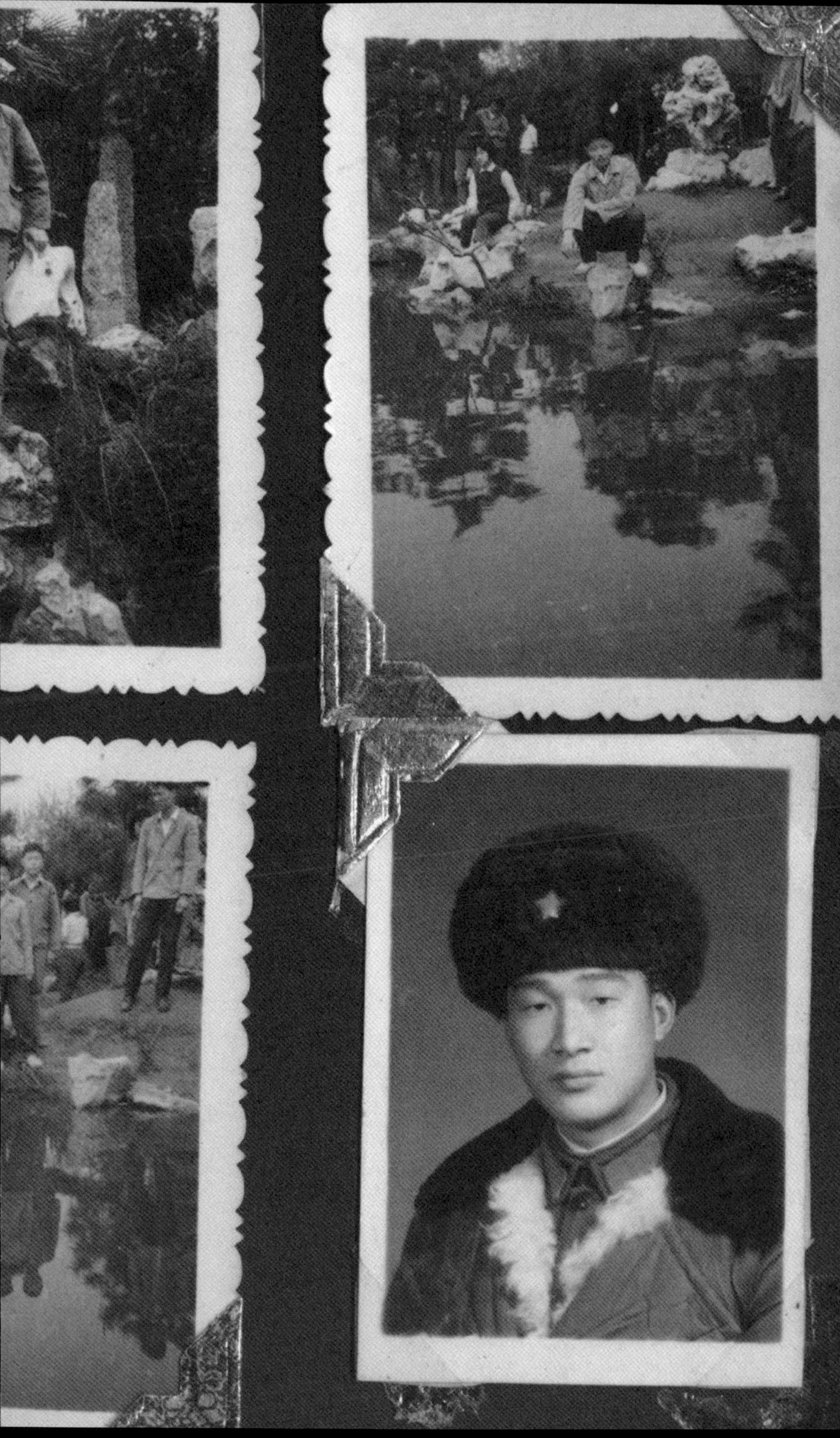

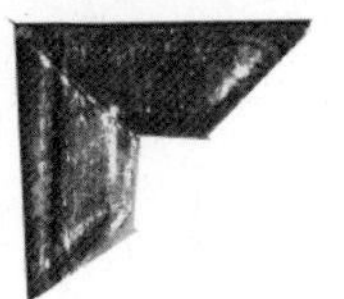

Bo's father had fought with the Kuomintang. Bo had never been red, never walked in the footsteps of the Immortals of the Revolution.

When he disappeared, I took over his position. It was my duty to do so, even if dissenters might criticise me. Father is close, Mother is close, but neither is as close as Chairman Mao. Maybe my memories would be happy now – on this New Year's Day – if people hadn't strayed from the revolutionary fold, from the teachings of the Red Red Sun in Our Hearts. I have heard it said that the children of the Immortals, the sons and daughters of our great leaders, have betrayed us, laughing at our struggle, at our amnesia. I dare not reply. I hold my tongue. In any case my silence does not matter. Those princelings are powerful beyond measure, reopening the canneries, building factories, speaking out in voices so loud it pains the ears.

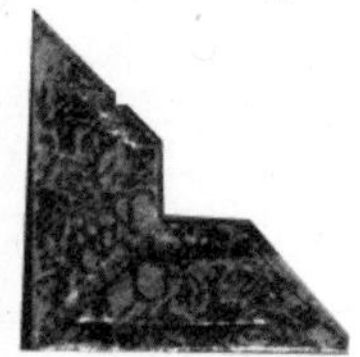

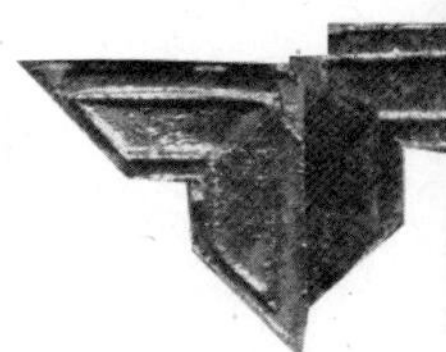

No family visits me here on Xiushan, the eastern island that will not let me go. My lovers and parents, sisters and brother are all long dead, or gone after the years in the camps. I see them only in the pictures in my head, and there I do not trust them. Once I tried to get out of this homely prison, to walk down to the old theatre and unearth my father's album buried beneath the green banks. I wanted to remember who I am, or rather, who I was. But the orderlies would not let me leave the home. They blocked the door and at night strapped me to the bed.

Today I sit by that barred window at the place where the land once fell away from our old veranda. I touch the glass as if to reach for the clouds that come and go. Beneath them sampans no longer cross the bay, families no longer gather for picnics, a silver screen does not fill my summer evenings with stories. Neither Akio, Bo nor the Great Helmsman himself walks along the cobblestone lanes towards me.

Instead the valley has been found to be ideal for an enormous dry dock, for Zhoushan's Yuanye yard and the Japanese Tsuneishi Group. Reform through labour has a different meaning now. Beyond the cranes, container ships and oil tankers slip off the floating factory and into the sea, sunbeams playing in their choppy wakes.

I hear the world is richer and happier these days. All I know is it is louder, so loud with so many people. But soon it will be again the year of the dragon, with body of snake, horns of stag, claws of tiger and scales of fish, and I will be reborn.

I look away from the land, and dream of becoming someone, and forget who I am.

At the weekend it was dead quiet in the archive. The phone didn't ring. There were no deliveries. At my desk I heard muffled whispers and thought for a moment that the curator had arrived, but there was no one at the front door and the kitchen stood empty, apart from the ghosts of the weekday staff. I often feel that a place is infused with the spirit of people who live and work in it, permeating the bricks and mortar in a kind of kinetic osmosis. It's the same for photographs of course. The camera captures an instant of life and encourages one to imagine the story behind it. At the same time the photograph reveals something about the photographer, and his or her relationship with the people who stood before the lens.

I take down from the shelves a mother's spotless memoir to her two sons killed on the Somme. Her handwriting loops and lingers beneath crisp pictures of her boys as children, as young men, smiling farewell from an open railway carriage window. I put the memoir back in its place and look again to find reverential pictures of Hitler's bunker, sexist press clippings from the 1942 Miss America pageant, and the album of an unnamed Polish clown during the Communist takeover.

I find myself choosing photographs that reveal a line of history that binds the century and shows how remarkable were people's everyday lives, as our own lives are today. I walk along the shelves filled with longing and curiosity, opening the folders, stepping into secret gardens, hearing men tell of having seen angels, and watching their stories take wing.

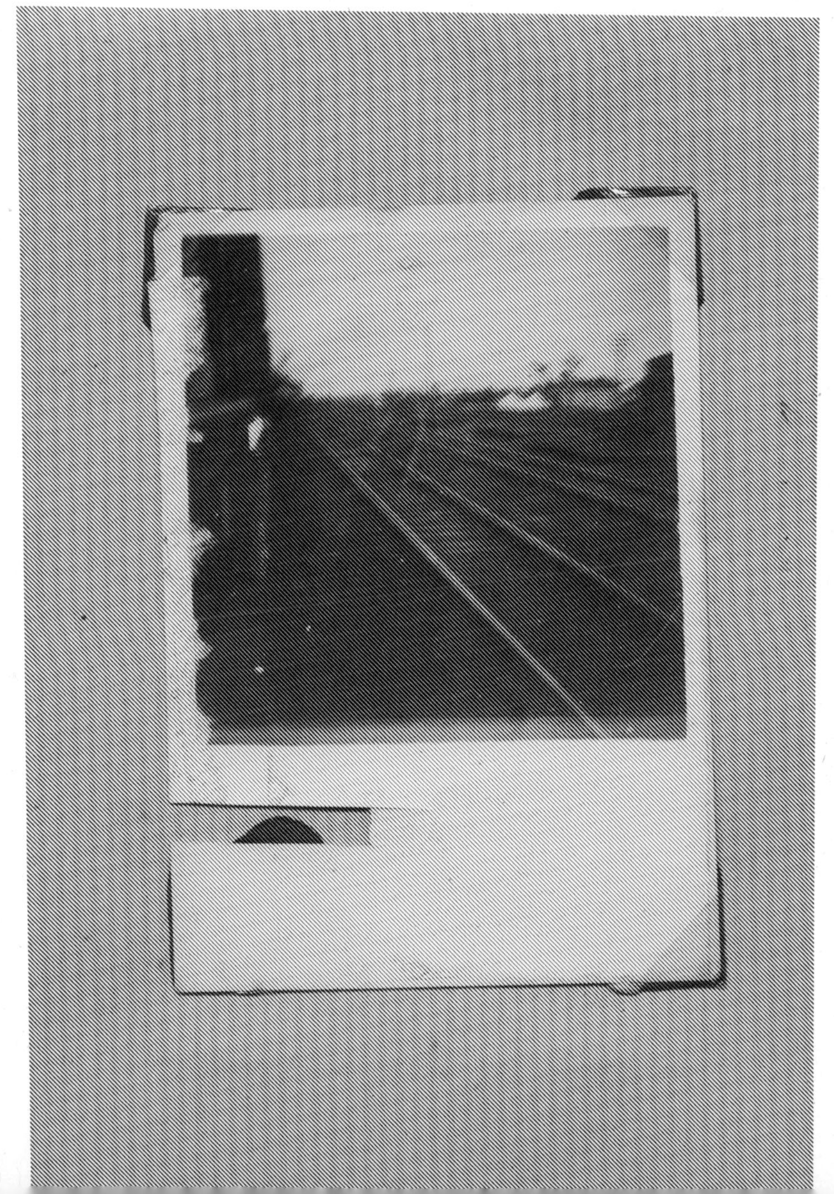

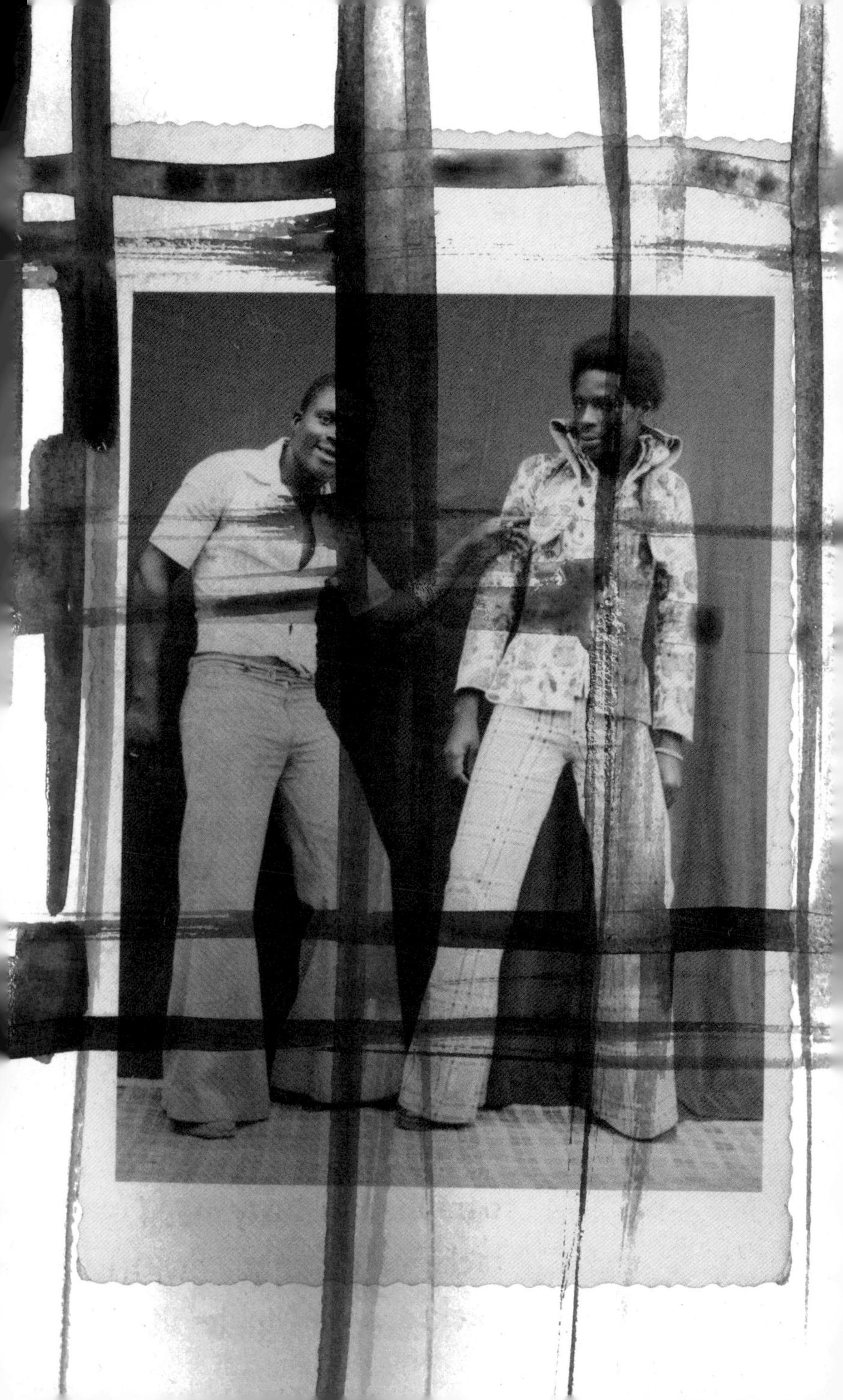

My Brother Mongo

Mbouda, Cameroon

06.06.1982

Do you hear it, my brothers? Do you hear the voice of the earth? Its call rises with the mist, breaks through the dawn, shocks awake the sleepers. Its lanky limbs crab out of the grassland. Its great, beaded abdomen crashes through the scrub. Its creaking claws clash and clatter, then pivot it toward the circle of baked brick huts. Women drop their cooking pots and run barefoot toward the trees. Children and chickens scatter in its path. Men cry like tinkerbirds and take flight in terror.

Alongside it – in the swirl of acrid fumes that spew from its terrible, metallic jaws – runs our own Mongo Nzebo, feeling the call in his blood, hearing the voices of the ancestors, at one with the living earth. At last.

As a child Mongo had been struck down by fever. He had writhed and burned on the hut's earthen floor until he fell through it. Deep in the ground a colossal elephant-masked eagle owl had caught hold of him. A winged palm nut viper had prepared to pluck out his liver. In his terror Mongo had cried out, 'O my fathers, do not gobble me up like a breakfast puff puff.' He promised the earth spider that, if allowed to live, he would honour them in the upper world. He pledged that he would build their effigies in clay and wood, that he would make mortals respect and fear them. And so the beasts of the underworld gave him back to the feeble surface dwellers.

When Mongo regained his health, he kept his vow. In his quiet Bamileke village he gathered twigs, snail shells and cane beads. He found a cache of old tins and a cast-off snakeskin among the banana palms. He borrowed clippers and paint from his builder uncle. An auntie who worked at the surgery gave him brokenbone plaster powder to make papier-mâché. He mixed it while squatting in the dust, winding strips of soaked bark around sardine tin bodies and slender wooden limbs. He worked shells and the wings of dead cicadas into his tiny sculptures. Then his father came home, held the delicate models in the palm of his hand, and crushed them.

Mongo's father worked as a bureaucrat in nearby Mbouda. He wore a European jacket and tie. He scoffed at the notion that the village chief could turn himself into a buffalo or leopard. He disdained native people like the Sawa who celebrated the gods of the waters on the banks of the Noun. He even forbade his wife from singing at funerals. As a member of St Joseph's pastoral council, he would never let his son build a pagan image.

Mongo's father embraced modernity in every form, for he feared the world. To him – a graduate of the Holy Spirit missionary school – our bright and raucous globe was a dark place filled with dangers: death, disease, mortal sin and, especially, bad drivers. Mongo's father took every precaution to protect himself and his family. His wife and son were to eat only tinned meat. They were to receive frequent inoculations, often for maladies unknown in Cameroon. In his briefcase he carried bandages, intestinal worm powder and a pad of blank accident report forms. He trusted in western medicine and bureaucracy, for they were backed up by the certainty of – respectively – science and the law.

Mongo's mother, on the other hand, placed her trust in the ancestors. She threw them morsels of food when her husband's back was turned. She studied the droppings of bearded barbet birds. Above all she tried to peep the signs from the earth spider.

Alas, my brothers, neither parent's wiles were of any use in

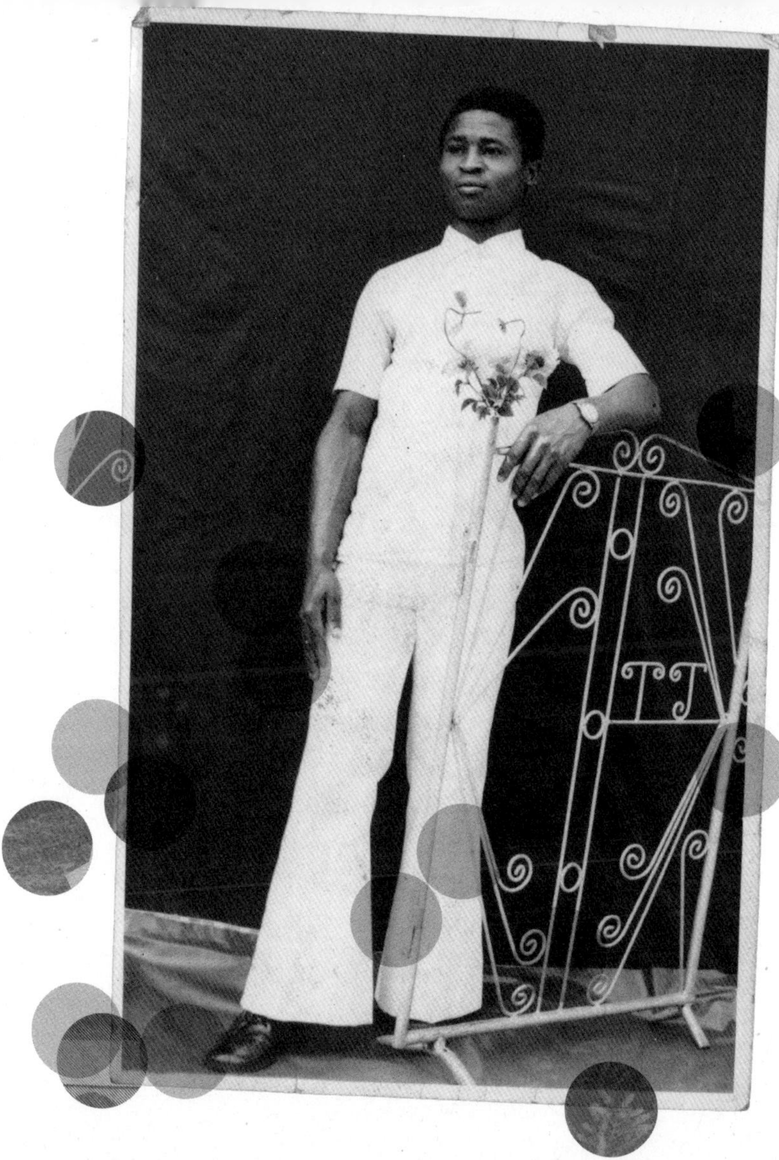

protecting them from life's misfortunes, their first-born twins having drowned when the Kumbo bus drove into the Bamendjing reservoir a few years earlier. Afterwards Mongo's father often heard noises at night.

Mongo's father had high hopes for his only surviving child, and

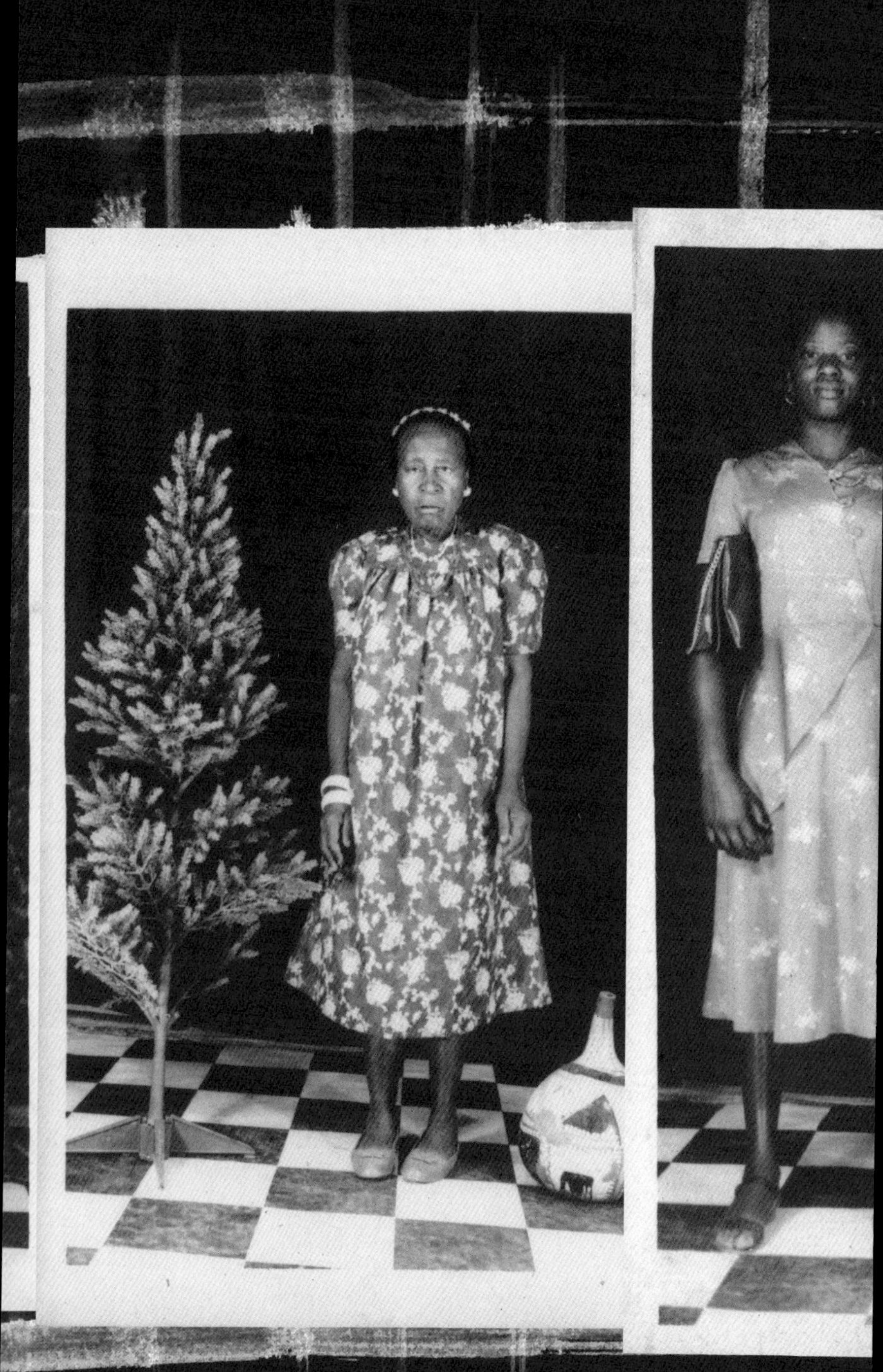

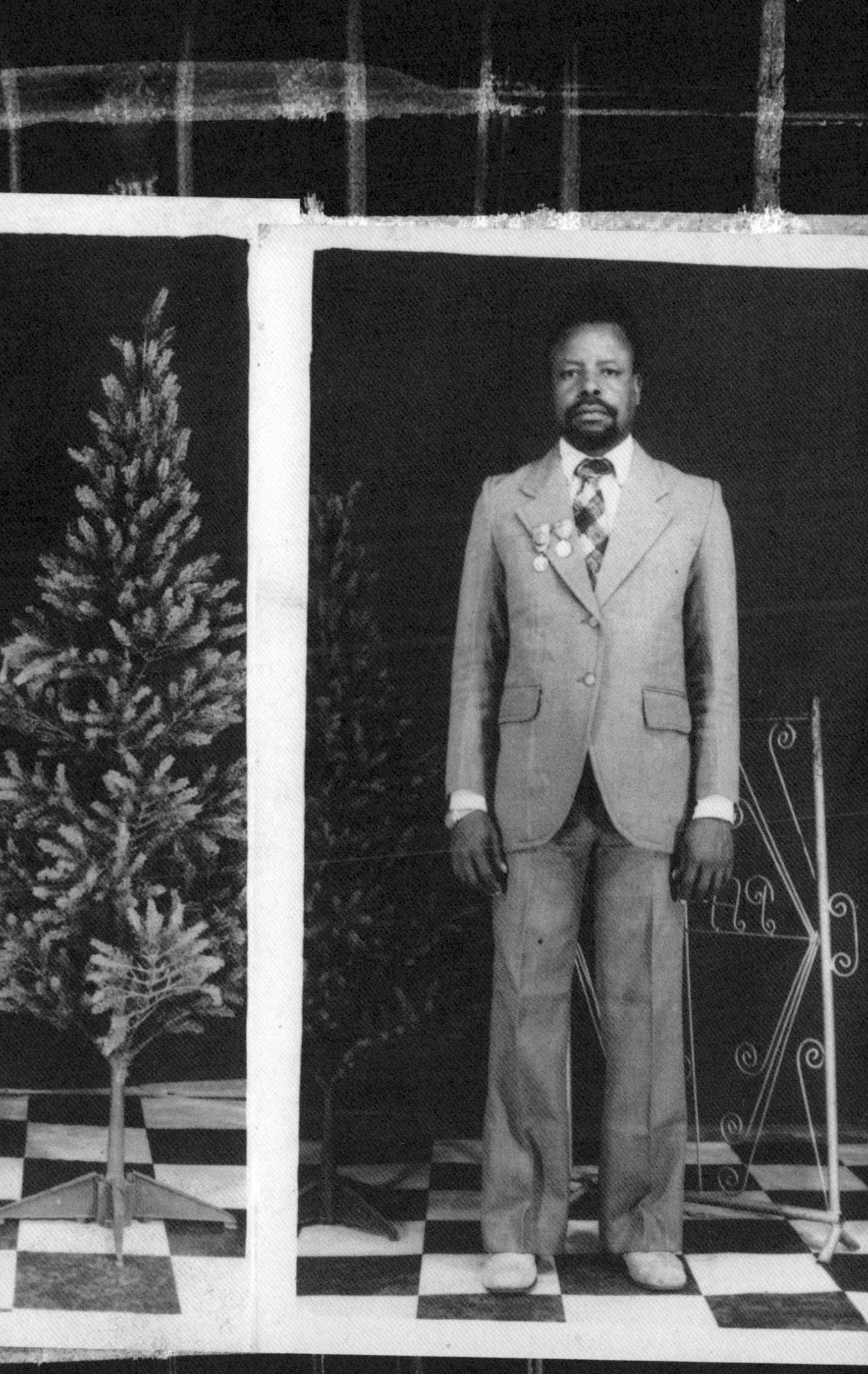

steered him towards a civil service career. Their private tragedy and the end of the insurgency brought with it an appreciation of a quiet life. Most evenings Mongo sat with his parents at supper, eating cornmeal *fufu* and Spam in silence, their peace disturbed only when his father sprang to his feet, flung open the door and stared into the night.

After high school, Mongo studied mechanical engineering. He did well enough at Mbouda's *lycée technique* to secure – with his father's backing – a junior position at the two-room regional sub-office of the Ministry of Transport. Success with his Drive Alive safety campaign brought him swift promotion, despite two fatal head-on bus collisions on the Bamenda road in his first week on the job.

He quickly moved to the Mechanical Worthiness desk, where he was charged with ensuring that every car, bus and truck in the region met the prescribed standards for the safe transport of people, baggage or cargo. The public's complete disregard for the law – as evident in the dozens of broken Citroën 2CVs, mangled Mercedes and bloody Saviem road wrecks locked away in a whitewashed compound behind his office – was never held against him.

To advance his career Mongo's father whispered in influential ears, gifted bottles of Johnny Walker to junior ministers and put his son's name down for both the ruling CPDM party and the Lions Club. He also drummed fear into Mongo, warning him again and again about archaic tribal traditions and sin, counselling him to avoid both pagan superstition and office romance. Not only would such weaknesses undermine his authority but also, under the General Regulations of the Federal Public Service (1966), the performance of sexual intercourse *with* a fellow member of staff *on* government property (eg a chair or desk) was the only offence that could lead to dismissal from the civil service.

Meanwhile in secret Mongo's mother scattered marked palm leaf chips on the ground and practised divination. Once every month she'd watch a tarantula emerge from its hole, examine how it moved the chips, and – as arachnids are believed to link the two worlds – foretell the future. At the spot where she'd buried the placentas from the births of her children she prayed for Mongo to find a suitable wife.

Mongo's heart was never in the work, but his success at it put him in debt – above all, to his father. In late 1970, the year that electricity lines reached Mbouda, he bought him a nearly new motorcycle, teaching him to ride it in the scrubland behind the market. Yet the gift brought more trouble than expected, as the Yamaha was far superior to the chief's own motorcycle. More than once did the chief egg on Mongo's father – trying, then failing, to outrun him. Unfortunately after one such speed challenge, on a tragic Christmas afternoon, Mongo's father confused the brake and accelerator controls and slammed into one of the new electricity poles, killing himself instantly.

Brothers, how his mother wailed, how the mourners whirled like dust devils as if to suck the dead man's soul out of the soil. The incident changed Mongo's life, of course, for it heralded the return of his long-buried nightmares. For almost 15 years his father's strict and rational mind had kept in check the subterranean spirits. Now they came back with a vengeance. At night he watched a winged viper spring from the earth to devour his twin siblings at the village bus stop. He saw bluebottle leopards stalk his father in the forest. As the old man raced away on the Yamaha, his winding cloth unfurled and the beasts caught hold of its end, reeling him in, eating him organ by organ. Now it was Mongo who awoke every night with a terrified wail.

Over time Mongo had matured into a big-boned, dutiful man of enormous earnestness. Few people noticed the uneasy look in his eyes or realised how fear and obedience had shaped him. Every day he hung his jacket on the office coat rack, arranged his papers with care, breakfasted on deep fried puff puffs and black coffee, then lost himself in his job. Along the Rue des Camions he inspected every garage and work pit. He measured innumerable tyre treads and counted countless brake pads. Mbouda's mechanics humoured him – offering him palm wine, knowing he was teetotal – but his superiors were less willing to play the game. The Deputy Minister of Transport (Bamileke Division) commended him for a long service medal, then ordered him to ease off with the copious reports as he was increasing the department's workload. Mongo was advised to take a month's leave but – in his desperation to be distracted from the dark – he refused to miss a single day.

One Saturday morning his junior clerk Miss Kareyce – a tall and slender high school graduate with a hesitant smile and single-minded ambition – knelt by his desk, looked into his eyes and ventured that he needed someone to look after his health.

'Mongo Nzebo, life is yours to make,' she told him.

Her concern did cause him pause for thought, or at least embolden him to spy on her at the market. After all he was a man, albeit a bamboozled one. When Miss Kareyce bent over the baskets of maize and yams he felt the blood pump hot in him. But he recalled his father's warning and resolved to remain pure. To deny the beasts, he had to keep the wild at bay.

In Western Cameroon the Bamileke believe that the dead can reach the kingdom of the ancestors only after nine years of mourning, and then by way of the world of the living. Mongo awaited the anniversary with chilling trepidation. He longed to be freed from his nightmares but feared that the exhumation of his father's skeleton would plunge him deeper into the shadows. But his mother prevailed on him – begged him – to play his part in the ceremony.

On the eve of the anniversary Mongo supervised the unearthing of the remains: sprinkling water over the grave, directing the diggerman, reaching into the rotted coffin. As custom required, he pulled his father's skull from the earth and brushed off the mud. He picked a

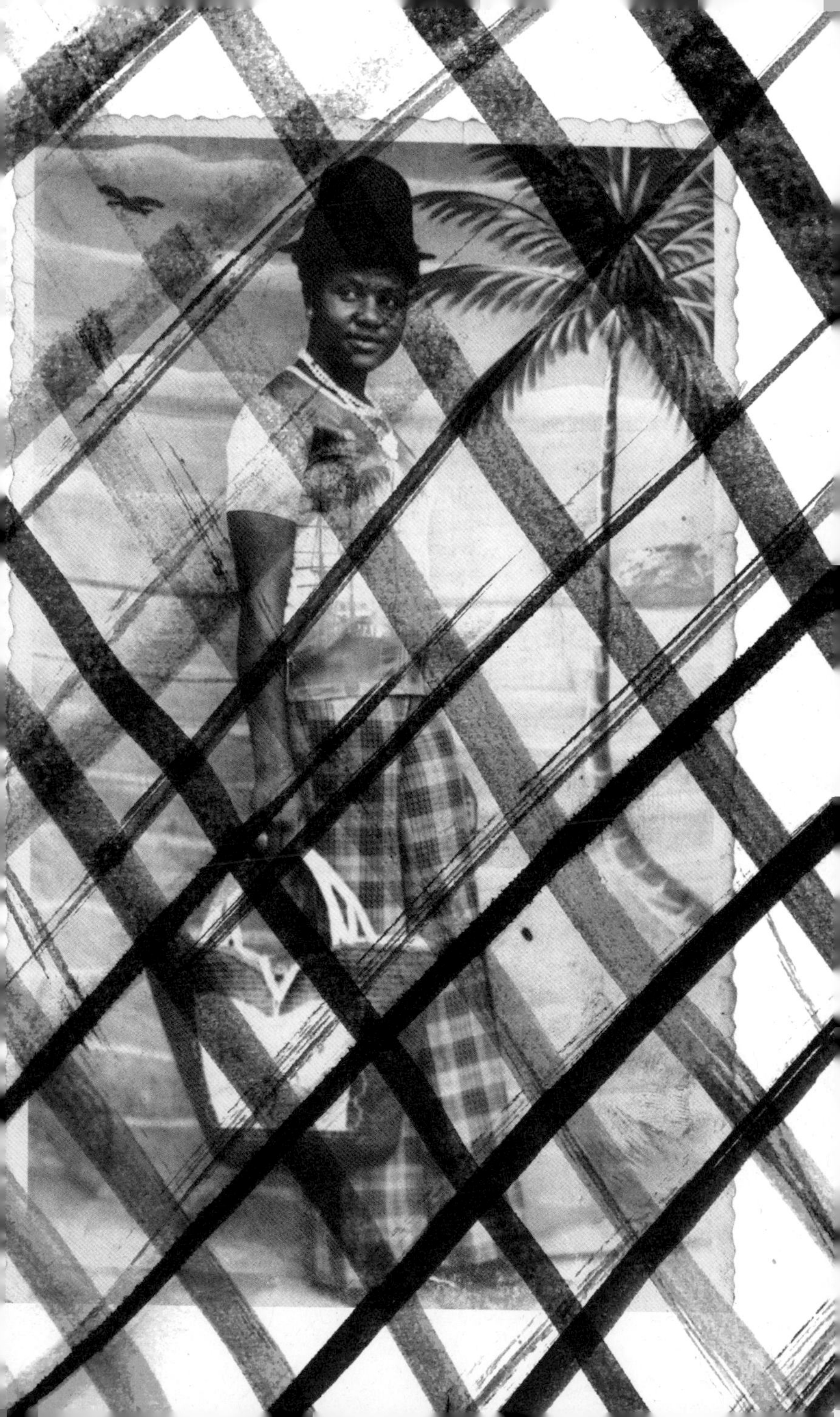

worm from an eyehole and placed the cranium in a metal bowl. Then he prayed to it, promising his father that he would forever follow the General Regulations of the Federal Public Service (1966).

'Listen clear Papa, I'll never stray into fairy tales again.'

Ancestral skulls are believed to bring good fortune, but their improper care can herald illness, infertility, even death for the bereaved. By following the old ways Mongo felt he was issuing a new kind of Mechanical Worthiness Certificate for his soul.

That night while Mongo slept, his father called to him. The old man's voice was soft and tender and it drew him towards a clearing in the forest. At its centre stood the Yamaha, beside a Christmas tree and above a tarantula hole. Mongo reached out his hand to his father, but then in a flash a silken thread lashed out to snare him and knocked him to his knees.

In the tangled dream Mongo cried, fell back, twisted onto his belly and clawed at the earth in an attempt to escape. But the arachnid's grip was too strong. It pulled him down, clasping him now with a hundred strands. Blood roared through his ears. Grit tore away his fingernails. He braced his foot against a rock. He grabbed for a plant and uprooted it. He seized a length of broken timber, and recognised it from his father's coffin. In horror, he felt his feet being wrenched into the hole. He scrabbled to save himself, kicking his legs until they too were bound in a web. He tried to find his voice, to call for help, but no sound escaped his lips. Only as his chest was heaved underground did he manage to arrest the vicious movement by bracing his elbows against the surface.

In that instant Miss Kareyce appeared before him. She gripped his hand so firmly that her own fingers and palm seemed to stretch and swell with the effort. In the dream he heard her say again, 'Life is yours to make, yours to make.'

Then the earth spider jerked him with such violence that his arms were wrenched from the shoulder sockets. They paddled at his side in ugly contortions and were levered above him as his head slipped beneath the surface. He felt the coarse walls of the tunnel cut and crush him. Around him he heard the earth whisper unfathomable sounds. He lifted up his mouth to catch a last gasp of air, and watched the patch of sky – and Miss Kareyce's tear-stained face – shrink above him as he was dragged lower, deeper into the earth.

Morning mist clung to the ground, pooled in the hollows, drifted over the grassland. Above the main road a hand-painted banner welcomed local and out-of-town mourners to the village, declaring *Bienvenu aux funérailles*. But my brothers, when Mongo awoke he didn't join the preparations for the funeral. Instead he left for town, knowing what he had to do.

In Mbouda, behind the locked double metal gate of the whitewashed Ministry compound, Mongo set to work cannibalising the old road wrecks. He did the same the next day and throughout the following week. He did not once go home to the village or answer his mother's calls. When Miss Kareyce reminded him of both his familial and civic duties (under the Revised General Rules and Regulations of the Public Service of the United Republic of Cameroon (1974)), he threw open the double gates, pulled her in to the compound and made love to her on the back seat of a 1957 Renault Dauphine.

At the same time local garage owners reported a rash of odd burglaries. Dozens of rocker arms, camshafts and klaxon horns vanished from their workshops. Three neighbours then claimed that their hens had stopped laying eggs. Next the deputy mayor blamed his daughter failing a geography test on the godless racket. But the thefts and noise weren't the only problems. A gagging, rotting odour had come to hang over the compound. Behind the double metal doors Mongo – and from time to time Miss Kareyce – paid no heed, hammering, welding and wailing day after day and through most of the night.

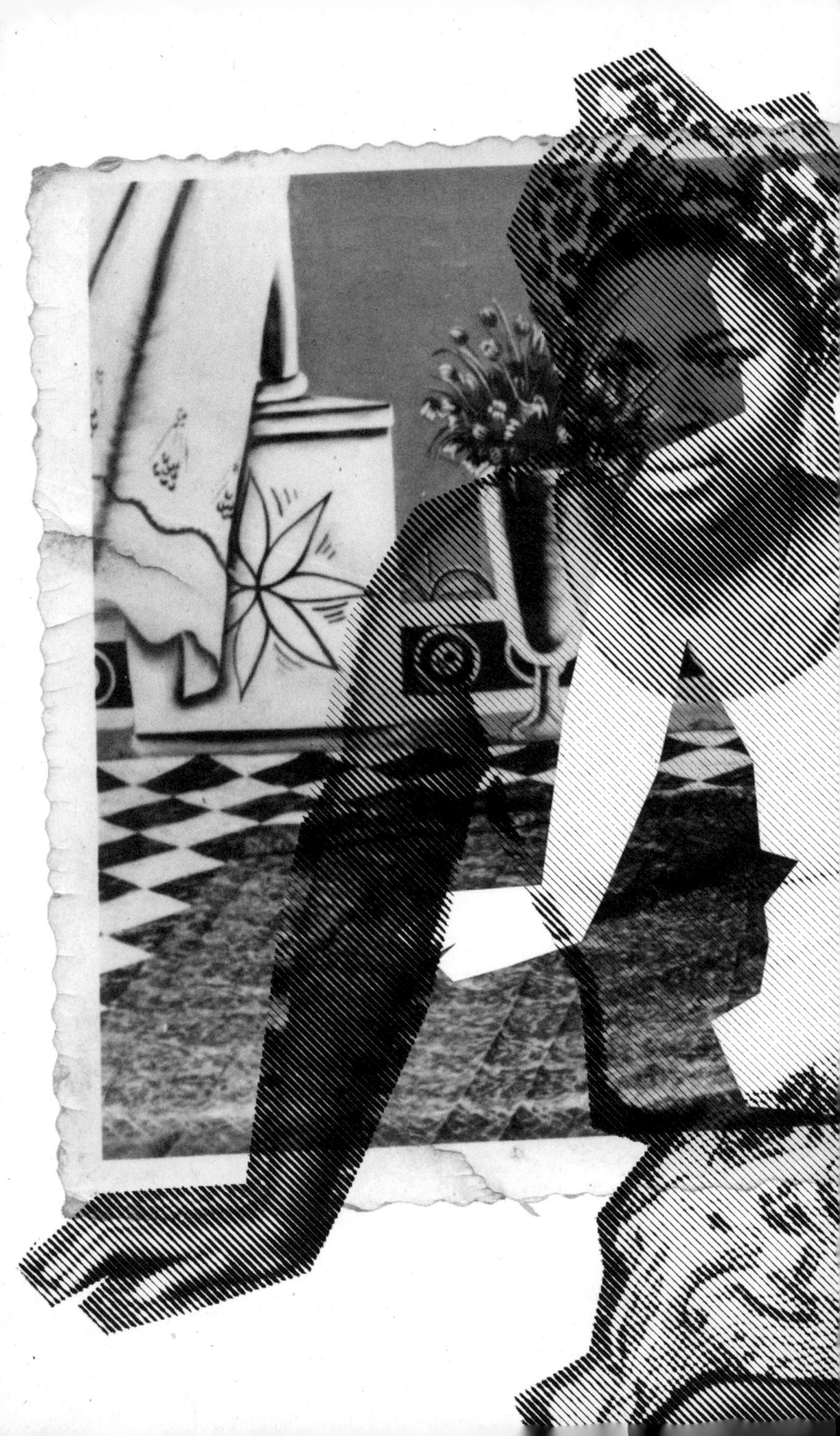

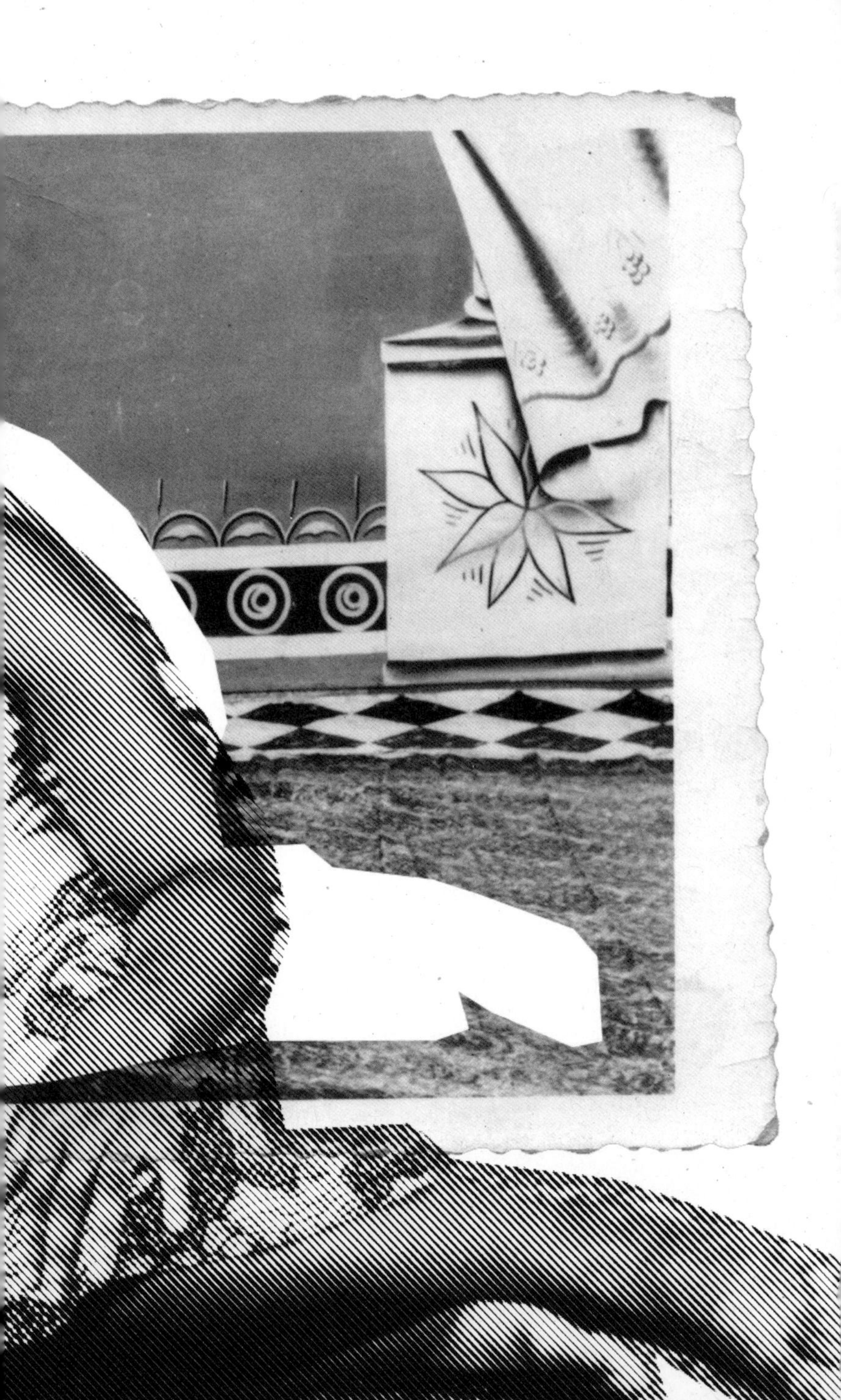

At home Mongo's mother delayed the funeral for another week after the discovery that her husband's unearthed skull had disappeared.

Ten days later Mongo emerged looking wild-eyed and grizzled, and collapsed in the street. Miss Kareyce manhandled him into a taxi and stayed with him at the clinic. She held his hand and heard the heartrending prognosis. The duty nurse didn't think he would last the night. Although she couldn't actually name the illness, Mongo's stratospheric blood pressure and delirious gabble foretold doom. The nurse suggested sending for a priest or, better still, a witch doctor.

In Bamileke's grasslands the dead are not dead, but live on in the hearts of the bereaved, in the family's home, in the earth. At last, after the long delay, the mourners gathered for the funeral. Their chief – who'd never again been challenged by a motorcyclist – fired shots into the air to open the celebration. Joyful chants echoed between the conical thatched roofs and across the maize fields. Barefoot boys played drums and rattles, marking the end of the grieving years. Village elders in formal white robes keened and stomped in the dust, drowning out the buzz of cicadas. Kuosi masqueraders danced in their beaded elephant masks and feathered headdresses, celebrating Mongo's father final journey. Only Miss Kareyce wept as the believers' tears were brushed away.

Then at the height of the festivities, the well-wishers spotted a strange parade of curious effigies. They emerged from the savannah, advancing in jerky mechanical movements: a slithering bat-winged cobra, a rolling pygmy porcupine, a three-wheeled fish with scorpion's tail. Piston arms had become greasy centipede limbs, timing belts were oily peacock plumes. Mongo's small animatrons – constructed from cast-off motorcycle parts and electric motors – congregated on the village square, trailing long tail-like wires behind them from sparking bus batteries. They toppled against carved doorways, marched into kettles of *cous cous* steaming over open fires. Together the villagers laughed at their cockeyed mechanics, mocking the feral creations, shivering with eerie premonition.

Suddenly a shrill siren call broke through the haze, shocking the villagers into silence. A dozen klaxons howled the monster's advance. A great, whirring colossus thundered out from behind the trees, pitching wildly, three metres tall and spitting fire. Three petrol engines crabbed its lanky, articulated limbs. Its huge, beaded abdomen crushed palm fronds and scrub. Its metallic claws pivoted it toward the circle of homesteads. Children and chickens scattered in the path. Barbets and tinkerbirds took flight in terror. Women abandoned their cooking pots and ran toward the trees. Black exhaust fumes spewed from its painted jaws. Cowrie shells and bells rattled off its black pads. Only the chief seemed to stand his ground, frozen on his beaded throne, staring with eyes and mouth agape at the skull of Mongo's father bolted to the beast's bonnet.

My brothers, the earth is full of voices. They clamour for attention, cry out to be heard. Before our astonished eyes Mongo sprints beside the roaring, spitting black beast. He feels the call in his blood, hears the voices of the ancestors, becomes part of the wild. At last he has freed them, and is one with them. He turns the canted, sideward steering wheel and watches his whirring, eight-legged earth spider miss a step, snap a wooden tibia, and fall onto the chief's motorcycle.

Thus passes the glory of the world: in noble enterprise, in opportunities seized, in the puny, stupid struggles of our daily existence. Laughing, weeping and ready at last for the miracle of being, Mongo Nzebo runs on into life – watched by the wide-eyed, single-minded, ecstatic Miss Kareyce.

As a child, I once made a cardboard-and-crayon atlas of the world, slipping imaginary lands between the countries that I knew. Africa was a crazy mosaic of mystery. China was a blank. Oddly-shaped states surrounded Brazil. The Balkans looked like a leopard's skin (I wasn't far off there). My world was at once a place known and unknown, observed and imagined like the maps of earlier explorers with mythical sea monsters and captions that read 'Here be dragons'.

As I grew older and became a travel writer, I began to people the map, filling the blanks with stories, confronting those sea monsters and dragons. Yet every journey reminded me of how very little I knew, and so kept me travelling, kept me redrawing my atlas. I came to perceive the world by rendering it into words instead of cardboard and crayons.

The past is like another country, yes, but old photographs do not simply throw light on a bygone age. Rather they can spark an animated dialogue between past and present, suggesting possibilities, evoking scenarios, bringing alive that other time. Who is in the image? What is Mongo hiding in his pocket? Did he and Miss Kareyce check into Mbouda's Motel Le Saree immediately after the picture was taken and make love for a week? Or did they just go back to the office?

Last night my hands shook when I wrote about Mongo finding the courage to build his mad machines. Emotions can live on if they're strong enough, and I am not impartial to his story, nor to that of the forgotten Chinese crone. There is something in them both: new beginnings, old victims, and above all the straddling of two worlds. If she could read her story, Qiao – that's the name I'll give to the crone – might now ask why I chose her.

'Why me? And why leave me in my misery?'

Perhaps I should have let her escape from her asylum. She could have found the album, run her finger along the serrated edge of the old prints, and wept. She could decide to become the author of her own circumstance. But then Mongo would have told me that our fate is an irrelevance, that the very meaninglessness of life forces a man to create his own meaning.

That's the difference between fiction and travel writing, of course. In fiction one is bound to tell the truth, whereas in travel writing one can make things up, or at least the writer must impose a pattern on a journey in order to establish its meaning.

The stories behind the photographs are like imaginary lands, places of the possible and impossible, shaped by fact and fancy, a world both as it is and as it might be.

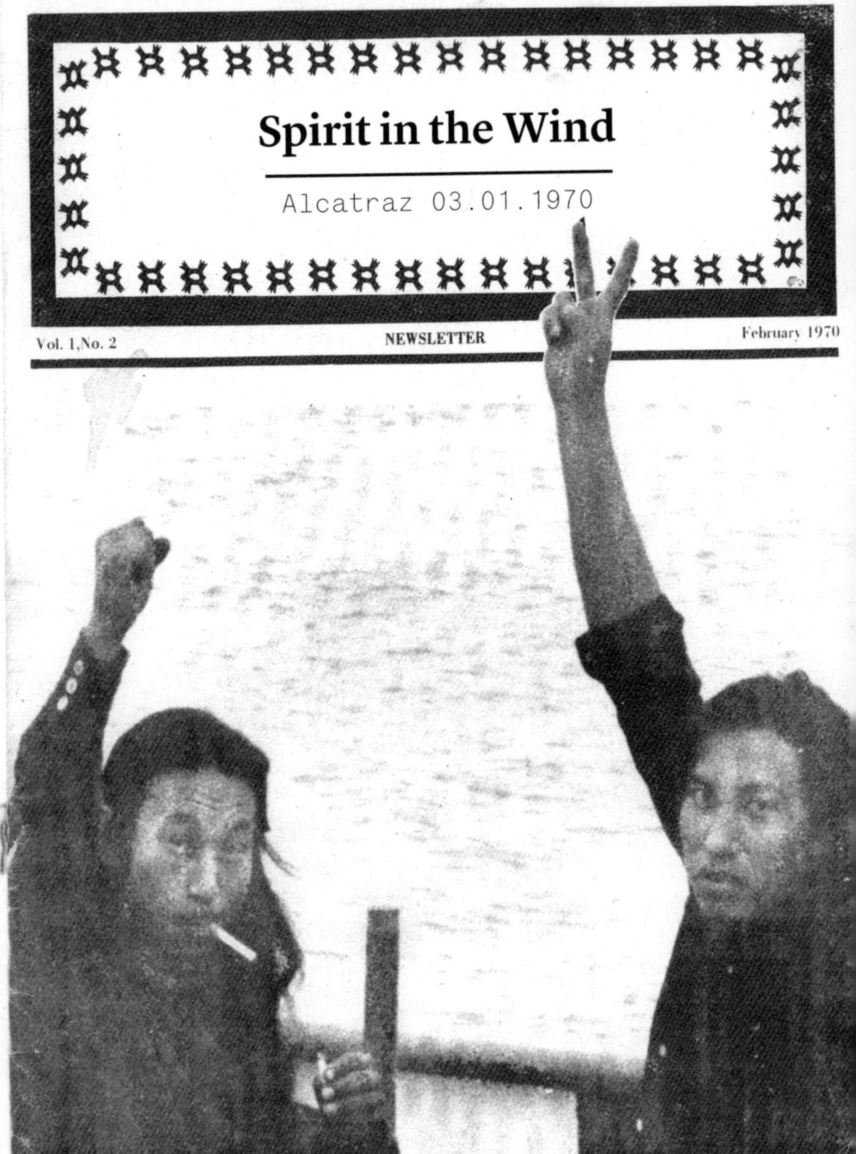
Spirit in the Wind

Alcatraz 03.01.1970

Vol. 1,No. 2 NEWSLETTER February 1970

Once upon a time our leaders were caged on Alcatraz, tortured on Alcatraz, left to die like dogs on Alcatraz. When the white man shut down his vile prison we claimed back the blighted island. Any abandoned federal land had to be returned to us, that was what it said in the Fort Laramie Treaty. All we asked was that the whites kept their word.

We asked, and we waited.

Have patience, they said, and we waited some more.

Six years on, we gave up waiting.

'The choice now lies with the leaders of the American Government...' declared the braves, muscled and feathered and standing shoulder-to-shoulder in front of the news cameras. At dawn they'd landed on the eastern shore and seized Alcatraz island for Indians of All Tribes.

'...to use violence as before to remove us from our Great Spirit's land, or to institute a real change in its dealing with the American Indian.'

We were at war.

On New Year's Day, with notebook in hand, I hitched over to report on the Occupation, knees quaking as the rebel boat outmanoeuvred a Coast Guard cutter. I felt charged as the cold and salty air stung my nostrils. Here was our new beginning, the birthplace of a true brotherhood that would cut through all the bullshit and lies.

At the island's pier I helped to lug donated food boxes up the ladder. I joined the drumming and dancing in the exercise yard. I interviewed LaNada Means about plans to build a Native American cultural centre. Kay Many Horse told me of the hard-as-hell offer to buy Alcatraz for the price that we were being given for our land – 47 cents an acre, to be paid in glass beads and red cloth. I walked the abandoned cell-house with dozens of other excited supporters. A freaking American eagle hung above the main door, around its neck a painted cardboard sign proclaiming, *This* is *My* Land.

My land.

It was a front page story.

At the end of the afternoon I was at the pier waiting for a ride back across the Bay when John Trudell, a Santee Sioux, collared me and asked me to stick around for a day or two. He knew that I wrote for the *Berkeley Barb* and wanted someone to help him start an island newsletter. 'People have to understand what we're fighting for,' he said.

I jumped at the chance to become a part of this amazing experiment, this resurrection of our people's hope and pride. I could file my *Barb* copy later.

Then as the last boat was about to pull away from the dockside, something made me suddenly grab for its gunnel. I don't know why I did it, call it intuition, but I was seized by an impulse to get out of there while I still could. Everyone around me stared like I was crazy, so I let go of the boat and made a joke of it. But my laugh was hollow.

That first evening the Warden's House was bursting with

activists: Chippewa College protesters, displaced Navajos, gaudy Red Power militants in headbands and feathers yelling, horsing around, eating home-roast chicken and buttery white bread. Richard Oakes and Wilma Mankiller argued back and forth about civil rights and big-shot attorneys. Joe Morris was cheered when he said the Longshoremen's Union would close San Francisco's ports if the Occupation was ended by force.

'Now let the Feds try to cut us off from the mainland!'

As the night and the debates deepened I forgot my misgivings. We were too determined, too emotional, and too loud to be scared off the Rock. The flickering lamplight caught in its glare hawk-eyed looks and firmly set jaws. I got out my notebook and began to question resolute tribal elders of patient countenance. I rapped with Blackfoot families with bawling children fresh off the reservations. I chilled a strung-out Huron teenager with bruised head and lacklustre eyes. All had their own stories to tell, but all had come to Alcatraz for the same reason. Annual household income for an American Indian family was one-quarter of the national average. Life expectancy was 44. Cesar Chavez had mobilised Chicano farmworkers. Martin Luther King had led the movement for Blacks. Now it was our turn.

Towards the end of the evening I slipped away from the warm brazier and fiery talk to write up my notes. Behind me the lamps burned like eyes in the windows, casting trembling glances and weird shadows across the old parade ground. A breeze was blowing as I walked down from the darkened lighthouse towards Baker Beach. In the dying light the island felt a strange and unsettled place: wild soughing pines, agave shivering in the wind, the cry of a disturbed gull or grebe. I felt the current move around me, heard the swell tumble and foam against the shore.

'You Ohlone?' a voice asked in the darkness.

I stopped, startled out of my reverie.

'Any Ohlone with you?'' added the man.

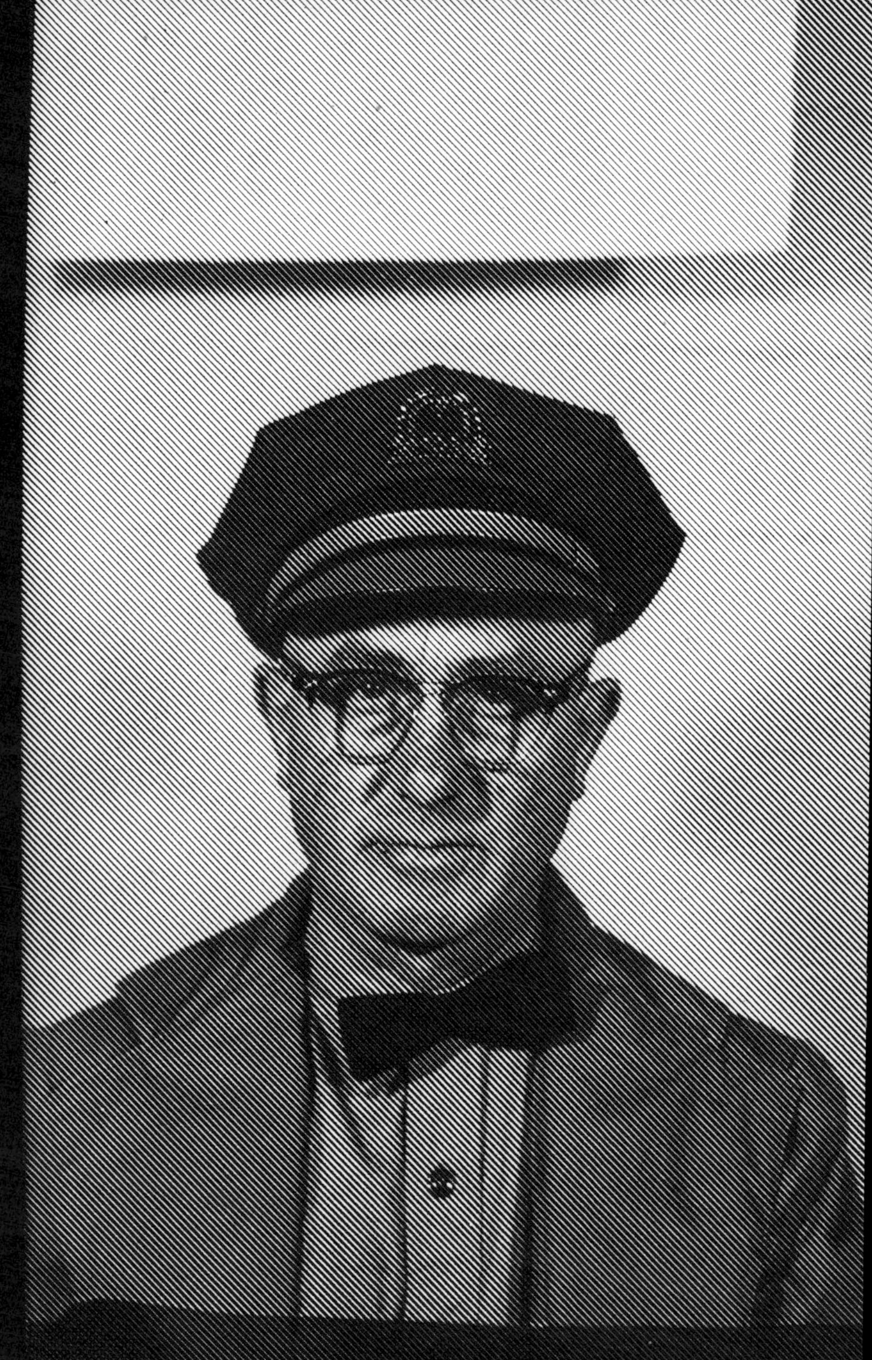

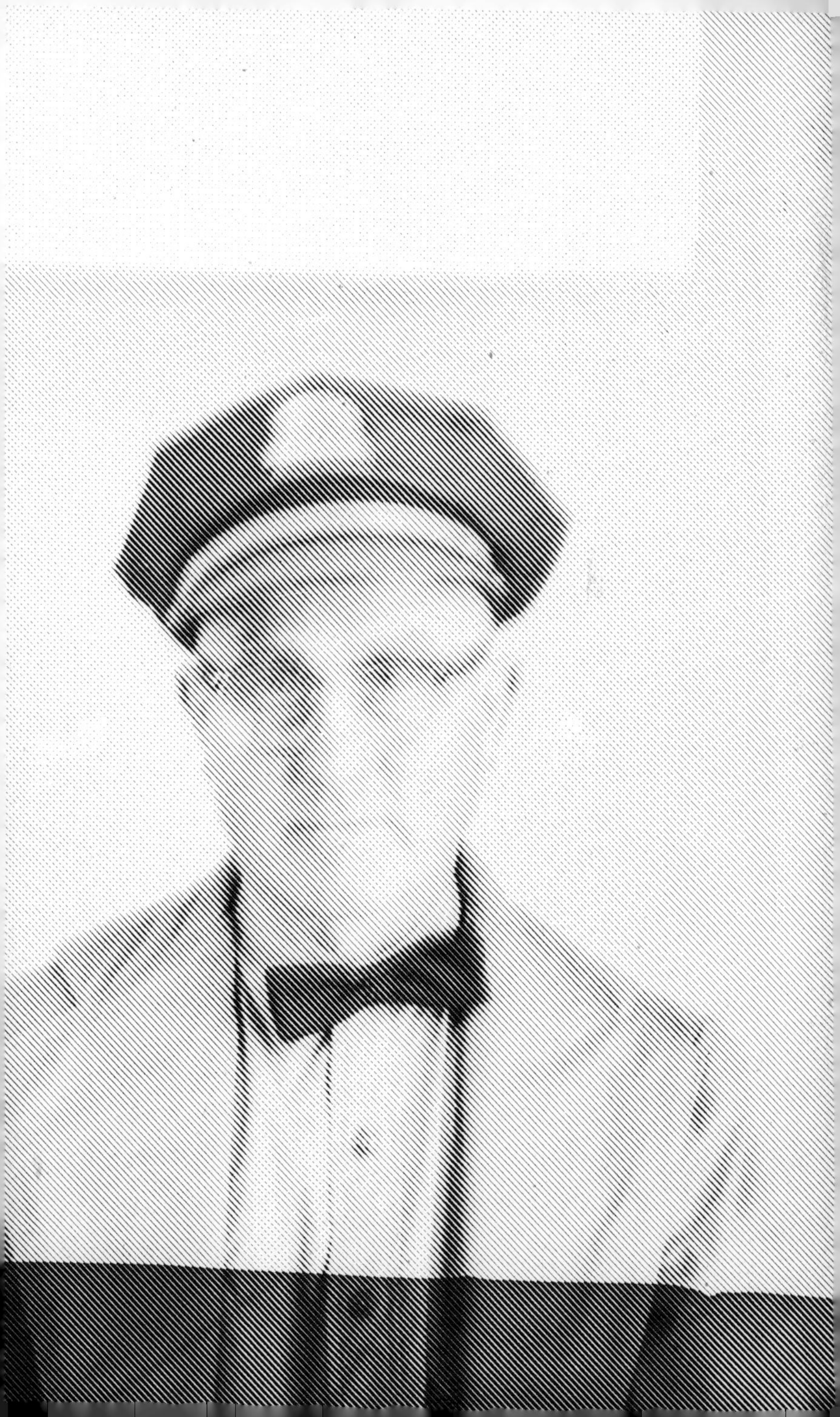

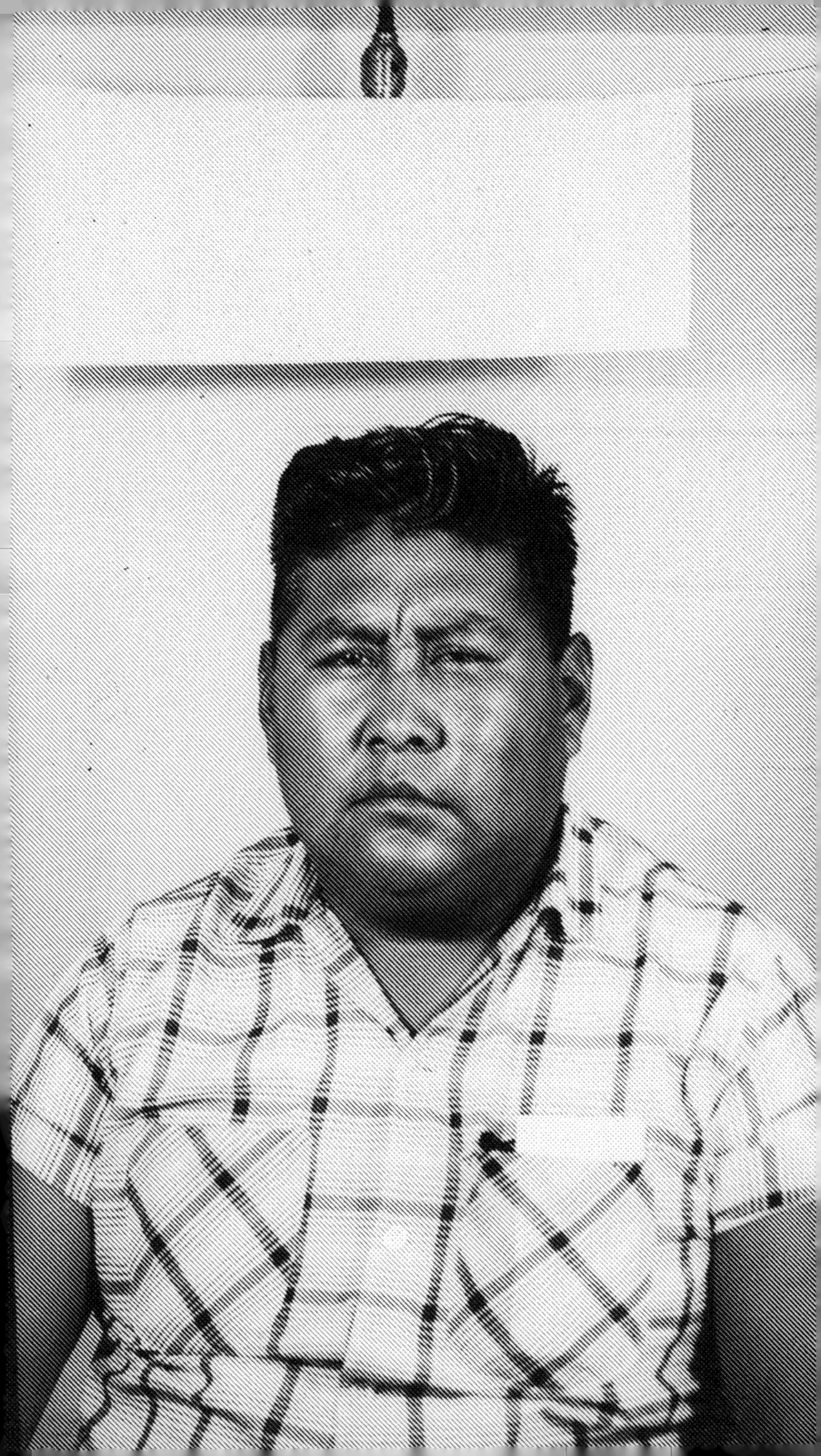

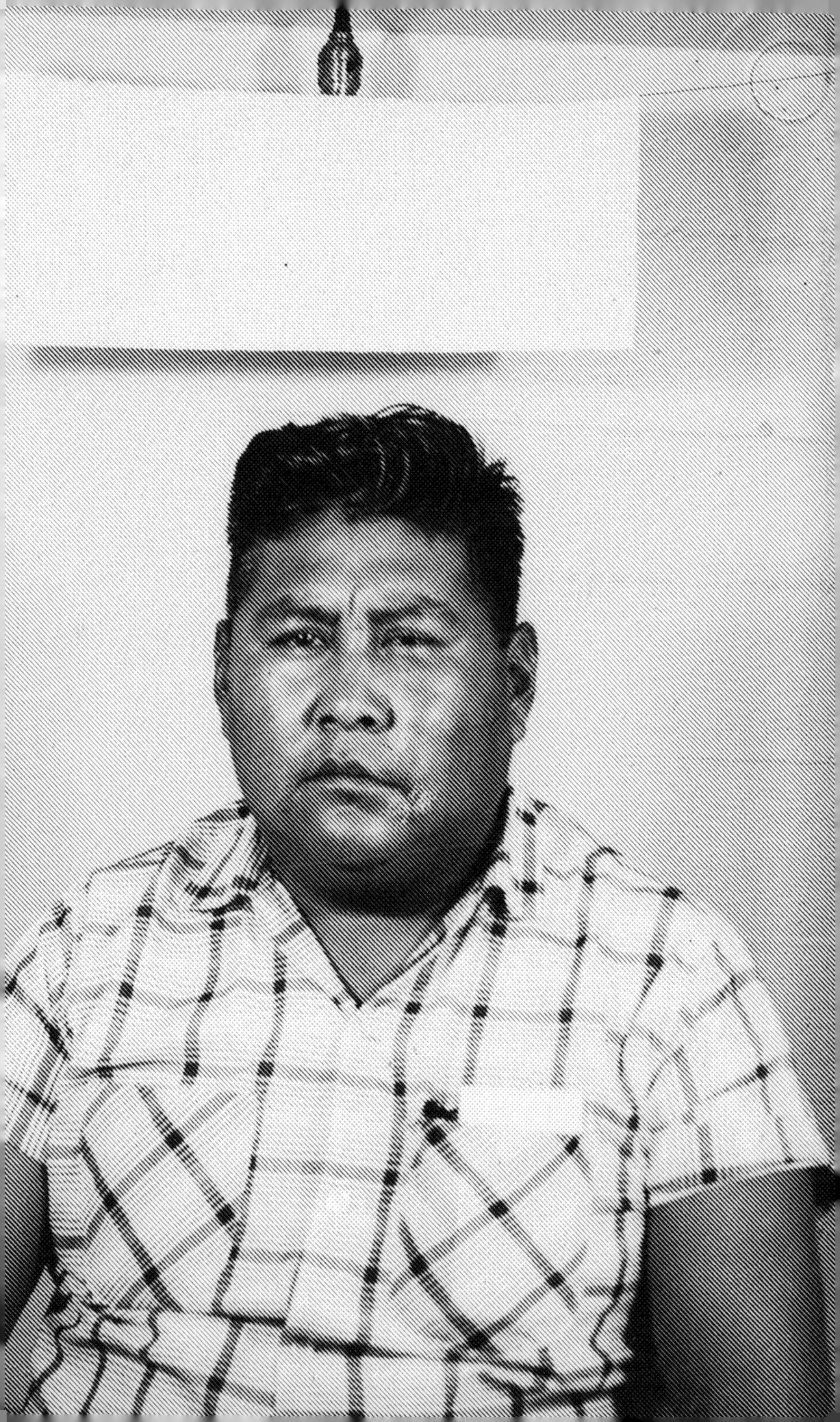

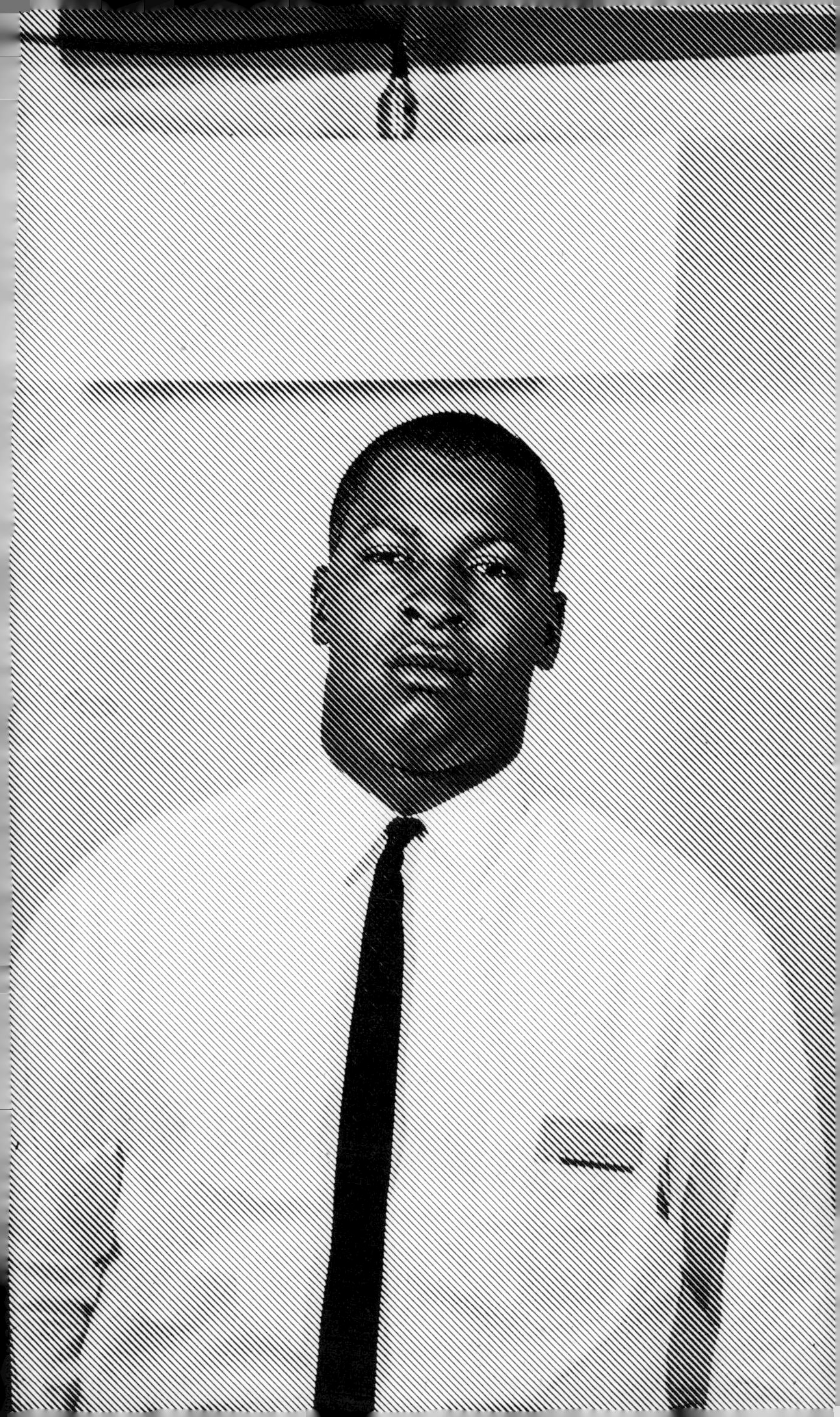

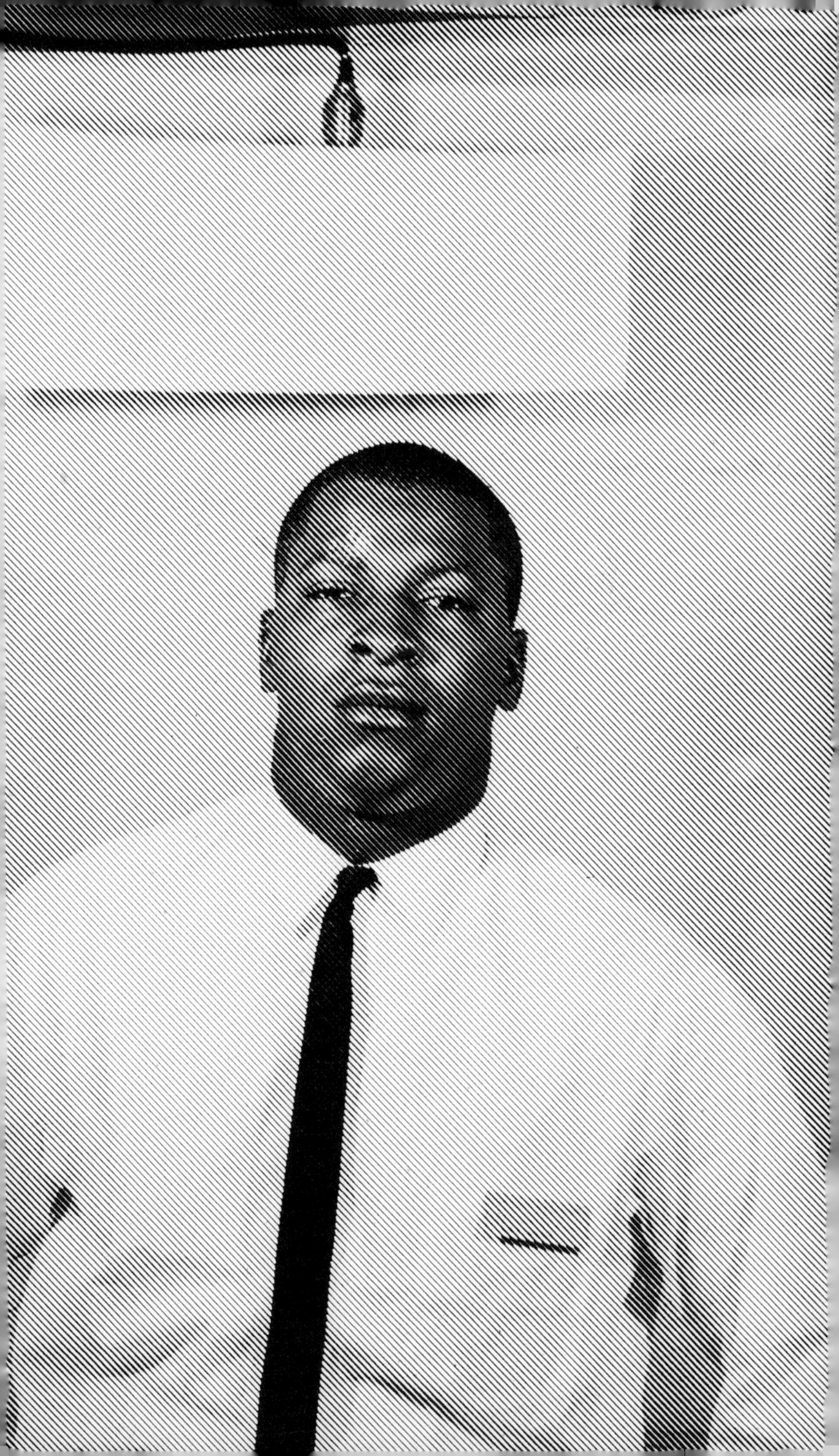

'Plenty of us inside,' I replied, finding my tongue. The Ohlone – my people – had once inhabited the whole Bay area down to Monterey. Some 26,000 Ohlone and Salinans had lived in the Northern Mission Area. Today only about a thousand of us are left.

'Ohlone never used to come out to this rock,' he said.

In the gloom I made out the pale contours of his face. He was a work-a-daddy old guy, big in stature, all but bald – and white, although he claimed later to be one-eighth Cree.

'Why's that?' I asked.

'Cause once on it, you can't get off,' he said. He sat on a rough stone seat, staring not at me but out to sea. 'In fact, only people to ever escape it were white. They made a raft out of rubber raincoats and went in the water there,' he added, tilting his head towards the old power plant. 'I figured you'd like to know, seeing you're writing about the island.'

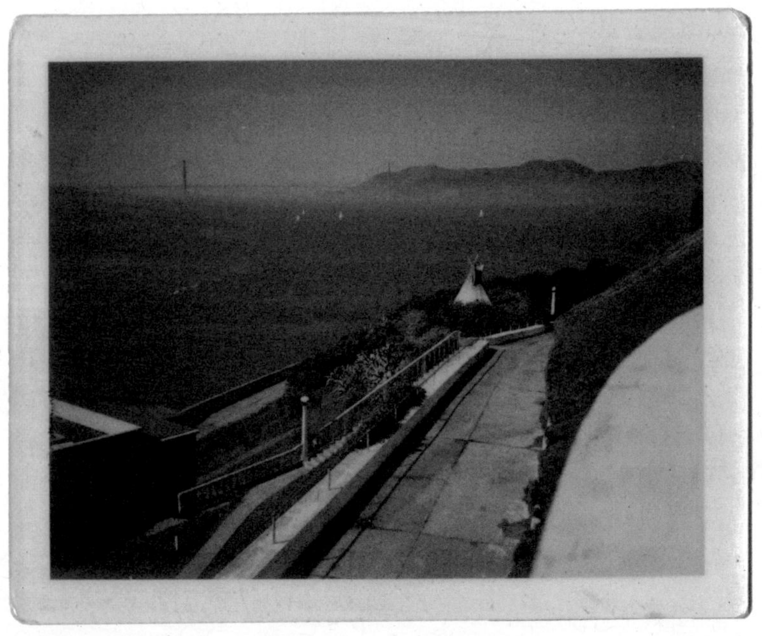

Next morning the wind was blowing even harder, driving us all a little wild. People stayed indoors, listening to radios, bickering. No one went out to clear the vines and weeds from the pathways, to put the tepee back up or even to fish from the pier. A few kids huddled around the electric heater at Mad Bear Anderson's Native American Studies class, until the generator ran out of gas. Spirits were lifted only by the smell of frying corn fritters.

Pop, the poker-faced white man, went about his chores and I followed him. I needed background for the article, to put Alcatraz in context, and he knew the history. Al Capone had been locked up here, he told me, Modoc and Hopi chiefs had died over there. He also let loose something of his own story. Born in Chicago, parents lost to TB, all his life he'd hated noise: his mother's blood-spitting hack, the metalwheel shriek of the 'L', gunfire in the Ardennes.

'I came out to the coast after the war and joined the Prisons Bureau in the hope of finding some quiet,' he said. But on Alcatraz he hadn't been able to get away from the clang of cell doors, the catcalls, the bells – until the prison was shut down and they kept him on as caretaker.

'Morris and the Anglin brothers went through that vent at the rear of their cells,' he told me, explaining the last convicts' escape route. 'They left papier-mâché heads in their beds so they'd not be missed at the night count.' He led me along the path the men had taken to the water and showed me the exact spot where they'd launched their rubber raincoat raft. 'No bodies were ever found,' he said.

Something about Pop both fascinated and unnerved me. Some aspect of his nature felt unfathomable. As far as I could tell, he'd sat out on his rock every night since the escape, even after the prison had closed, watching the currents, watching the swells.

'But what do you do out here?' I asked him, looking across the angry, wind-whipped water.

'Wait,' he said. 'Just wait.'

A skiff rolled and pitched across the churning black water,

a lonely figure at its stern. As we looked, the man drew a finger across his neck.

'Fisherman,' Pop said, his voice flat.

I confess I love my sleep. Like, I'm no good after an all-nighter. I avoid shooting the breeze until dawn because I know how bad I'll feel in the morning. Both that first and second night I turned in early but hardly slept.

When I got up on the Saturday, Alcatraz seemed to have turned against us. From first light the Rock felt unmoored, adrift in a heaving mass of water and wind. The foul weather sank us into edgy gloom, our rancour magnified by the cold prison walls. Then a thirteen-year old girl – the spokesman's stepdaughter Yvonne – fell down a three-storey stairwell inside the Warden's House. In the afternoon a Coast Guard cutter broke away from the cordon to take her body ashore, along with Oakes and his wife Annie. No one else was allowed to leave the island.

Next thing a gull flew against a kitchen window, hitting it so hard that it left a chilling, down silhouette of wings on the glass.

By evening I couldn't bear to stay indoors any longer and went out into the storm.

Pop wasn't at his rock, but something – a mottled grey shape, like a body floating in the sea – caught my eye. Curiosity overcame fear and I clambered down to Baker Beach, whipped by branches, battered by the wind. The waves had pitched the shape against the shore. I picked my way across the lip of slimy stone above the water's edge and reached out to touch it.

The body jerked away and slid away into the deep. In horror I stumbled back, tripped and was falling when Pop caught me. I'd not heard him approach, just as the seal hadn't heard me.

'It's a seal!' I yelled to him above the gale, laughing in relief and shock. 'It's just a goddamn seal.'

'Get inside,' he said.

In my cell – improvised like dozens of others into a bedroom – I lay down and shut my eyes. Again I couldn't sleep. Instead I listened to the gale moaning through the broken catwalks and ghastly stairways. For an hour or two I tossed and turned in a vain hope of slumber rescuing me from my imagination. But the blood kept throbbing in my ears, and the crazed waves roared around my brain.

Somehow I got it into my damn head that I needed to look outside. With no electricity, no light of any kind, I started to feel my way along the bars. I knew I should stay put, but I couldn't stop myself. I felt drawn toward the exit. I blindly followed the bare, damp walls. Finally, I threw open the door to the outside.

In the ghostly darkness savage, scalloped sheets of rain beat against the island, wave after wave of them as high as the sky. They rose before me in terrible, towering, unearthly shapes that swayed, as if alive, as if scanning the crumbling buildings, searching the barren rock. Then a curtain of the storm reached towards me and I slammed the door against it, shaking with fear.

'Sleep well?' asked Trudell the next morning. He seemed unmoved by our captivity, oblivious to the forces gathering around us. 'That was some storm.'

As the wind had dropped, a group of braves had begun putting up the tepee. Their voices rang in the still, washed morning air and then paused into silence. They'd found long, jagged tears in the skin of the tepee, as if it had been ripped open by some enormous animal. Then the voices rose again, but in anger now as they blamed the damage on each other.

One raised his fist.

Another pushed a third man to the ground.

In the kitchen the burners would not light.

Over cold coffee Trudell talked through plans and politics, spelling out how to launch the newsletter. My brain was so fried that I hardly heard him. And my heart sank when I learnt that no

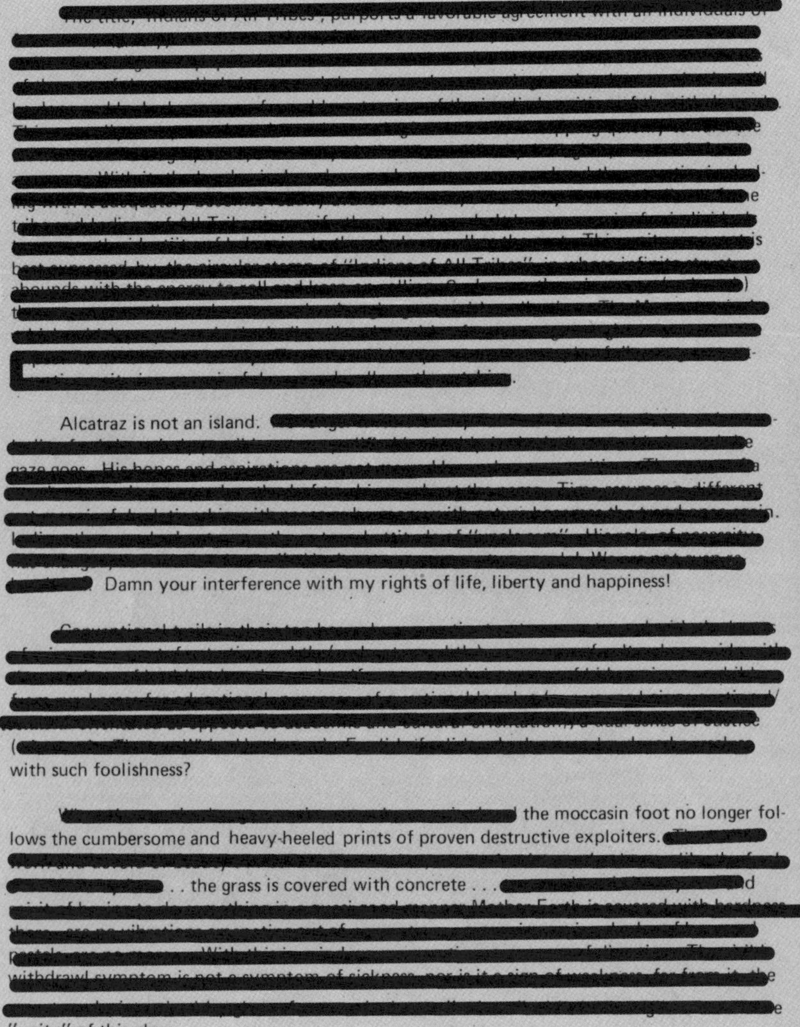

ALCATRAZ: THE IDEA

Alcatraz is not an island.

Damn your interference with my rights of life, liberty and happiness!

with such foolishness?

the moccasin foot no longer follows the cumbersome and heavy-heeled prints of proven destructive exploiters.

. . the grass is covered with concrete . . .

"unity" of this glow.

Page 2

We , have expressed our willingness to Lead.

from foolishness and moments of weakness,

This is the Indian direction,

ALCATRAZ THE IDEA AND ALCATRAZ THE ISI AND MUST ALWAYS BE IN HARMONY.

GUEST EDITORIAL

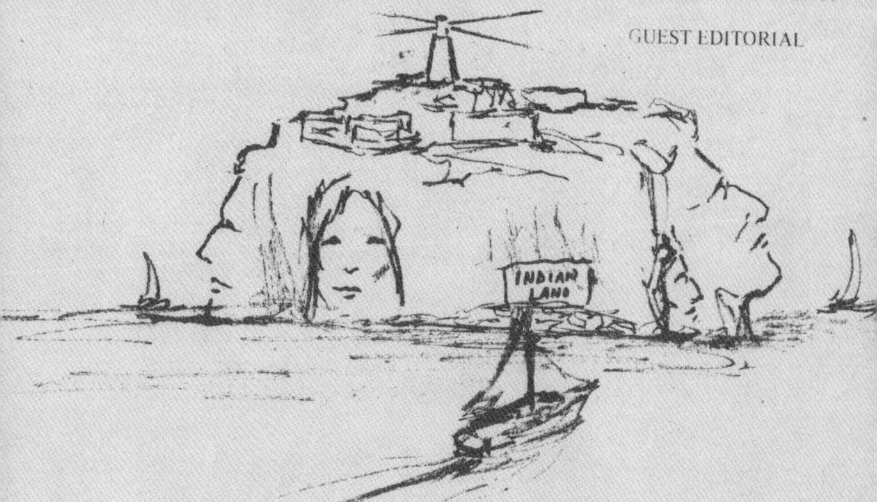

boat would be allowed out that day. The Feds were tightening the noose, offering to evacuate everyone or no one, trying to break our resolve. I looked across the glass-smooth bay and wondered if I should swim for it. Morris and the Anglin brothers, the cons, they had made it, probably. For God's sake, the city was hardly more than a mile away.

I went looking for Pop and found him on the clifftops at the island's north end. Below us cormorants and pigeon guillemots nested on the cliff face. Water – so benign in daylight – shuckled between the stones at its base. I told him what I'd seen in the night. His expression remained unchanged.

'Don't trifle with it,' he said.

'I've got to get out of here,' I told him.

'Don't show your fear. Never show your fear.'

•

As the sun dipped toward the horizon a dull hum began to echo around the island. At first the sound was so low that I figured it was all in my head. Then I thought that the generator had come back online. I laughed with relief, imagining for a moment that the telephone link would soon be restored, that the whites had given in to our demands. But no boat had arrived, so there was still no fuel, and in any case the sound wasn't coming from the powerhouse.

To keep myself sane I tried to locate its source. I walked from the north end to the parade ground and down to the tide pools. But no matter where I stood, or how I held my head, the humming surrounded me, rising up out of the water itself.

No one else seemed to hear it.

At the pier one of the island dogs wheeled around and around in a tight circle, as if in an invisible cage. Half-a-dozen Iroquois drank from brown-bagged bottles at the foot of the lighthouse. Three Yurok Indians from Del Norte County smashed up a broken government pickup.

Maybe in the morning a boat would reach us.

At dusk I looked for safety in the crowd, joining the rowdy evening pow-wow in the chapel, and turned in late as if to shorten the night and hurry on the dawn.

In the dark I awoke with my heart hammering. A heavy weight was pressing on my chest. I felt a hellish panic rise in me. I was suffocating, gasping for breath. I struck out at the blackness. There was nothing in my cell, nothing on top of me, yet I knew I wasn't alone. The demonic humming raged in my ears. Terror gripped me and I scrabbled for the flashlight I'd liberated from the office, shining it in every corner. Nothing! Nothing! I dragged myself to my feet, and ran out into the echoing hall, yelling for help.

Outside, the hum had become deeper and angrier. Away behind the Warden's House the dogs were howling. I shone the light up into the sky, back down at the sea. In its beam the swells coiled back on themselves, rolling into alarming, horrible shapes. I saw torsos, arms and legs take form in the cold water. Waves peaked into skulls, then washed away. Bodies rolled towards the shore and broke on the rocks. Wild, living seas rushed around Alcatraz, surrounding it, engulfing us.

No one else was awake. Pop wasn't at his lookout, but I knew he wasn't indoors either. I ran across the bare parade ground towards the beach, stumbling on the stones, scrambling down the rock face, cutting my hands on overhanging branches. At the shoreline I could hardly hear myself shout his name. In the shallows the humming came from every side. I played the light over the rocks, across the water until its beam caught the outline of his shoulders, about to slip beneath the waves.

I ploughed into that hellish water, bitterly cold and furious. I caught Pop around the chest, and tried to yank him back toward dry land.

'Leave me!' he shouted, hardly breaking his step.

He was bigger than me and doubly heavy with the weight of his

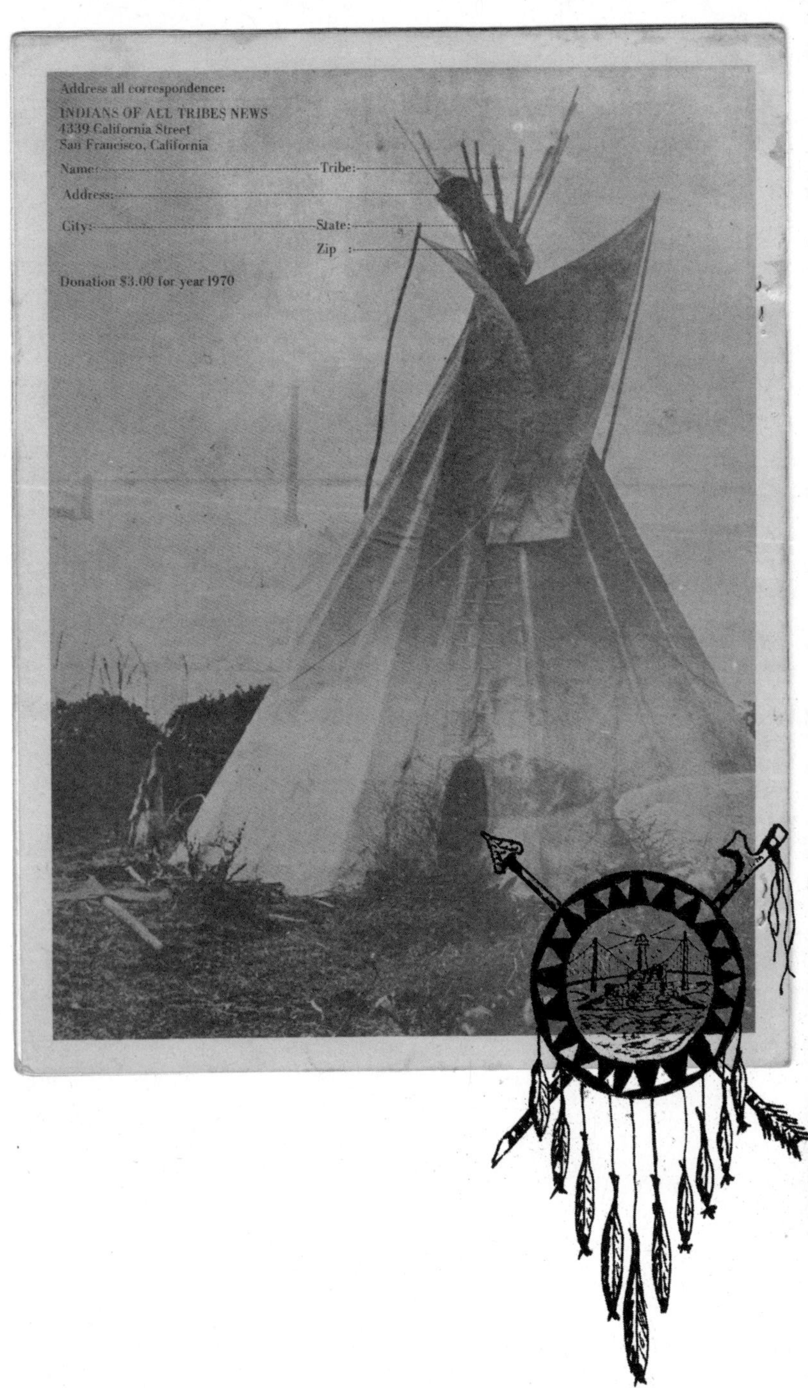
Address all correspondence:

INDIANS OF ALL TRIBES NEWS
4339 California Street
San Francisco, California

Name:--Tribe:------------------------------

Address:--

City:--State:------------------------------

Zip :------------------------------

Donation $3.00 for year 1970

soaked clothes. I pulled him back again and a wave broke over us, sucking us both under. The noise was deafening and disorientating, his yells muffled underwater.

'Let me go!' he screamed when we broke the surface.

He was too strong, too determined. In seconds the cold began to sap my strength. I started to lose my grip. I couldn't hold him back. He broke away, pushed on towards the deep. In that moment I knew what he – the watchman, the sentinel – had been waiting for.

Suddenly in the waves a corpse was floating before him. Pop sprang back in recognition, falling against me so that we both went down again, our wheeling limbs flailing against it and each other. A white silence of terror grasped me, deafening me, slowing us down until we were all but frozen.

Then we heaved ourselves up and back, our eyes fixed on the grey, bloated body in prison uniform. We fell onto the stony beach gasping for breath, trembling with cold and shock. When I could hear again, I realised that the terrible humming had stopped.

'They have him,' said Pop. 'Their sacrifice.'

I didn't sleep again that night. Instead I found a change of clothes and stayed on the rock. At dawn I watched a lone boat make its way to the island, the rising sun catching its wake as it outmanoeuvred a Coast Guard cutter.

As I stepped on board to head ashore, the waves sucked and hissed under the bow. Across the bay a seal, mottled with white and black spots, rolled among the swells.

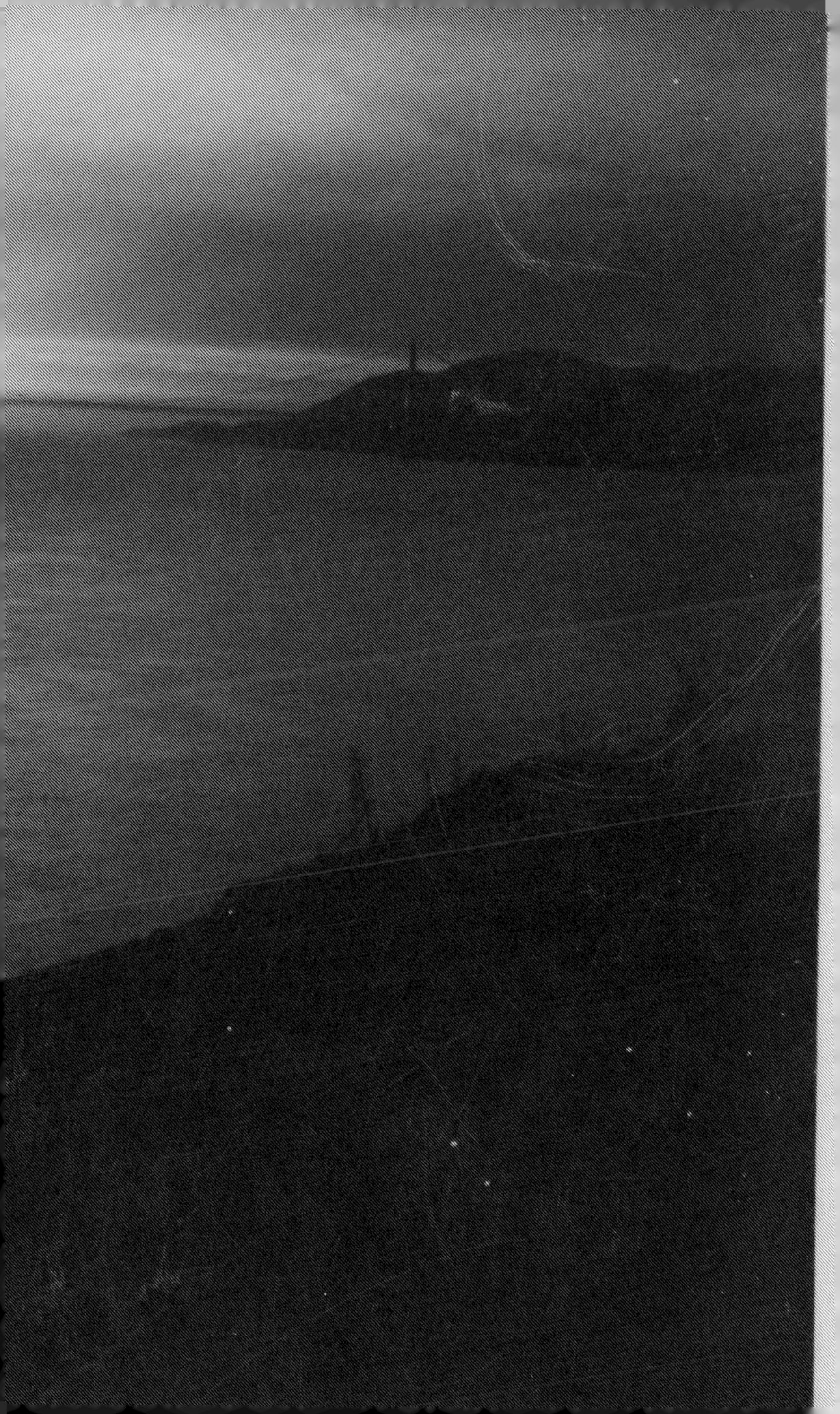

‘The most terrifying fact about the universe is not that it is hostile, but that it is indifferent,’ I heard him say as I stared at his photograph. He took a last pull on the cigarette and added, ‘However vast the darkness, we must supply our own light.’

Stanley Kubrick said those words in a 1960s interview. This morning I retyped and edited them (a little). He’s gone now of course, like almost everyone in this book, as I will be too, although not quite yet. That’s him on the next page, standing beside the camera and laughing with Peter Sellers, living on even though he hasn’t drawn breath in almost 20 years. It’s no fluke that Kubrick died within a couple of weeks of Qiao, when the Chinese New Year closed the 20th century.

I had found the production stills from *Dr Strangelove*, the Cold War comedy in which an insane general triggers nuclear holocaust, on a shelf beneath the archive’s high glass dome. On a wide oak worktable I laid out two dozen photographs of director Kubrick and actors Sellers and George C. Scott. In the film Sellers played three roles including President of the United States. Scott played General Buck Turgidson. I’ll never forget the scene where he imitates a low-flying B-52 on a bomb run. Or when Slim Pickens rides a warhead to Armageddon.

In a crew shot I identified the assistant director Eric Rattray, continuity person Pamela Carlton and an unnamed ‘script girl’ with stopwatch in hand, on the warpath. Everyone was playing a role, everyone had a story. I couldn't tell them all. I had to choose one story, in one space, in one time and - as movies do - make a little bit of it immortal, to give us forever, until doomsday.

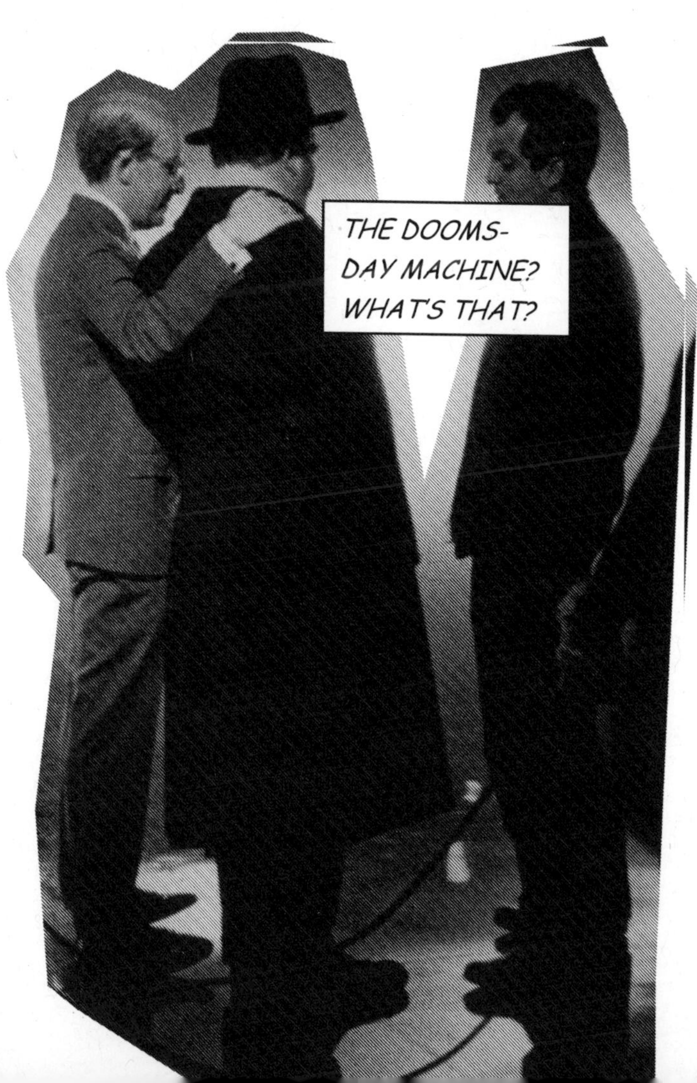

Strange Love

Shepperton Studios

28.02.1963

In the War Room: a ring of light, a green baize poker table and 26 military men gambling with the fate of mankind. We are in a dark cathedral, a bomb shelter at the end of the world, a two shot on 50mm T2.3 Angenieux lens.

'The Doomsday Machine? What's that?'

Peter is playing President. He's on the hotline to the Soviets, facing Armageddon. He's wearing the grey suit and charcoal tie. The key light glints off his bald head. In front of him is a notebook binder entitled *World Targets in Mega Deaths.*

Don't rush it, Peter. Enjoy it while you still can. Your timing is so good on the set. And in bed, I suppose. If only it had been better in the bloody car this morning.

The Doomsday Machine? It's 'a device that will destroy all human and animal life on earth'.

Today.

At the cut the crew uncoils like a rusty spring. Sparks yelp up at the catwalk, start moving lamps along the gantry. Carpenters resume their hammering. Gaffers whine for a tea break. I don't bother looking up. I just stay calm and quiet and jot down the scene's timing. A script girl's job is to help monitor continuity, to watch for costume changes and jarring jumps. It's a trainee position, the stepping-stone to becoming the crew's mother hen. I'm meant to be objective, to stand above the fray, not to get horizontal with Peter bloody Sellers. I don't pay him any attention, even though the bastard is now laughing. He's walking off the set without so much as a glance at in my direction, laughing.

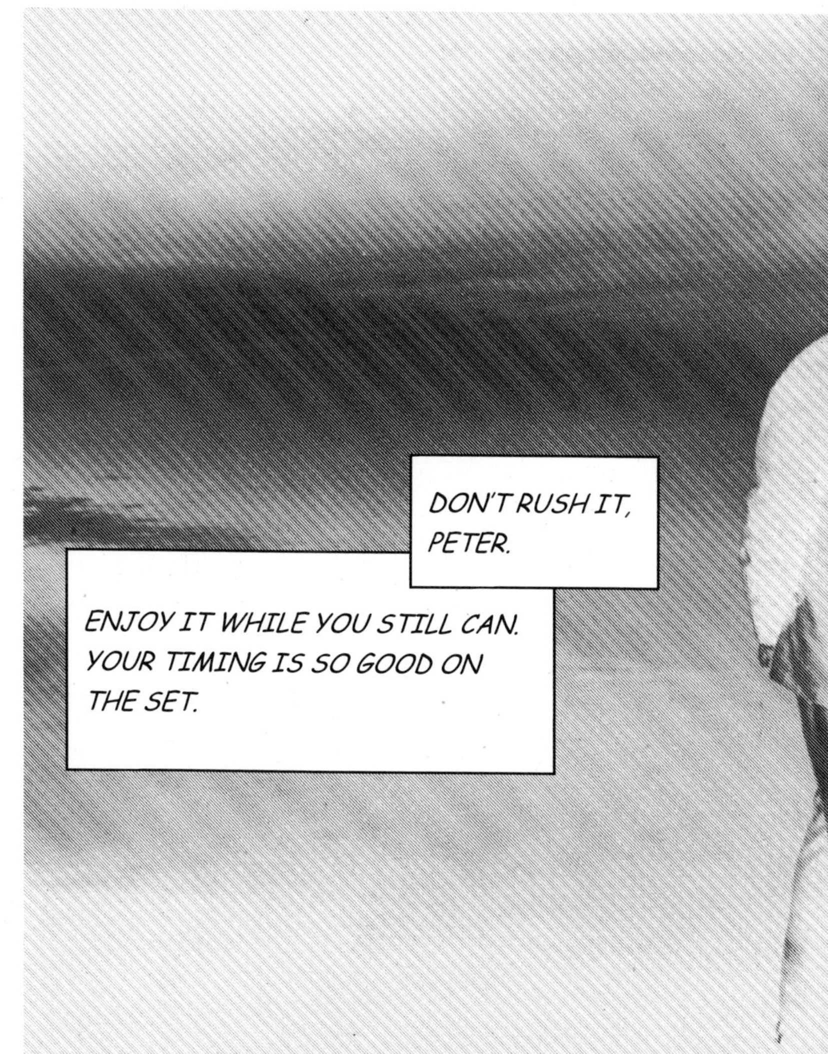

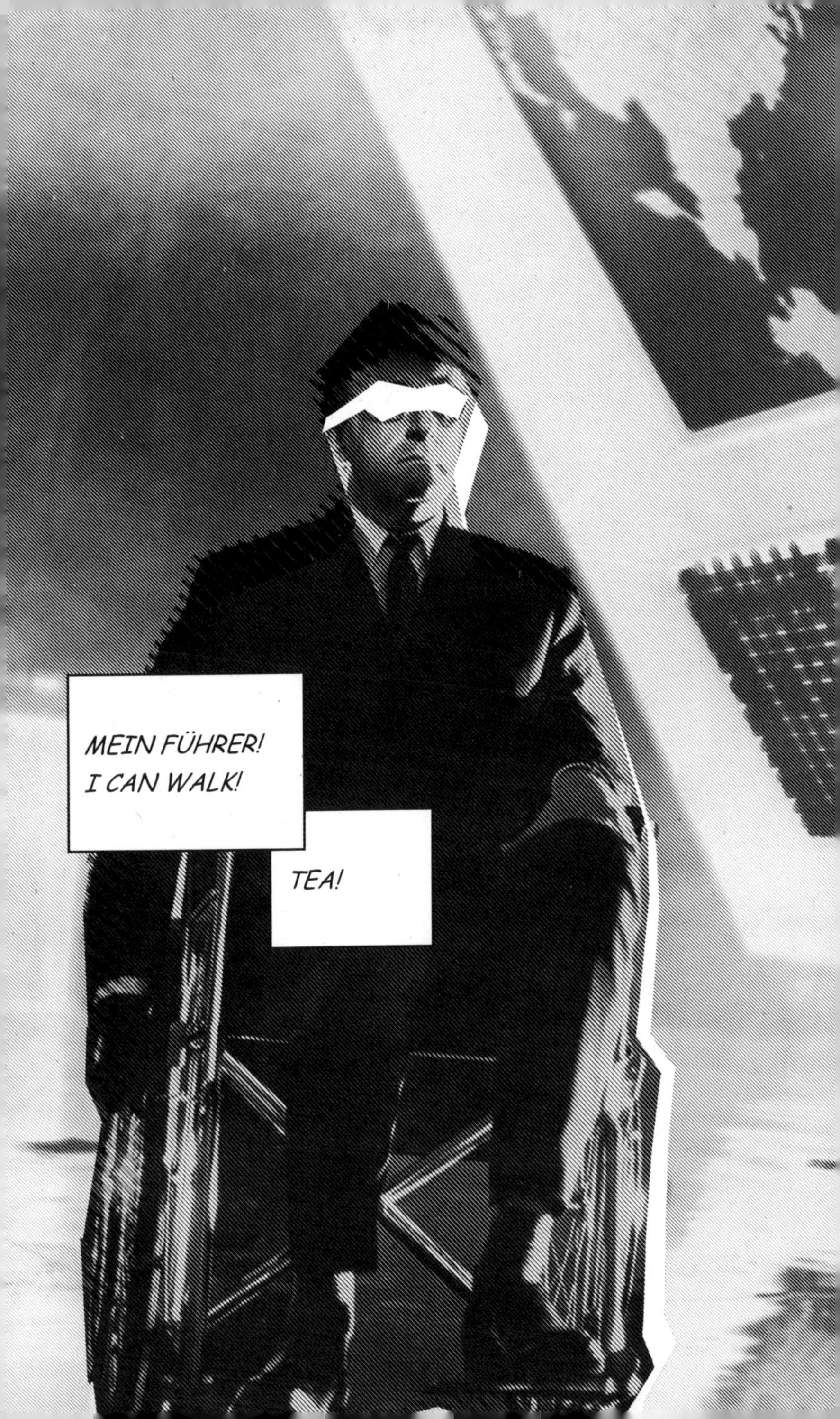
MEIN FÜHRER!
I CAN WALK!
TEA!

I could kill him. By rights, I should kill him.

'What's the next shot please, Mr Kubrick?' Stanley's assistant Eric is shouting, right in my ear.

I don't know how anyone can think in this racket. There's too much noise, both inside and outside my head. A film set is the most pig-headed, most dishonest working space ever devised by man. I hate the sham of it, the stupid illusion, the squalor hidden behind the scenery, and above all I hate what goes on behind the dressing room doors.

That's why I must act. Why I must do something. But what? I must stay calm, must not let them see me hurt. I sharpen my pencil to give myself time to think.

'We'll do the reverse shot on George,' calls Stanley, interrupting my thoughts.

MR SCOTT, YOUR
CLOSE-UP IS NEXT.

George.

Dear George.

George C. Scott: Broadway star, Obie winner, actor with the biggest soft heart and most explosive temper. I should have had a drink with him on that first night and saved myself this grief. I'm not unattractive – dark eyes, long hair, figure rounded in a pleasing way. He wouldn't have led me such a merry dance. He's nice to me today because he senses what happened, like the whole damn crew. I never can keep a secret, not on or off the set, not even at the end of the world.

George is backstage at the chessboard. He's been planning his move for thirty minutes. Stanley never told him that he used to play for money. Stanley walks backstage, scans the chessboard, makes his move.

'How in hell did I fall for that?' asks George.

George hadn't seen the trap. Neither had I.

This whole sorry business is like a screwball chess game. There's a clock and you make your moves within a certain time. If you don't, then you forfeit, even if you think you're ahead. A smart player with three minutes on the clock and ten moves left will spend two minutes on the first move, because she knows that if she doesn't get it right, the game is lost.

But I won't be losing this game, despite my idiotic first move. I'll not be a victim again. I take a deep breath. At the next set-up I will get as close to Peter as I can, closer than ever, right beside the camera. I'll have my stopwatch in one hand, and my revenge in the other.

Where did this strange love begin? With the Bomb, with the Wall, with Hitler. Stanley had optioned the book for $3,500, adapted it straight, and asked me to time the script. But even I could see the first draft didn't work. Every time Stanley had imagined a scene, or tried to put meat on the bones, he had to leave things out to keep it from being funny. It was around then that I told him the story about Hitler living in Liverpool.

Back before the 1914 war, Hitler had a half-brother in Toxteth. He stayed with him on Upper Stanhope Street for a couple of months, playing chess, standing on the terraces at Anfield and – from what I'd heard – feeling rather happy with life. Of course he wasn't Führer then. I told Stanley that's why he later bombed Liverpool and Coventry, because men always destroy the things they love. Stanley laughed at that – even though he didn't believe me – and went back to the *Strangelove* script. He started to put absurdities at the heart of it, like Strategic Air Command's motto being 'Peace is Our Profession'. Slip on a banana skin and annihilate the human race. That's how it began.

Then Peter came on the scene.

Camera is in position but lights aren't ready. Lights are never ready. Plus the photo spots are blistering the screens again. Ten miles of electrical cable snakes behind them. The air conditioners make a racket between takes. I can't stand the noise but Stanley likes the look of the screens: square electronic maps above the giant circular table within the triangle of the War Room – menacing, claustrophobic, jarring into pitch-black space.

I wish the whole thing would go up in smoke.

On this last morning Peter and I drove through the studio gate behind Stanley and Ken Adam, the art director. The top was down on Ken's red E-type. Stanley says he and Ken get more work done in their thirty-minute drive from London than during the whole rest of the day on set. He likes to hear Ken's war stories. Heinie the Tank-Buster was Ken's nickname, because he'd been born in Berlin and was one of only three German nationals in the RAF, flying Hawker Typhoons. He didn't know about Hitler in Liverpool either.

'Eric, this light rig has to come up a couple of inches,' Stanley tells the assistant director. 'And where's Ken Adam?'

The chess game is a way to keep George calm and focused during the downtime, while he runs through his lines. He treats them like gospel, gets them word perfect every time. Unlike Peter. This morning Peter was so morose – not because of me, that'd be a pretty lie – that Stanley had cleared the set to rehearse with him until his mood brightened. 'A device which will destroy all human and animal life on earth' tickled them both, and Peter started to ad-lib the line. He rewrites half his dialogue this way, feeling it through, letting ideas click. Once the camera's rolling he'll improvise again, until he

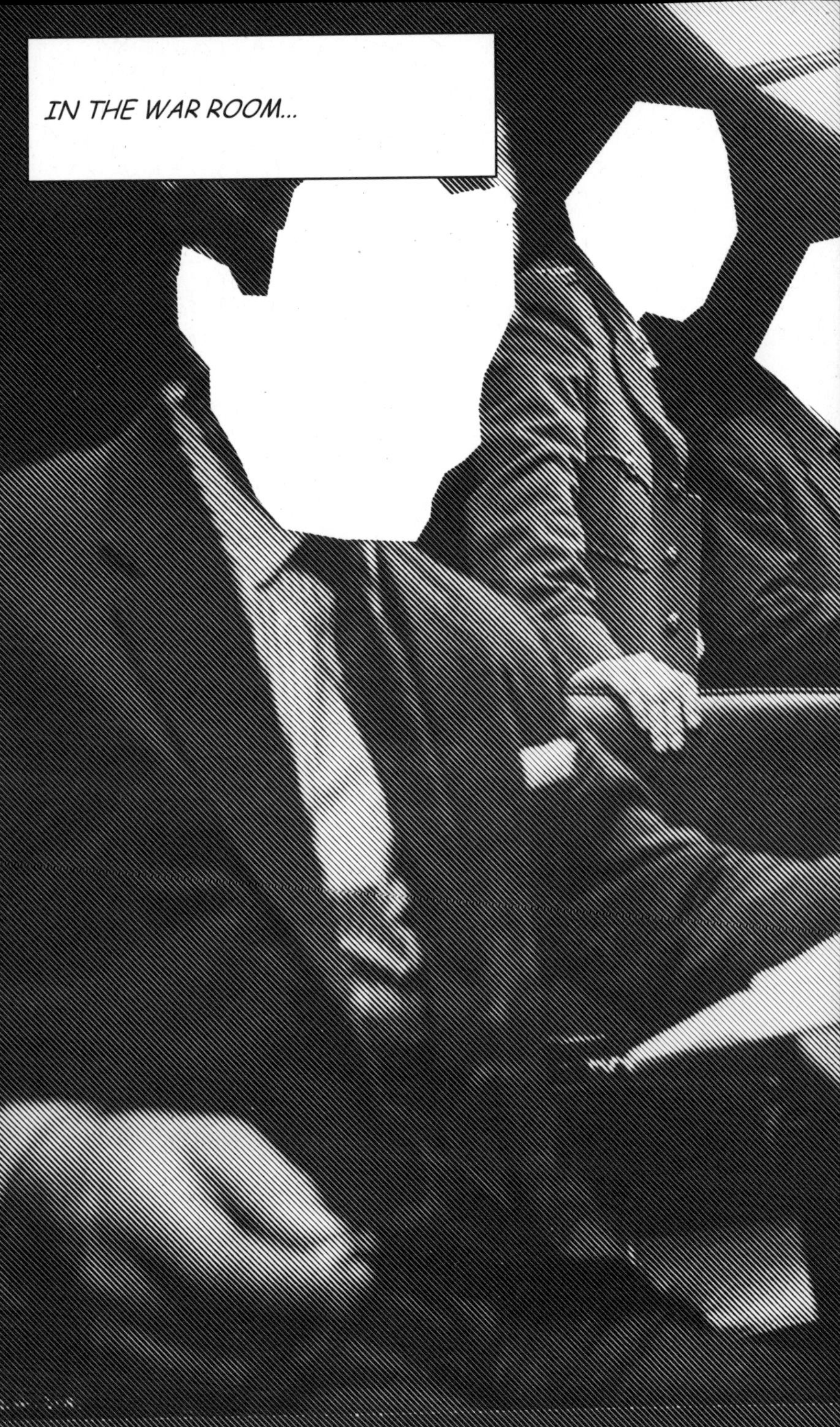
IN THE WAR ROOM...

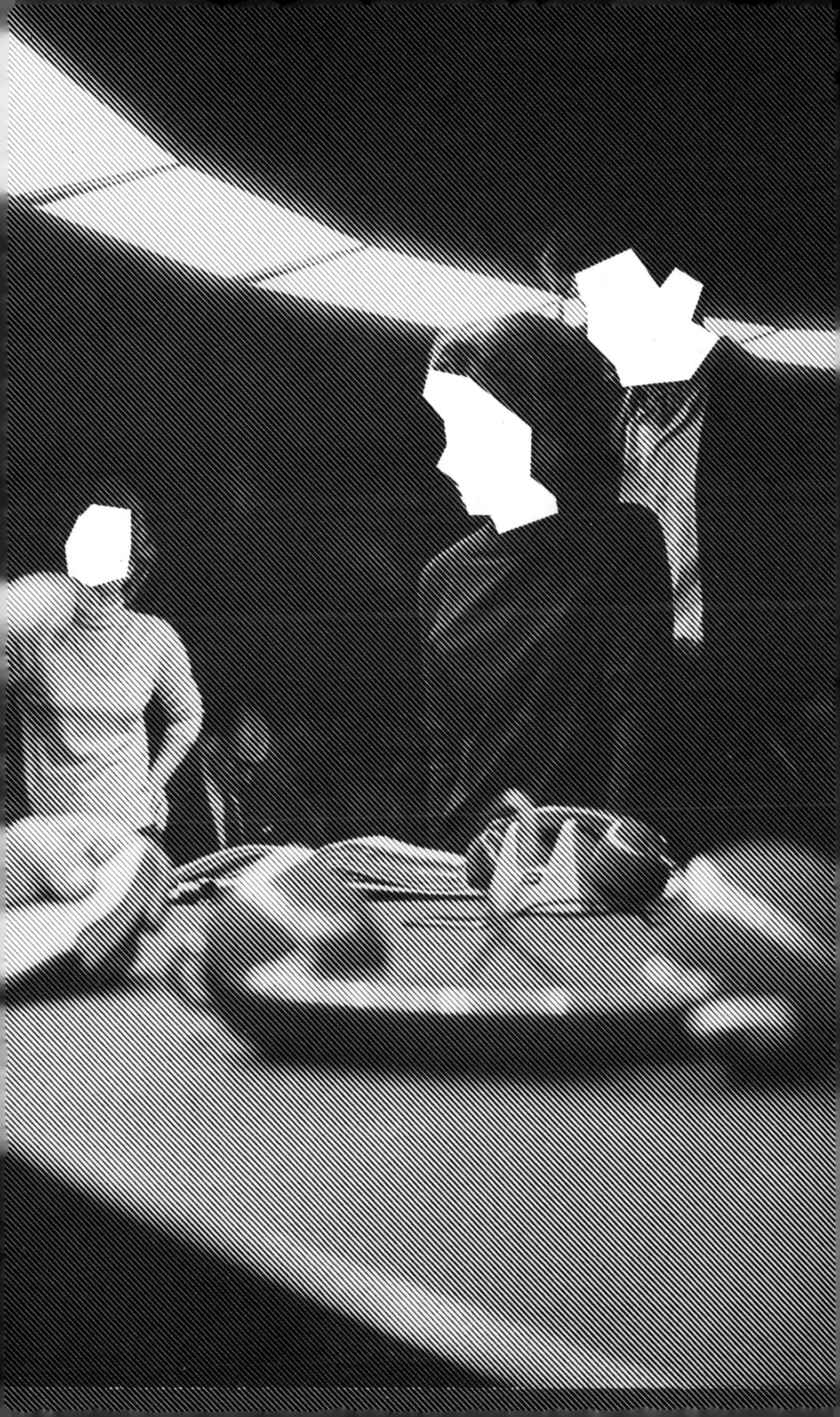

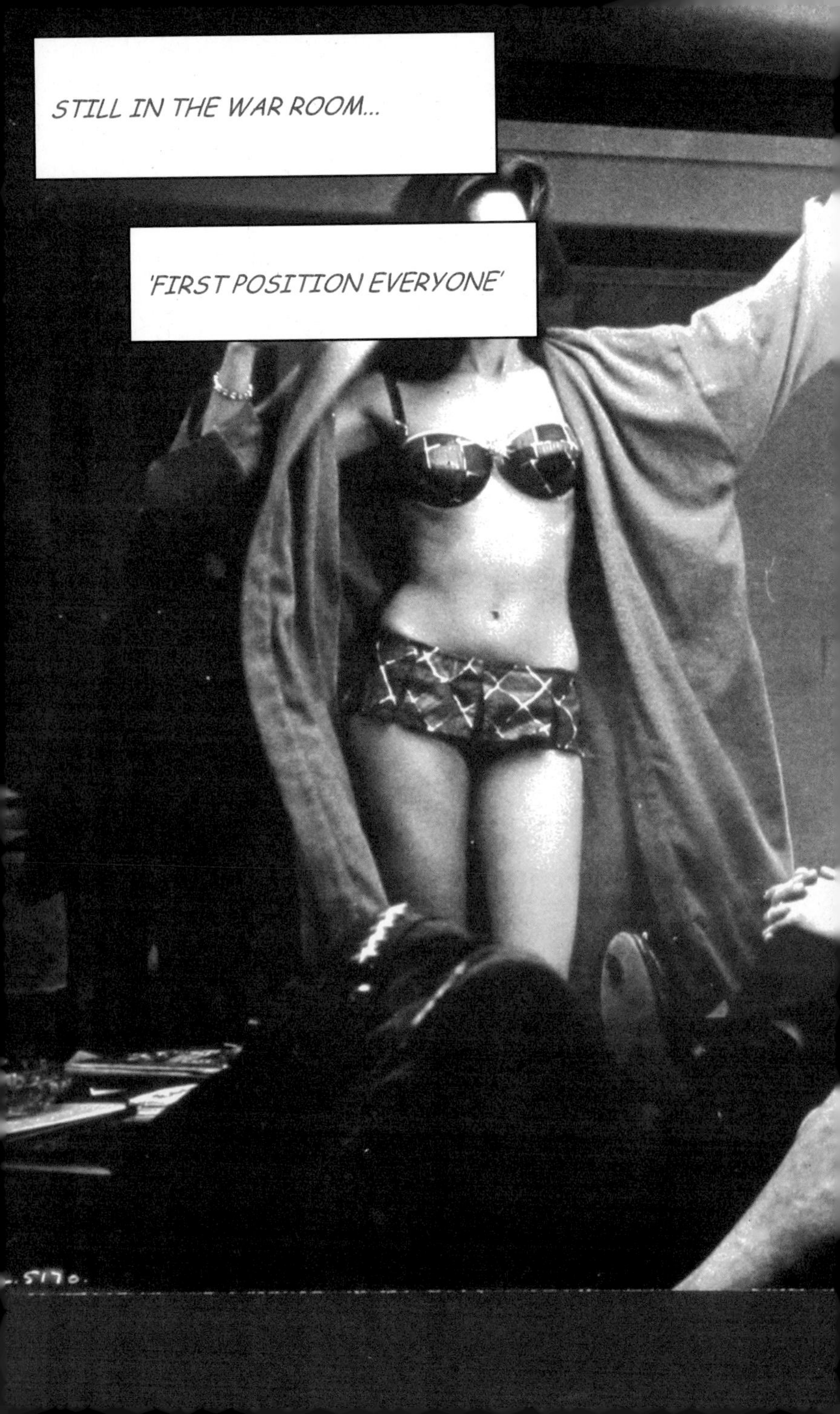

STILL IN THE WAR ROOM...

'FIRST POSITION EVERYONE'

HELLO. WHERE IS EVERYBODY?
LET'S DO IT

reaches a kind of comic ecstasy. It's beautiful to see, that ecstasy – while it lasts. Third take is best for him, before boredom kicks in and kills his performance.

Last night Peter told me the only time he's really happy is not when he's with Anne and the kids, not when he's preparing a part, and not with me, but in the moment he's doing the shot on the floor. When that moment comes out of him, and he's done it, that's the time when the achievement – the full feeling of achievement – comes to him.

That's how he invented Strangelove's accent, in the moment. When I told him about Hitler in Liverpool he started goose-stepping around the bedroom in his boxer shorts like a mad wind-up toy, shouting 'Mein Führer! I can walk!'

How can any woman not love a man like that?

'Tea,' calls Eric.

The barn-like stage doors swing open and daylight pours onto the set as sparks and gaffers shimmy down from the overhead rigging. The crew bunches around the tea lady with her battered silver urn and plates of flaccid cheese rolls.

'Hello? Where is everybody?' calls Stanley.

He's pacing the floor. He can't stand our English set-clearing ritual – union tea breaks at 10 and 2, lunch at the pub, crew ready to knock off by 5. We're already six days behind schedule.

'Eric, I need to see Ken.'

Ken is on stage 2. He's been playing in his mocked-up B-52 cockpit for hours. Boys and their toys. Apparently the FBI now think Ken's a threat to national security because a couple of air force men said it was a perfect copy.

'Where the hell is Ken?' shouts Stanley.

George has made his move. N–QB3. Knight to Queen's Bishop 3. Tea breaks tick him off too.

'Sometimes while waiting for these guys to finish their goddamn tea my life loses all meaning,' he says to Stanley.

I watch Stanley as he looks at the board. He's calculating. QB3 isn't a strong move, doesn't threaten, allows a timely Na5. I've never let on that I play chess too.

'English coffee tastes like cat's piss,' adds George.

'What time will we run the rushes?' Stanley asks me.

The most terrifying fact about the universe is not that it is hostile, but that it is indifferent.

'Sparks?' calls Eric. 'Are we ready to go?'

At last. I can't stand this waiting any longer. It's now, or never. Plus George has moved again. White to Qa4 taking a7 pawn. Now it'll be Ra8, Qxb7 and the end of his Queen.

'First positions everyone.'

'Camera's ready, Stanley,' says Eric.

Light's good. Sound is ready. I am ready too.

Stanley is at the camera. George is in position. And Peter is back

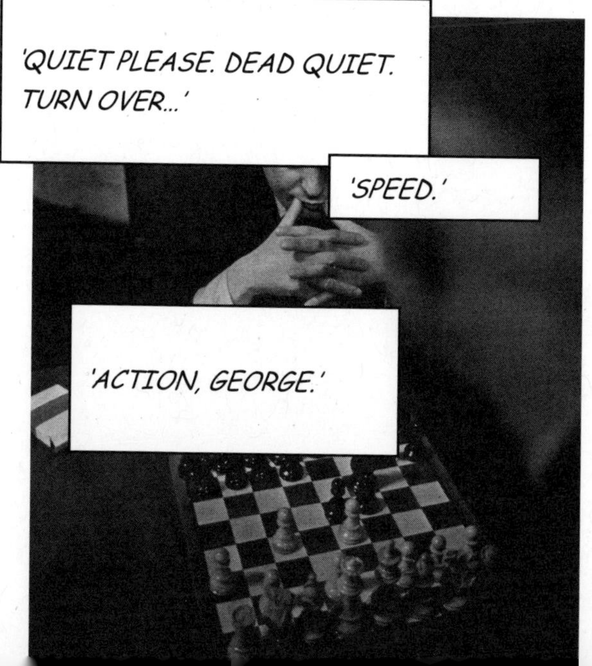

on the set, beside me. He touches my shoulder, the bastard. He's calling me *his* script girl, it's so demeaning. I feel his breath on my ear. My pencil couldn't be sharper.

'Let's do it,' says Stanley.

Yes, let's do it.

'Quiet please. Dead quiet. Turn over...'

'Speed.'

'Action.'

The camera whirrs. Sweat glistens on foreheads.

George C. Scott turns to Peter and says, 'Mr President, we stand at the threshold of history.'

The bomb is about to drop.

The tip of my pencil flashes under the studio lights.

I lift my arm to strike.

At that same moment, as the B-52s stand poised at their failsafe points and a white Queen threatens to take the black King, Fate makes its move. High above the Shepperton stage, a gaffer misses his footing on the lighting rig, a loose plank wobbles and an arc of stewed tea leaps from its chipped mug to fall in a twisting spiral onto the script girl and Sellers. Her hair is ruined, his bald head is soaked and – as she springs forward – the course of lives is changed forever at that strange point where love meets art.

'Cut!' shouts Stanley in fury. 'You can't fight in here. This is the War Room.'

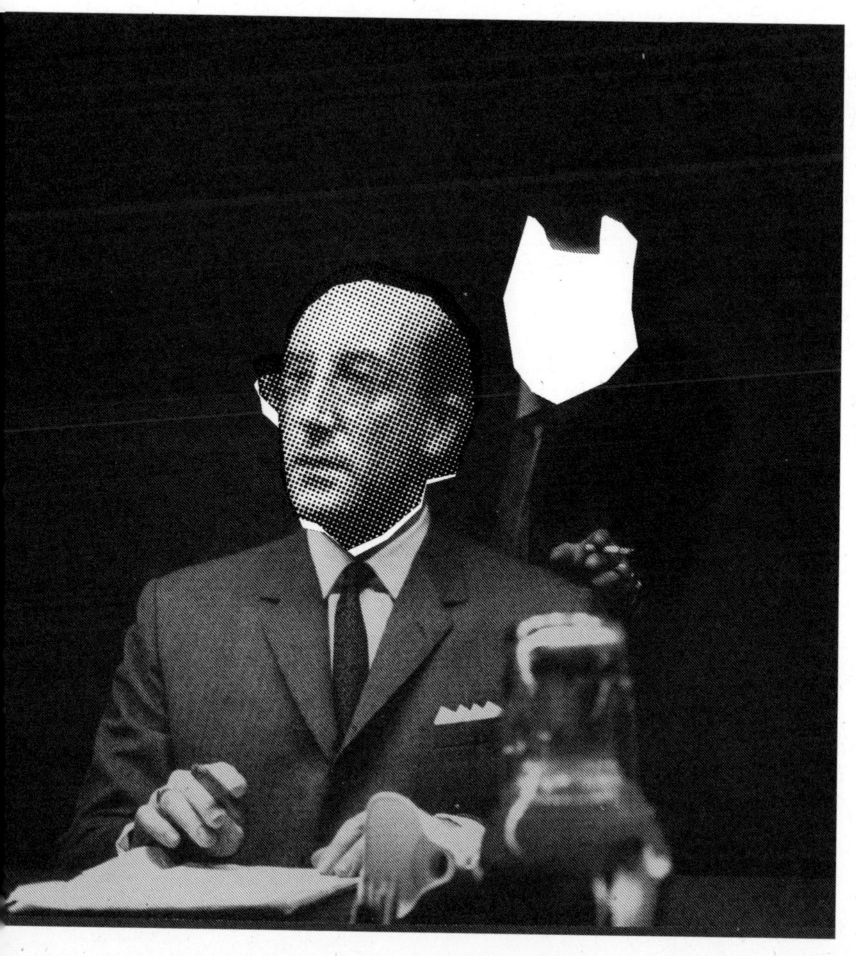

One day in the archive I found a most mysterious album. Instead of photographs it contained hundreds of locks of women's hair. Through the 1940s and 1950s an unknown Ohio hairdresser had collected her clients' curls and braids, mounted them with care in cellophane packets and added comments and names.

'A friend of long-standing. She endured my wild experiments while I was learning the beauty business.'
Miss Hilda Stark

'She has snappy brown eyes, pink cheeks and a smile for everyone.'
Mrs L.N. Owens

'Wanna know what is so rare as a day in June? A natural blonde - and here she is - blue eyes and all.'
Miss Dorothy Tham, 396 Watson Street

All the hairdresser's clients were white. All have now moved on to that great beauty parlour in the sky. But some had been alive in the year that a local black man was arrested - wrongfully - for raping a child, and white rioters burned down the City Building to find and lynch him.

Several years ago an Akron undertaker came across the album and invested hundreds of hours tracing the hairdresser's clients. At the back of the album were pages of his funeral home letterhead, on which he had printed their birth and death certificates, drawn family trees and noted new addresses. I was curious to know why he would bother to do such a thing, but when I rang him he was abrupt and refused to answer any questions. He claimed to have bought the album on eBay, from 'someone out-of-town', even though the hair salon had been only a few blocks from his parlour. He said that he'd sold it to the archive and washed his hands of it. He ended the call.

His reticence made me even more puzzled. I made another call to the States and learnt from an old friend that Akron had been a deeply divided place in the 1950s. All America's tyre makers - Goodyear, BF Goodrich, Firestone - had been based in the town, and workers had been drawn to the city from West Virginia, South Carolina and Mississippi. I was told that the whites had come off southern farms with their old prejudices, and that the black incomers had lived in the 'projects' - subsidised housing developments - on North Street. No whites went near Wooster Avenue or Howard Street. No blacks went to the white bars or neighbourhoods.

In the 1960s race riots would tear through run-down East Akron, but until then blacks were treated like dirt, abused, even murdered. I researched the unknown hairdresser's story until no more facts could be distilled - and then, with the cagey undertaker in mind, I discovered a life.

Hair

Akron, Ohio 05.08.1954

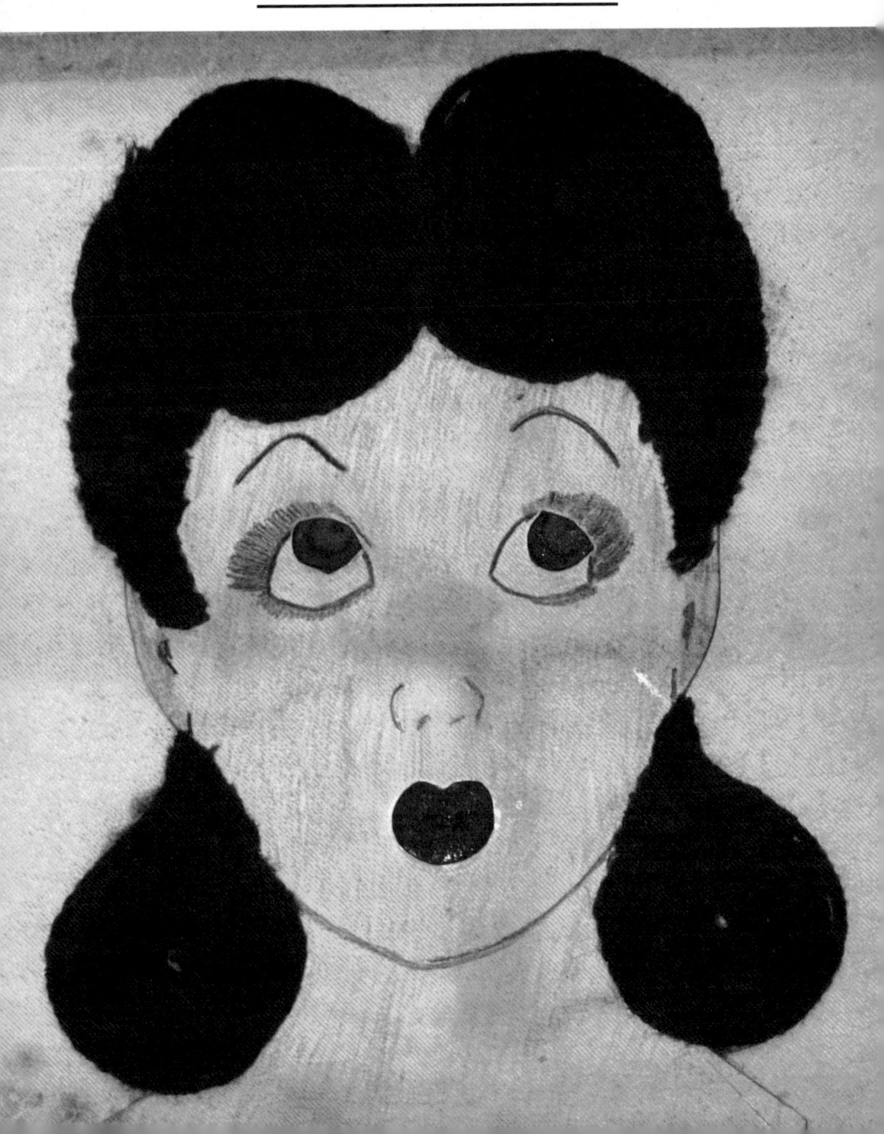

I fix the features, it's what I do best. I shaves them, men and women both. I wash their hair, taking my time, reading the strands between my fingers – thick and dickty, thin and wise, tangled and mean. I close the lips through which no word will pass again. I cleans the eyes and shut them tight. Then I set myself down on a stool and open my bag.

Any fool can use cream and a rub of rouge. Me, I'm smart with wax. I soften it in my palm, shape it with a spatula. I use it to hide missing skin, to dress a bullet hole, to veil the rope burn from hangings. I gives peace to the mother of a battered baby. I makes the victim smile again. I brings them poor souls to life for one last moment, brushing bruises and jaundice out o' sight and memory. Mister Leon calls me an artist and I thank him for it, but in truth all that I does is stand between the living and the living that died, like I always done.

Back home in Issaqueena County, Daddy was a sharecropper. He worked the land, bought on credit, sunk in debt. He and Mama did three jobs a day, night and day. Only time they took off, apart from the Sabbath, was payday. Daddy would set on the porch and lie up a mess.

'Wait a minute Conrad, let me put a dime in your dollar,' he'd say, straining against the other menfolk to tell a tale.

'Lightning comes when angels look in the mirror,' Conrad'd lie.

'And thunder happens when rain barrels roll across Heaven,' Daddy'd lie back at him, hollering and laughing.

Sometimes the women'd stop to break breath and sing with the men,

'Oh, oh
I won't be long here.
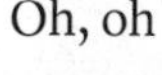
Oh, oh

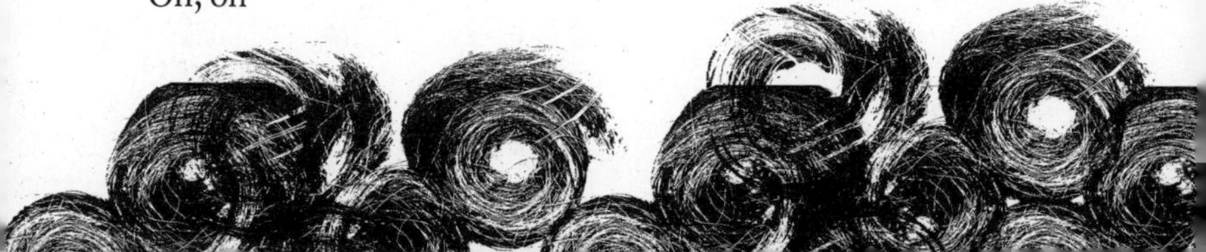

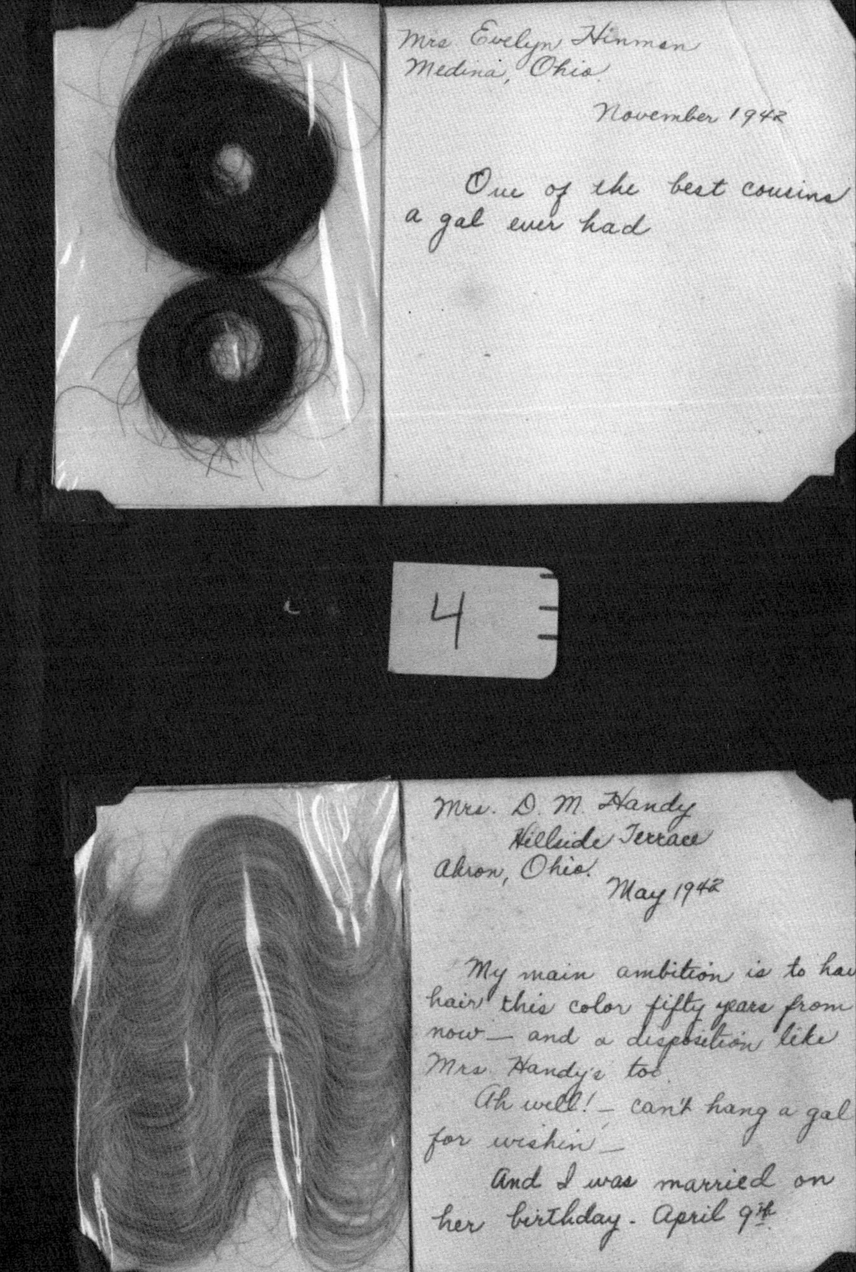

Mrs Evelyn Hinman
Medina, Ohio

November 1942

One of the best cousins a gal ever had

4

Mrs. D. M. Handy
Hillside Terrace
Akron, Ohio.

May 1942

My main ambition is to hav hair this color fifty years from now— and a disposition like Mrs. Handy's too.

Ah well! — can't hang a gal for wishin'—

And I was married on her birthday. April 9th.

2

Mrs. L. S. Baechtel
949 Amelia Ave.
Kenmore, Ohio.
November 1942

She had visions of me in a beauty shop in Virginia – Nice work if you can get it.

5

Mrs. Felix Dorraugh
1610 Hillside Terrace,
Akron, Ohio.
July 1942

3

Dark gonna catch me,

Dark gonna catch me.'

No surprise then that I began to learn about the Work on that porch. It came up out of the stories, or the stories out of it: God and Devil, root doctors and mojo bags, cures for swellings, and midwives who'd call a new-born's spirit. In them days few folks could afford a needle doctor, fewer still had time for one. Daddy broke his leg when I was thirteen years old. He could not work and the debt collectors took away our mule. That was when Mama first sent me out with a swamper. I gathered herbs and roots, shells and bones, for conjure. God used magic spells and mighty words to create the world in six days. At home I cared for Daddy and he done healed that old leg in six weeks. Above the cooker I set a jar filled with honey and St John's Wort for sweet works. But as there's a dark side to life, 'specially on a plantation, I puts beside it a break-up jar of vinegar and goofer dust, which is dirt scooped out of a grave.

That's where the hair thing started, of course. Hair is full of power. Just one strand can be used to put the roots on someone. Never throw hair in the trash, I told my sisters and brothers. Never wash it down the drain. Birds and rats might steal it, use it to build nests, bring on headaches, or worse. Much worse. The more I learned about the Work, the more I kept quiet. For everyone knew about the spells and recipes, knew they was part of us, part of where we'd come from.

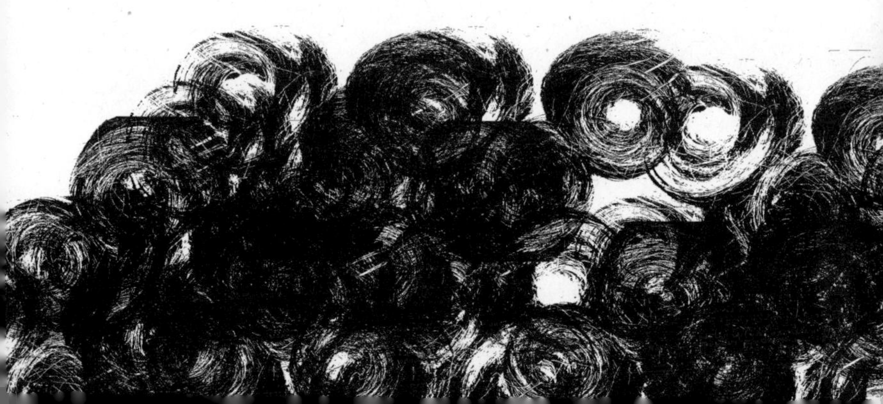

Hair, that was the first thing I loved about Leroy. His hair was silky and shiny. He didn't cut it short, grew it long. First time I saw him he was walking out with a girl, walking along Deer Creek like he owned it. Pride's not a honourable quality, but there and then I wanted Leroy as my own. And that was how it would be.

Maybe I oughtn't have done what I did. Maybe I should have stopped myself. But sometimes I just cannot. Sometimes my head gets all hot and my sight goes all anyhow and I do stuff that others mightn't do. I followed Leroy and the girl and picked a pinch of dust from a footprint of each of them. I mixed his with a dog's hair, hers with a cat's. I buried them in my special place, at a crossroads of the paths of the seen and unseen. Two days later Leroy and she started to fight.

They broke up the week before he was called up, and I was there to catch him when he fell, to be the girl in his heart for the whole time he was away at the war. He done got my name tattooed on his arm. On the night he left Issaqueena County I took a lock of his hair and braided it together with my own, gave it to him to keep him safe, to bring him back to me.

Land shapes the people, and people shape the land. If you don't treat it right, it shakes you off like a dog shakes off fleas. Leroy came back, but not to stay. He wanted off of the land and out of Mississippi. We

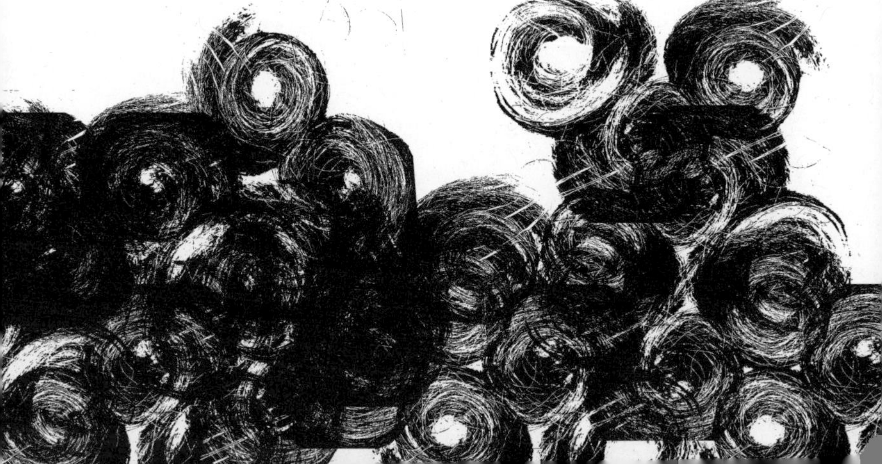

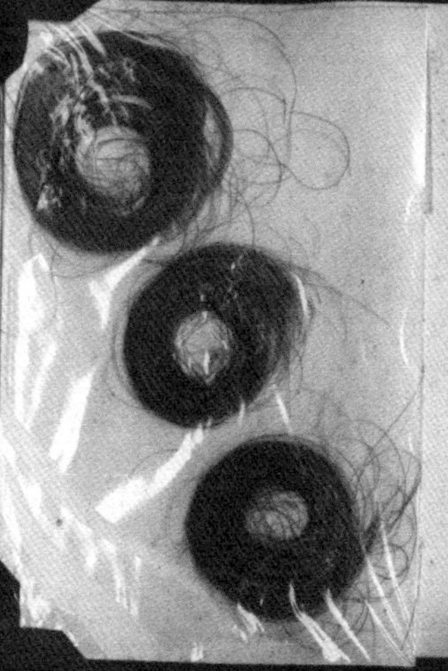

Mrs. Kathleen Williams,
1723 Honodle Avenue,
Akron, Ohio.
June 1942

"Katie"

Moved to Des Moines, Iowa
June, 1943.

We hate to see you go, but
best of luck!

27B

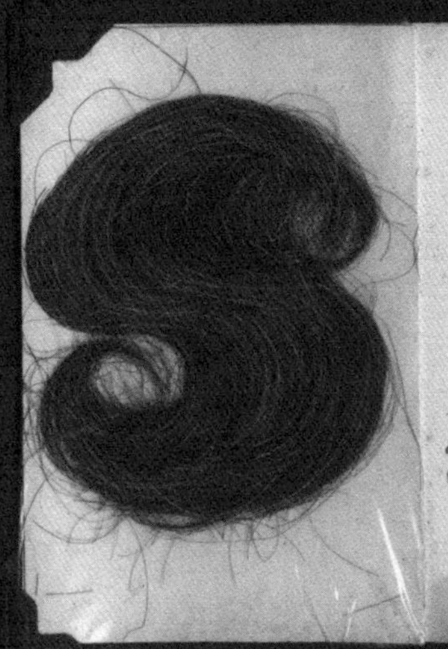

Mrs. William Bonfield
766 Caddo Avenue,
Akron, Ohio.
June 1942.

Our next door neighbor an
were good friends in spite
of that!

Mrs Betty Cliff
282 Malasia Road
Akron, Ohio.

October 1942

Nice red curls huh?

28

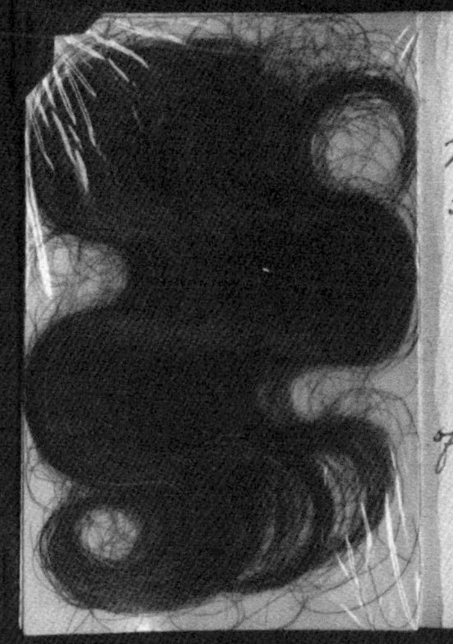

Mrs. Daisy Timms,
557 St. Leger Avenue,
Akron, Ohio.

July 1942.

I wish I had her sense of humor—

30

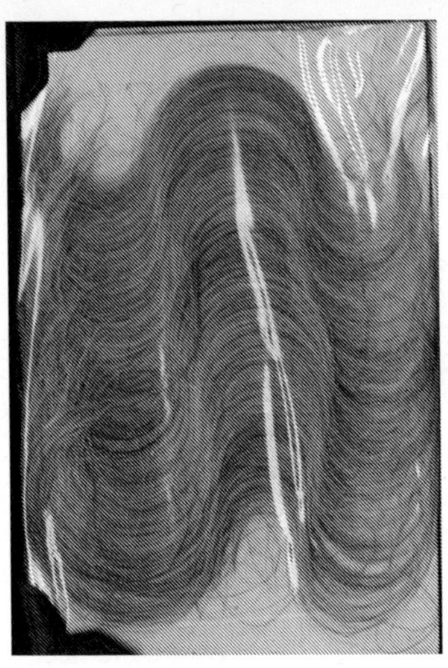

married at the First Baptist Church and pointed our toenails north. Our honeymoon was spent on the backseat of a Greyhound. A buddy from the army had said there was opportunities for New Negroes in Akron. Summit County they called the place, because it stood on a summit, because from it half the rivers ran north to the Great Lakes, and half ran south to the Tuscarawas, down the Ohio, into the Mississippi. All the world's rubber companies were set up in Akron.

Leroy found work on the line at Goodyear, earning $75 a week (whites made $90 depending on overtime). The money was good, so good we celebrated every Friday with a Banana Split. That first summer at the Dairy Queen we'd stand in the same line as whites. No water fountain said 'Colored Only'.

'Life's different up here,' Leroy would say, proud to have fought for America in the war, proud to be one of the first Negroes at the plant. 'We's all equal now.'

Oh, oh
I won't be long here.
Oh, oh.

In Akron I didn't get no baby, not that year or the next, not even after a mess of recipes. At the projects we came to have anything a body could need: nice stove, refrigerator, new radio. I got pretty clothes and three pairs of shoes. But my real wishing came to nothing. My arms felt so empty. I ached to have a baby. And the more I was wishing, the more often Leroy'd come back from work and just fall asleep, dead asleep, in the chair. Them Ohio winters got to be so cold and dark.

Man got physical strength and he can beat a woman, but woman got something stronger. She got three keys: one for her heart, one to the kitchen and one to the man's future. Without them no man can survive for long. So when Leroy went missing I figured I knew the reason. I couldn't give him a son, no, but I weren't giving him up, 'cause I knew, like it says in Corinthians, without love we're nothing. Nothing. I went to his buddy's place. I went to the Dairy Queen. I walked along Howard Street where no lady goes. I hung around the Goodyear gate and spoke to everybody, yet nobody done seen him there or anywhere else. In our room I took nine red candles, wrote his name three times on each, washed them in Van Van and lit them while calling out his name. Still he didn't come home.

I had a steady job at a beauty salon over on Cuyahoga, but without Leroy's pay I needed more to get by. I started a home hair cutting service, only to end up rubbing a little white lady's foot, massaging it, then making her tea in a china cup. Her feet weren't her biggest problem. Whenever I cleaned her kitchen she made me save the dishwater, even though she had an abundance of money.

Next lady I worked for had the filthiest house I ever saw. I scrubbed it top to bottom, polished all the floors with Johnson's Paste, and when I was done she told me I was the worst maid in Christendom. When I reminded her I'd come to cut her hair, she told me to get my you-know-what out her house. She never gave me one nickel, and I walked away.

But the ache didn't go away. At the end of every day I'd open the door to our room, praying that Leroy would be waiting in the armchair saying, 'Sugar, I don't know what came over me. Let's go back home now.' Because for sure that's what I wanted to do, deep in my heart, to float away down the Tuscarawas to the Ohio and down the Mississippi. Only Leroy he was never there.

When I was a child I believed an undertaker carried the dead underground, carried them down into the earth and handed them over to God or Devil. In a way I'se still believing it today, although Mister Leon sure don't.

'When we die the lights go out,' he told me at the interview. He wore a black three-piece. His collar had wing tips. His hands were as white as the belly-feathers of a screech owl. 'There is no life beyond the grave. There are no ghosts. The dead are dead.'

But I knew it weren't true.

None of the other girls at the labour office wanted the job, saying I was crazy, going down into the cellar of that big old house, working among all those stiffs, cleaning up after a mortician. I just told them that the sun rises and the sun goes down, even in Ohio.

On North Main Street I kept his fixing room in order. I set his tools in neat rows. At first when Mister Leon worked I went upstairs to dust the viewing room or rearrange the flowers. But then he needed another pair of hands and called me down, and so he saw that I had the touch. It weren't too long before I was helping him to wash faces and hands, to clean the dirt and blood from under the fingernails of mechanics and farm boys. I'd bend and flex their arms to ease rigor mortis. I'd massage their legs as Mister Leon pumped the embalming fluid. Our work weren't done for the dead, he said. He thought they was beyond caring. He worked for the living, for that last look into the open coffin, to give a memory picture to last a lifetime.

It came natural that I started to help him with the grooming, by virtue of me being a beautician. In the morning at the salon I'd pluck and perm the living, straightening their hair with hot combs or shaping it into curly bobs, then in the afternoon in the funeral parlour I'd spruce up the dead. I'd rub massage cream onto foreheads, apply a dash of red to cheeks and chin, brush brown cosmetic onto eyelids. Hair was dried and combed, loose strands stuck back on with rubber cement. Lips was Vaselined and sealed. I'd glue the eyes shut.

In that North Main cellar I looked into the face of the father of six who'd lost his job and hung hisself in the woods, not to be found before the start of hunting season. I stared at the redhead divorcee who'd put on her wedding dress before mixing Drano into her 7 Up. I combed the hair of car crash victims killed in a second, and cancer sufferers who'd slipped away after twenty years. I met people who'd died of sorrow, the corners of their mouths so down-turned that it was impossible to set them into a smile.

Later, upstairs, the great and the good of Akron would weep and wail, never suspecting that it was an angry Negro woman who'd helped to keep their dearly departed alive in their minds. Angry. Maybe it was because I was angry, because I'd got no man, got no child, that it also came natural to start collecting again: whiskers, hair clippings, crescent moon slivers of fingernail. I'd fold them into a Kleenex, slip them in my apron and take them back to my room. Here lie the remains of Jessica White, of Jeremy Fitzgerald, of Ernst Wagenknecht, and I'se holding on to them. I ain't letting go. Once I even stole a tooth.

Death awaits us all at the end of the road. So worst for me were the little babies born dead or soon dead, brought in from hospital ward or nursery crib, whose journey had been cut short. I cared for them with a mother's love, brushing colour onto their pale cheeks, leaving their mouth a little open as if they was only sleeping. When we lay them in their tiny caskets with a little rattle or teddy bear, it was like burying the future. I'd weep beside them for a spell, whisper them an old lullaby, before the lid was closed and screwed down forever.

I say worst of all, but that was before the police brought in Leroy. Mister Leon didn't handle Negroes of course, but he had a reputation for drownings, and I overheard the Chief ask him as a favour. I believed them until I saw the body. The police didn't want a black mortician to see the truth. On account of how terribly Leroy'd died.

I alone recognised him, recognised him from his damn tattoo, recognised him despite the rope burn from the lynching and flesh torn away by the river rocks. A group of nine southern boys had dumped him in the Tuscarawas with hands tied behind his back, dumped him and watched him splutter and sink. And the police knew. And they wanted no investigation. As if to say, there ain't no discrimination here.

Mister Leon let me prepare the body only because if he didn't, I told him, I'd tell the newspaper. He gave me mastic to fix the jaw, plaster of Paris to repair the fractured bones, a steady hand to piece together his skull. I wanted to make Leroy look good, so good. The living who have died wait for us in the next room, sending messages from time to time if we keep them in our hearts.

Folks say that when it rains at a burial, God wants the dead's tracks washed off the face of the earth. But it weren't Leroy's tracks that needed to be washed away. When I buried him at Glendale – alongside the Millers, Robinsons, Saalfields and Sherbondys, all the old white Akron families – I listened out, listened out for him to tell me what to do.

And I heard him.

At the very moment I was burying Leroy, over on Caddo Avenue a woman was soaking in her tub, listening to *Amos 'n' Andy*. She reached for the soap and knocked the radio into the water. Mister Leon collected her shocked blue body from the weeping family along with a few effects, whether for the viewing or to go in the coffin they didn't say. Among them was a photograph album that held no photographs. The lady had been owner of the East Akron Beauty

Salon, and inside her album she kept notes on her top clients, along with snips of their hair.

There before my eyes was a living part of Miss Hilda Stark, brunette and 'friend of long-standing'. 'She endured my wild experiments while I was learning the beauty business,' the lady hairdresser had written.

Next to Hilda's hair was part of Dorothy Tham – 'a natural blonde... blue eyes and all' – who lived at 396 Watson Street. Beside her the hairdresser had clipped a lock from Mrs Mabel Handy's head with the words, 'My main ambition is to have hair this color fifty years from now – and a disposition like Mrs Handy's too. Ah well! Can't hang a gal for wishin'.'

On the black pages were brown braids and red curls, split ends and Miss Dorothy Yocum, 'a very little Miss' who 'tried so hard not to cry when she got a "kink" in her neck under the permanent wave machine'. The album gave me white Akron, and the ingredients for conjure.

After the funeral was done, I went to City Hall with the names and addresses. I looked in the public register, found who was each woman's husband and brother, learned the birthdates of their sons. I discovered who was related and who had skipped town. I knew the right recipes – how to render a woman infertile with goofer dust and a guinea fowl egg, how to break up a family with sulphur and black mustard seed, how to kill. It didn't matter that I wasn't sure of the identity of the murderers. I'd put a last drop of Leroy's blood on a Bible and placed it at the north corner of our room, the formula that never failed to bring justice. I had all I needed.

When I was ready, once I'd selected the names, I began the Work. I bought nine cow's hearts from the butcher. I slit them open and put inside each a piece of paper on which I'd written a name nine times. I stitched each one back together with a strand of hair and 18 steel needles, then dropped them all into a big jar of bad vinegar. At

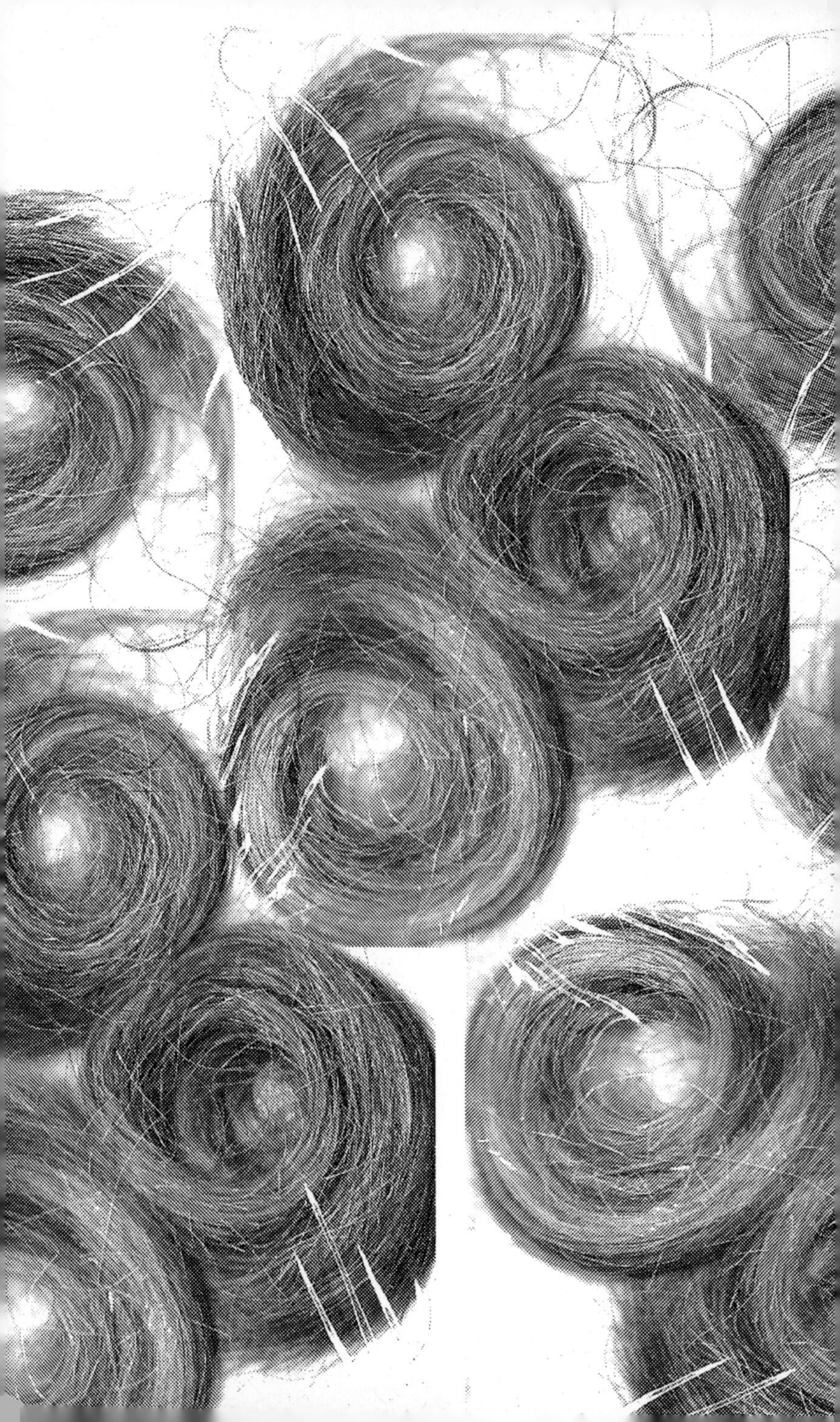

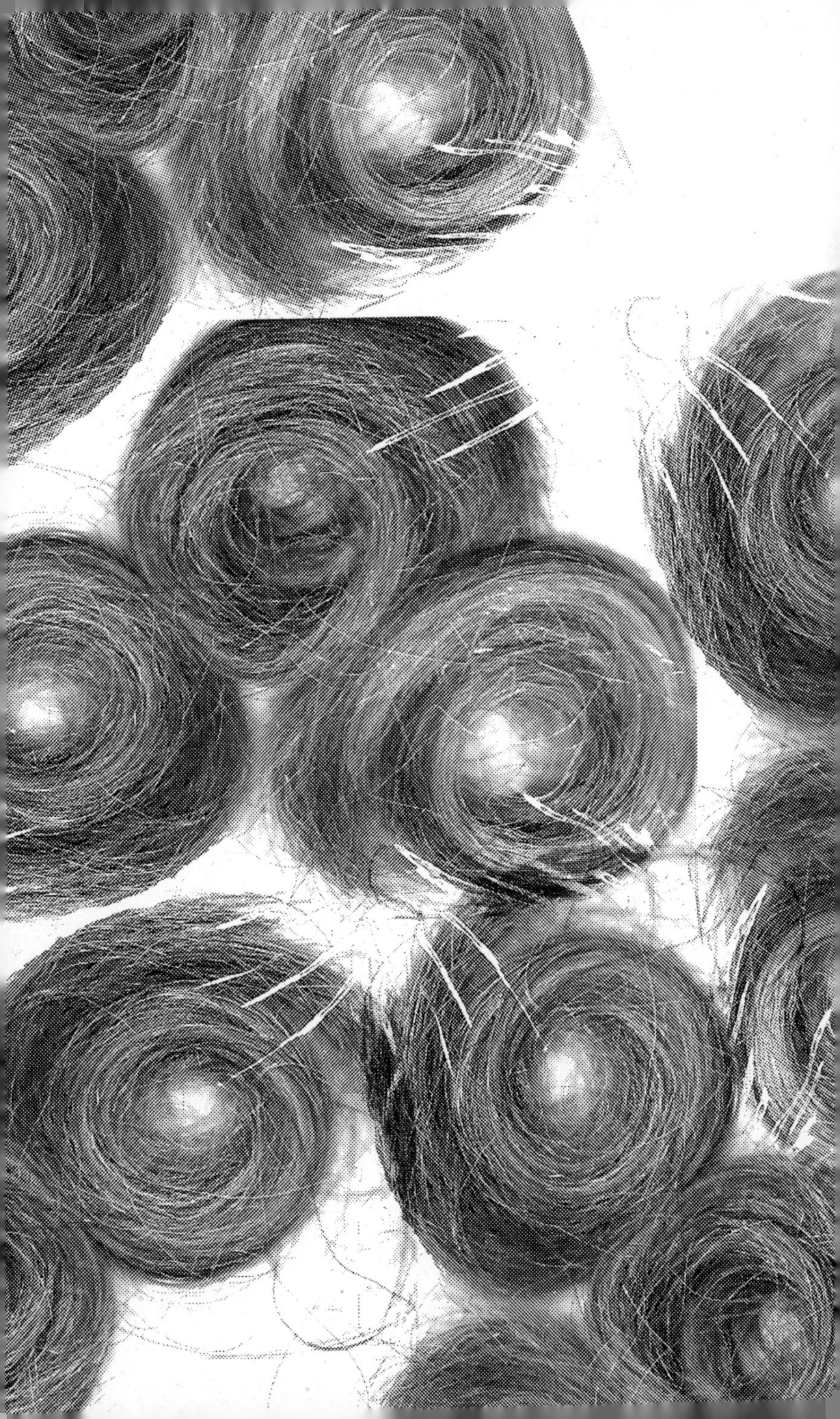

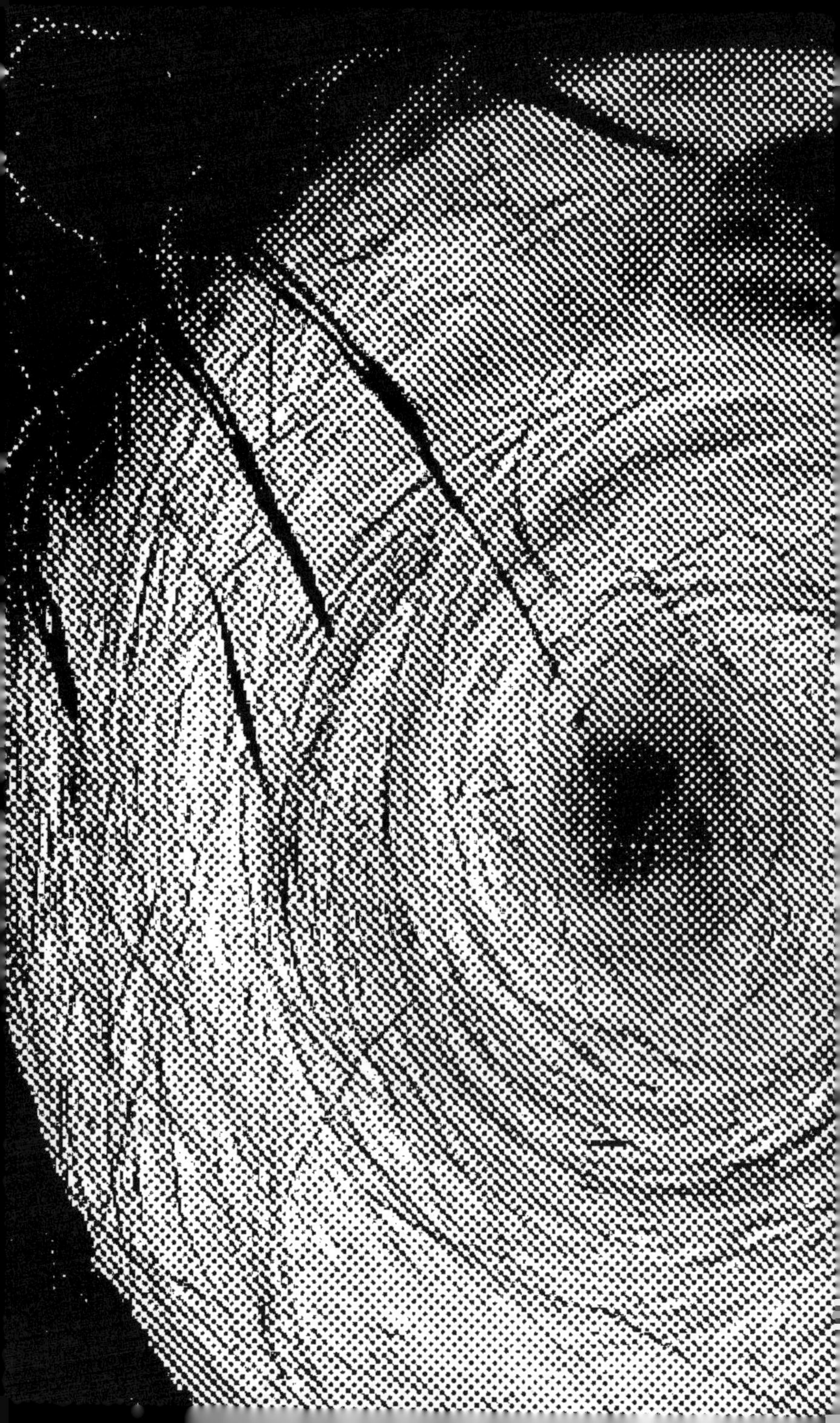

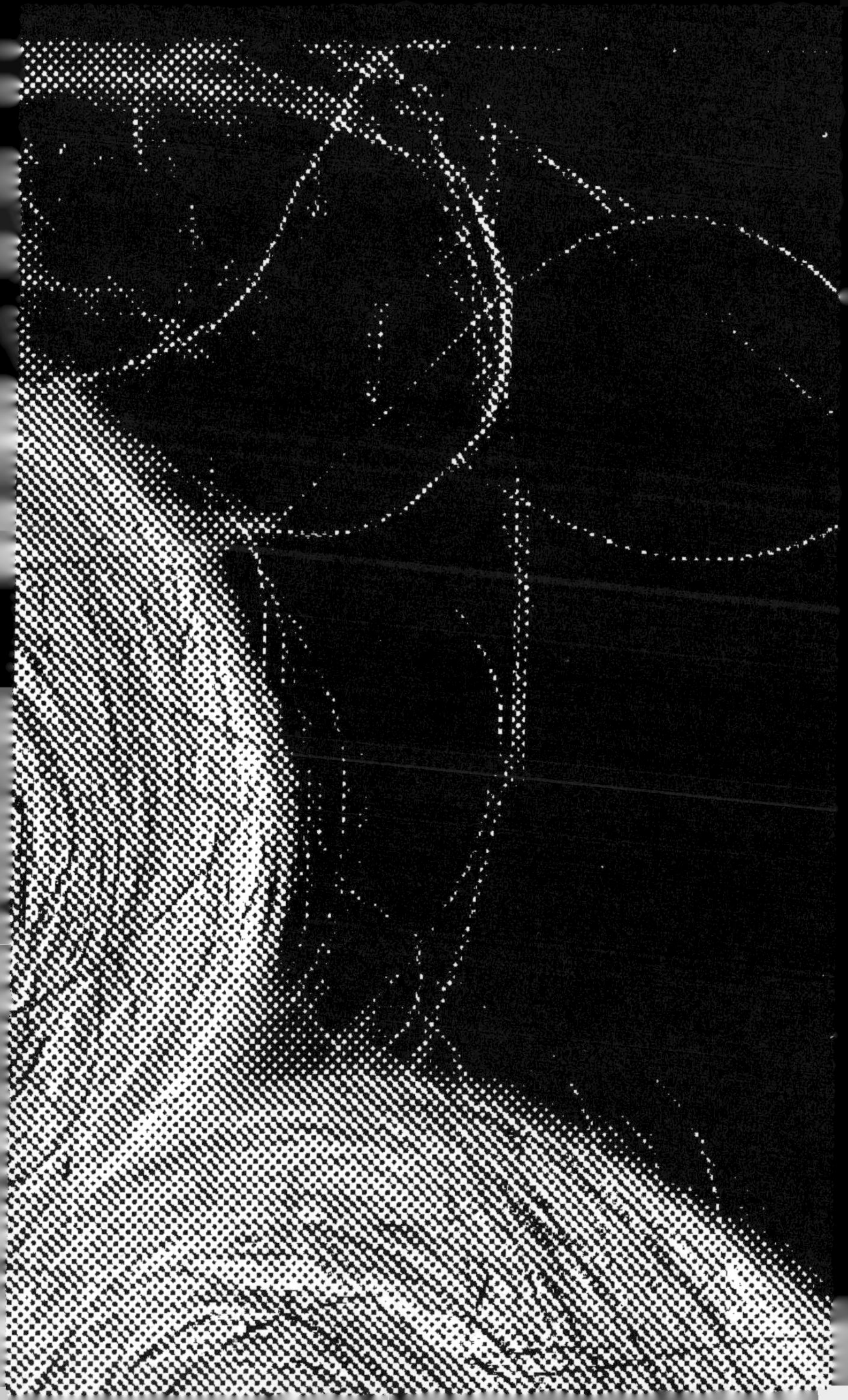

nightfall for the next nine days I called out the names, while shaking the jar and telling it what I wanted it to do.

At midnight on the last day I lit a black candle then snuffed it out. I unscrewed the jar. I took out the hearts one by one. I walked to each murderer's house, and at each I buried their heart breast-deep in the yard. To kill.

Anything may conjure and nothing may conjure. Moses was the first man to learn God's magic, both for good and for bad. In 40 years he learned ten words, so hard were they to know, and from them he made the ten holy commandments and ten terrible plagues.

I'd intended to go home when I was done with my conjure. Nothing held me to the north, apart from pain. Oh, oh, I won't be long here. Oh, oh, dark gonna catch me. But I didn't go straight downtown to the bus depot and catch the first Greyhound to Jackson, because Devil done laid a trap for me at the last house.

On its porch was a stroller, and in the stroller was a baby. A little, living baby. It was August and the air was hot and his parents had put him out to catch a breath of cool night air, then fallen asleep themselves in front of *Gunsmoke*. The TV was still on, still turned up loud. Nobody heard me climb the steps. I picked up the child. On the walk to North Main I kept to the shadows. I let myself into Mister Leon's mortuary by the back way.

In the cellar I held the baby in my arms for a few moments. He were so warm, so white. I sang to him real soft, like my Mama used to do to me, 'The river run wide, the river run deep, O, bye-o, sweet li'l baby, that boat rock slow, she'll rock you to sleep, O, bye-o, sweet li'l baby...'

I sang until the child slipped off back to sleep.

On the table there was a casket. It was an airtight Hillenbrand, occupied by a Goodyear manager who'd choked to death on a chicken bone. Occupied and sealed. His funeral service weren't to be an open coffin affair. Burial was scheduled for nine in the morning.

I found me a screwdriver. The screws weren't difficult to undo.

Maybe I oughtn't have done what I did. Maybe I should have stopped myself. But my head got all hot and my sight went all anyhow and then I too was asleep. I don't know for how long. I woke to the sound of footsteps on the stairs, coming down to me, coming down to the cellar. And there was no baby in my arms.

I always ended up staying late at the archive. I tried to be disciplined in my approach because time is limited and precious, yet I lost all track of it. On Saturdays I'd catch the last bus home. I love London at night - the empty streets, the clutching couples, a single bedroom light glowing in a row of silent houses, the smell of rain or autumn leaves that goes unnoticed during the day. I usually sat on the upper deck and watched the city slip by, longing to seize it all before it's too late.

Almost every Saturday on that last bus - the 00:16 from Kensington High Street - I'd see the same young woman on the upper deck. She was not yet thirty, with high cheekbones and wild red hair that tumbled down her back. She probably worked as a waitress or shelf-stacker in Covent Garden, near the start of the number 9's route, for she looked dead tired and dozed throughout the journey, except once when her mobile rang and she spoke into it, in Czech I think. I took to sitting behind her, to watch the way she laid her head against the bus window, to see the rise and fall of her shoulders as she breathed. Night journeys - even those as short as the dozen stops between Kensington and Hammersmith - can engender a strange intimacy between travellers.

Looking back, I'm not sure why I did what I did. It wasn't a spur of the moment thing, for I'd taken the scissors from the archive. They were in my pocket that evening. While the woman slept, somewhere near Brook Green, I took them out and snipped off a tendril of her hair. Of course she woke, turned in her seat and started yelling at me. She was livid. Her eyes were jade green.

In the morning back at the archive I made a cellophane sleeve and slipped the curl gently into the Akron hairdresser's album.

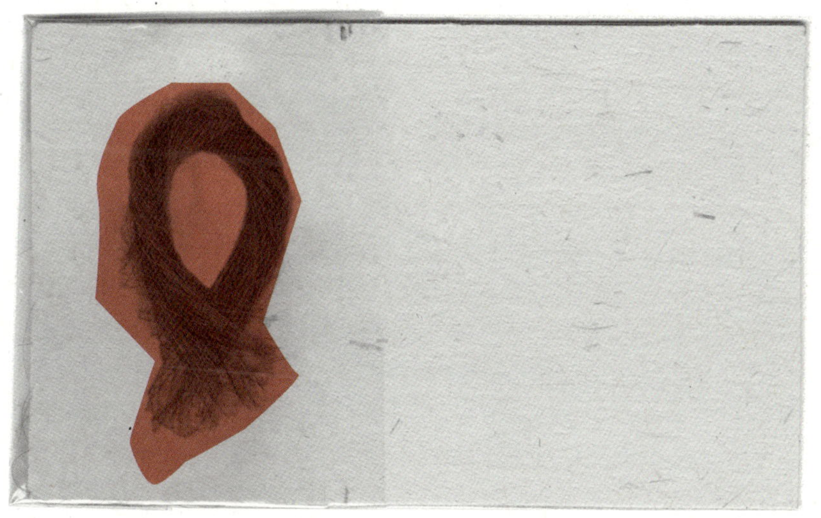

Boots

Raseiniai, Reichskommissariat

Ostland 22.06.1941

FIRE.

Fire under the cowling, licking the nose, ripping towards him. Red-hot flak hits the engine, bursting the fuel line. The pilot twists and turns like the Aero itself, writhing in his own body, going down, down.

Must get lower, mustn't ditch. Don't want to bail out.

The flames look too thin to be hot, too beautiful to kill. A blazing sheen ripples across the dull, torn fabric. Now it's on the wings, around the struts, at his feet.

HELP ME!

No one can hear a cry at a thousand feet, nine hundred feet, eight hundred feet. He's pushing the stick, trailing smoke, plunging towards earth. Behind him Andre is already a ghost, eyes bulging in his goggles, fighting with the belts. He is yelling. He wants to jump but can't. The pilot doesn't hear Andre above the scream of the dive. Or his own scream.

More flak. They're still firing at us. Too late to jump. Andre should aim now, drop the 400 pounder now, NOW onto the leading Panzer IV which rolls like a phantom out of the morning mist. But he's looking everywhere except at the sight. Poor bloody Andre, torn from his mountains to this godless open plain, never more than a step ahead of the Germans, now above them in a fireball.

I WON'T DIE.
I WILL LIVE.
WE WILL LIVE.

The pilot senses the heat now, catches the stink before he feels the burning flesh. He yanks at his legs but they don't move. His right boot is jammed under the rudder pedal. He struggles but cannot free his foot. Pull back. Pull back. His arms jerk, convulse, clamp the stick. Blood roars in his ears. It can't end in this flatness, he tells himself. It can't end after all the running, all the flying, all their effort.

The Panzers are everywhere, so there's nowhere to put down, nowhere to hide, not a tree to be seen between Berlin and Leningrad. In the open cockpit the flames are all around him. Fire cyclones around his limbs, singeing the wool of his flying jacket, searing away his eyebrows, torching his hair.

IT'S THE END,
THE END.

Mothe...

Then he sees the trees. There's a wood, right ahead. How hadn't he noticed it? It's a miracle, and somehow he levels the biplane and lifts it above the thudding flak, over the howls of gunfire, towards cover. A last round shatters an aileron, yet he steers his two-seater directly at the tallest pine, slicing off its tip, arresting the Aero A.11's forward motion. The impact tears off the port wing, rips him from his seat, snaps him clean out of his flying boots. As he's lifted up he's shouting back.

'JUMP,
ANDRE!
JUMP!'

He's out of the spinning, exploding aircraft. He's crashing through the bristling branches. He's spiralling his smouldering arms, falling down, down like a burning angel. He thuds, crumpled and barefoot, onto the forest floor, into silence. Silence.

EARTH. SAP.

He smells before he can see, cannot place himself. In front of his eyes there's a pattern, but it means nothing. Check control wires. Watch for wear at pulley points and fair leads. Grease and lock turnbuckles. He's in the Tatra Mountains in the summer after flight training, head down in the sweet soil. Pine needles are sharp against his cheek.

Andre my friend, it's time to wake, to walk. We're due back in Levoča by nightfall.

He tries to make walking movements, thinks he's walking, doesn't move.

Don't you love the view of the peaks, of the trees? There are so many trees. He blinks but cannot focus, blinks and wants to rub his eyes. He's lying under a branch, moves to shift it, realises that the branch is his arm, broken. Pain pulls him back into himself, searing, exploding like a starburst shell.

GOD. GOD.

He's not in the mountains. Where is Andre? He slips back into darkness.

Overhead a sickle moon glints through the pine boughs. Dot dash dot dot dash. He wakes trying to decipher the code: attack, hold your station, Roger, Control, maintaining altitude. In front of him the pattern is moving. There's dirt in his mouth, his eyes. This time he manages to focus, makes out a moulded scoop of glass, recognises it as the broken lens of a landing light. Inside it are three ants, trapped at the bottom of the upturned lozenge. They are trying to escape, trying to climb up its smooth glass sides, sliding back to the bottom. The ants keep climbing, keep falling. A minute passes, then an hour. The pilot stares, unthinking. The ants cannot escape. They stop trying, crawl towards one another and settle in a circle.

Dawn again. He's on his back, on a bed of moss, alive. With his good arm he feels to see if he is whole.

CHEST.
COCK. LEGS

IT'S THE END,
THE END.

EARTH. SAP.

MUST REST.
MUST RUN.
MUST GET OUT.

THIRSTY.

GOD. GOD.

READY?

His limbs are so heavy, like stone. He can't move his neck. But there's no blood. Nor boots.

He remembers the German attack on their airfield: the diving Stukas, the tracks of the tracers, the Yaks going up in smoke. His Aero survived only because it was parked away from the rest of the squadron, not being Soviet. He and Andre alone got off the ground, with Andre still clutching his black bread breakfast. Together they had nursed the Aero halfway across Europe via Poland, to internment in Romania, then freedom in Russia. She was lost but he can still fly, still fight, if he can get back to the Soviet lines. In his mind he tries to picture the chart, to plot a course to the coast. He has to make a splint for his broken arm. Where is Andre? He stops thinking, sleeps.

Now he's running. He doesn't know how he's been able to stand, how he lashed the splint. In the woods he'd heard voices, made to shout out, then realised that the voices were German. The wreck of the Aero hung above him in a cradle of branches as if unwilling to fall finally, fatally to earth. The infantrymen were looking for it, looking for survivors.

THINK,
YOU FOOL.

He dragged himself away from the sounds and crouched in a thicket of scrub, hardly daring to breathe. They found the plane but not him. Not him. He strained to hear but couldn't make out the words, couldn't tell if they had found Andre too, if he was still strapped to his seat.

When it fell quiet the pilot made for the edge of the trees. Across the plain as far as the horizon nothing moved. No tanks, no men, not a bird. He didn't question it. Instead he took a bearing from the sun and started running, keeping low to the ground, the wheat stubble knife-sharp under his bare soles.

I WILL LIVE.
I WILL LIVE.

He crosses the battlefield and moves beyond. He guesses it is a hundred kilometres to the coast. Twenty hours walking. Must keep moving. After ten minutes his head is throbbing. His pounding heart rocks his whole body. At the edge of a field he scrambles into a ditch to catch his breath. Call it thirty hours he says to himself, then slips back into blackness.

But in his mind he is still running. He imagines movements that his limbs do not make. The afternoon sun is hot on his face, as it was in the Tatras that last summer. They had climbed Východná Vysoká, spent the night overlooking the Great Cold Valley, eaten grilled trout in front of the fire. Andre was more than like a brother, until the pilot had told him that he was getting married.

'Maybe it's time you found a girl too,' he'd teased. 'It'd be a picture-postcard double wedding.'

'I don't want any girl,' Andre had said.

'Let's make honest men out of us both,' the pilot had replied, reaching out to touch his friend's cheek.

The prickle of insects stirs him from his reverie. He brushes them away as Andre had brushed away his fingers, and feels for the first time the open blisters. His face is scorched, wet with puss. His feet are cut and bleeding. The taste of the trout becomes vomit in his mouth. His stomach heaves. He retches into the ditch.

MUST REST.

MUST RUN.
MUST GET OUT.

THIRSTY.

Beyond a far field lies the house. It is unexpected, sod-covered and ramshackle, an ugly, lumpen mound of earth. After God had made the world he made the poor, domed hut from leftovers, thinks the pilot. With its low turf walls and rough tree-trunk frame it does not even seem to be of Europe. At least it offers cover, sanctuary. He crawls as much as runs to the knotted door, pushes it open and falls into the ground.

Darkness, silence, bed. He lies on a mattress. Around him a dozen low candles stretch away to infinity. The floor is a void, veiled in dirt. There are no windows.

I must have passed out again, he imagines. I am saved. Saved.

Who's there?

The smoky light catches a man's face, a plaster white mask adrift in space. As it moves towards him the pilot makes out a strange, slender, stooped figure. Its jerky movements bring to mind an arthritic marionette. Behind it hangs a small mirror, turned to the wall.

'Are you ready?' the peasant asks him.

READY?

The pilot thinks he is dreaming. He lets his eyes close and tries to ignore the pictures that come and go behind them: Andre, the high blue sky, the mask. He needs to gather his strength to breathe. In the slow, timeless movement of his mind he feels his body labour. He sees that the peasant wears a collarless wedding suit – black, worn and frayed.

'She was hiding in the cellar,' the man says, his voice high and far away, as if speaking from long ago. 'I came for her, gave a coin to her family – paying the ransom, *vykup nevesty* – and I was given their son dressed as my bride.'

Andre, my friend.

The pilot needs boots. Boots and water. He must get out of the bed. He tries to draw up his dead feet and realises that he cannot move. He hears the man say, 'I played the game, lifted his veil, feigned shock and called out, "Where are you, my love? Where have you gone?" Then we smelt the smoke and heard the screams.'

The pilot turns his head sideways, peers blearily into the abyss.

In broken Russian the man tells him that the wedding had been arranged according to the old ways and the saints. In a clean shirt he'd knelt in all four directions at her door as a sign of respect. He'd drunk the charmed water from her last bath. He'd agreed not to look upon her face until evening. A maiden seen is copper but the unseen girl is gold, he says.

'She would be dressed in red *sarafan* with golden trim and a bride's crown. In our bed, she would be mine, would have been mine, and all would have been properly done, if I hadn't lied.'

A lifetime ago at the knotted front door, the groom and guests had laughed at the game, while below in the cellar hiding place a candle had touched the hem of the bride's dress. Her long, trapeze-shaped gown had leapt into flame, and the girl in her terror had spun around, fanning rather than extinguishing the fire, dropping cross and icon, knocking over the round *karavai* loaf and cheese. Her muffled screams had lifted through the floorboards, through the hatch covered by a carpet.

WE ARE COMING. TOO LATE. TOO LATE.

In the dark, stifling room a kind of coldness takes hold of the pilot's body. A lump rises in his throat as if he is overcome by deep sadness. Above him hangs the old man's hollow, familiar face, whispering to him like a lover. 'The dead stay dead, have mercy upon us.'

'All that I love is lost, all whom I meet disappear,' he goes on. 'One by one my father, my mother, my wife-to-be, my fellows, never to return. In the end no one remains but me, and you.'

Suddenly the man begins to mewl, gripping the seams of his trousers, pulling at them, his wedding finery revealed as drab dirge-clothes. The mean, earthen house echoes with the mad wildness of grief. It rings off the beams, rolls across the fields, moans through the far, high mountains. Around them the dozen candle flames shiver with its force, rising and spiralling together as if in some elemental empathy. Within them at the head of the bed, the man is holding the mirror, slowly turning it towards the pilot, breathing into his ear.

'Now look,' he says. 'Look.'

The pilot struggles not to look, to escape, but he cannot free himself. His head thrashes but his body does not move. In the rush of heat he feels beads of sweat prick across his forehead. He tries to tear at his clothes. He smells the burning. Another scream reaches his ears, this time not from the man but from his own doomed, fatal dive. He is falling, falling. Dying. Lord, have mercy upon us. There is no forest. His foot is gone. The flames engulf him. He sees the reflection in the mirror.

'LOOK.'

On the open plain the infantrymen picked at the wreckage. The smouldering Czech-built Aero A.11 was a reconnaissance aircraft, converted to a light bomber at the start of the war, brought down on the first day of the invasion of Russia. Half a second before impact it had clipped a dwarf pine, the only tree in the wide bare field south of Raseiniai. Its fuselage had arched and its wheels been driven up behind the navigator's seat. The canvas had been incinerated, exposing the craft's frail skeleton. The navigator's body was still on fire, the skin on his face charred into a horrible, sorrowful scowl. The pilot seemed to have been trapped when the upper wing collapsed upon him. His safety harness hadn't been released. In the intense heat his flying suit had become welded to his body.

For the young Germans it was an unpleasant detail. One of them lit a cigarette. Another raised his Leica to his eye. Once the flames had died down they would bury the bodies, boots and all.

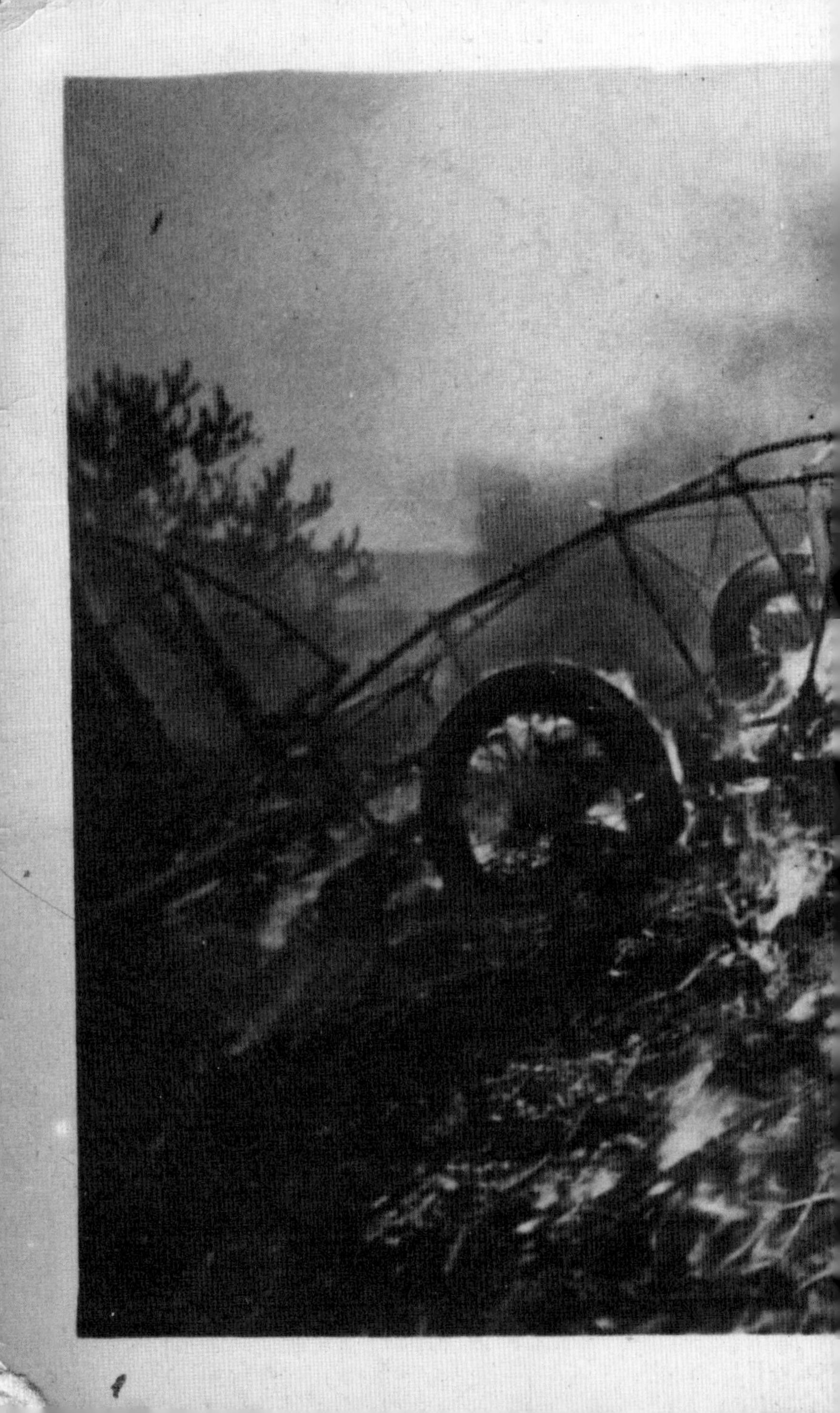

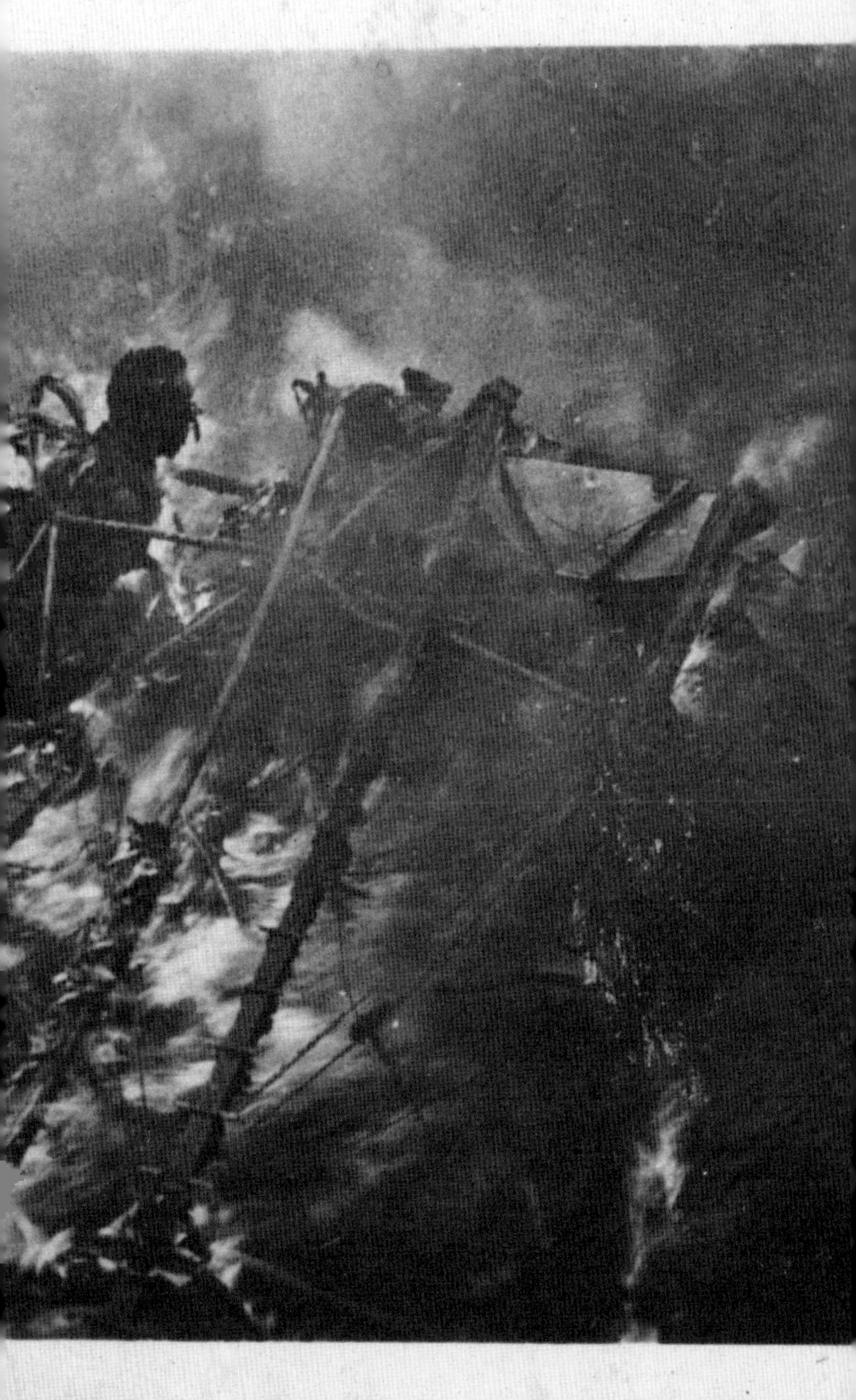

After the incident on the bus I started sleeping at the archive, in secret. I'd spend all weekend there, clearing up only early on Monday morning. In truth I don't think the curator would have minded. In a strange way I felt he already knew. I still heard those muffled voices, and sensed that it was him talking in the next room or on the other side of a door. At times I felt that I was being watched. I even took to imagining that there was something preordained in my presence there, as if fate had dictated it, as if it could have been predicted by a clairvoyant or priest. I was uneasy with the thought, for I wanted to believe that I was making the journey rather than the journey making me. Nevertheless I always got out of the archive before the staff arrived for the working week, and left no trace of my stay.

It was during my fifth or sixth weekend that I began to merge the albums together. I make no excuse for my actions. I'd been given the key in trust, I know. I respect the sanctity of the individual, of course. Yet some of the folders - photographs of victims of Soviet famines, an album begun by a Wehrmacht soldier and completed by his widow, a collection of Burmese brothel tokens - spoke of such loneliness, such loss. It came into my head that, as the only surviving record of individual lives, these men and women should not be alone at their end. I didn't want to cook their stories in fiction, giving them grand Hollywood finales - boy meets girl, triumphs over evil, lives happily ever after by the sea in Brittany - but I did want their common actions to have, in the black-and-white reality of the archive, a last, enduring moment of imagined significance.

So I started mixing War Ministry casualty lists with a rabbit hunter's diaries, pasting portraits of Soviet commissars into a 'Most Secret' British MI9 album, slipping a photograph of a pretty Japanese girl into the personal effects of the Enola Gay's bombardier.

At first I didn't know what to think about the morality of this work. The function of writing is to explode a subject, to transform it into something else. In the archive there were so many lives and so many endings, and the more I came to know, the more I felt a sense of both dwarfing immensity and subtle realisation. I was like the photographer discovering something about himself through the people before his lens. I opened album after album, overcome by a raw yearning to draw together the disparate strands. I couldn't bear to accept that life was a purposeless drift of events. I trembled as the individual stories took shape, as I looked for patterns in the narrative, as I grasped for meaning in the journey.

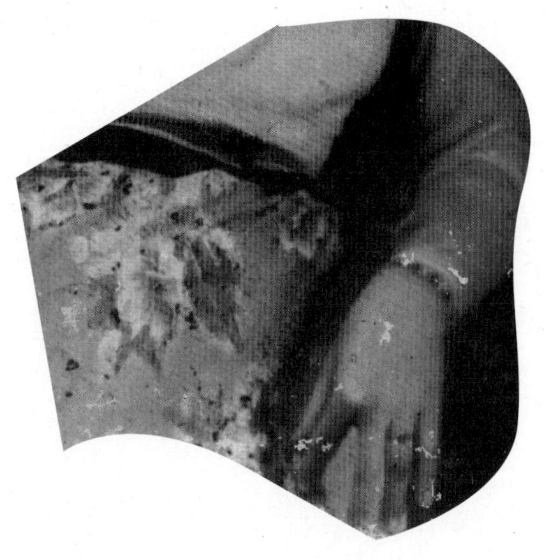

All That is to Come

Rangoon, Burma 28.03.1931

Crack of gunshot. Hush of feet on blood red stones. Su twists into the churning crowd, curving sunwise around the gleaming stupa, as the world turns. Incense and cordite spiral into the air. White jasmine blossoms and smoke encircle holy Buddhas. A child grasps her father's hand, slips into his arms, weaves herself around him, and dies in the evening heat.

Time is a wave that rolls out from the centre of the universe. Today curls around the fingers of the hand. Yesterday wheels into tomorrow. Around the great Shwedagon Pagoda, Su aged six skips between sun-baked paving stones. In the same moment she is five years older, reading the future in her best friends' palms, comparing birth times, looking for signs. At fifteen Su sees the signs and spins stories around her, the youngest and most popular fortune-teller on the temple's Eastern Stairway. She moves not with the forward march of hours but across them, as if in the space between the hands of a clock. She is also 23 and alone – her father having joined the rally – and terrified by all that is to come.

Let all beings be peaceful. Let all beings be safe. Let us die, and be born again.

For Su divination begins as a game, as young and green as the new leaves on an old banyan tree. She plays with voices and time as other children do with dolls and dreams. The game teaches her a way to trust a broken world.

'Yours is a fine hand,' she says.

And 'Your market stall must be sold between April 21 and July 31.'

And 'Your success springs from the head; you will prosper through academic work.'

The left hand reveals an individual's potential. The right hand shows what can be achieved with it. Long fingers denote delicacy. Small fingernails belong to the envious.

'People met in November will be friends for life. Your lucky numbers are 1, 3, 5 and 6. Number 8 brings misfortune. Your stone is sapphire.'

Like every palmist born and yet to be, Su comforts the bereaved, eases the ache of the lonely. Her father had the gift and she inherited that which was once natural to all beings, in the great circle of life. Her father who she loves more than tamarind sweets, more than the first rains of the monsoon, more even than the stars. Her father who advises her as she lights their lamp, 'Su Su, *Tha Mee*, tell people what they need to hear. Give them hope.'

Every month at the full moon the faithful gather around Shwedagon's gateways. In the dusty light they mount the long, pious steps, kneel before wide-eyed Buddhas and look out over Rangoon's treetops and parade grounds. Then they pose their questions to the mediums who wait beneath the acetylene lamps. What is my future? Does he love me? How can we be rid of the British?

All that we are springs from our deeds. All our futures are determined in this moment. In the timeless night the breeze stirs the tinkling bells atop the pagoda.

Su's first clients come to her from the local townships, then from nearby towns such as Bassein and Pegu, in time from as far away as

Mandalay. Word of her skill spreads across lower Burma until even the English catch wind of it and the wives of close-buttoned colonial officers join the queue, sitting self-consciously on the squat wooden stools as their sun-burnt husbands huff behind them.

'When I lost my daughter I lost my faith,' confesses one Englishwoman, tailored and padded despite the heat.

Su takes her hands and holds them. 'I sense the guardian of her soul.'

'You can sense her?' the woman asks under her breath.

'When I hold your hands I feel a shiver on my forearm,' Su explains, brushing the hair on her left arm. 'That tells me that your daughter still lives in your heart, that her soul is with you.'

'For God's sake Frances, hurry up,' interrupts the husband, a District Superintendent out of uniform, eavesdropping, mocking, impatiently pulling on a cigarette.

To many, Su doesn't look the part. She isn't old, troubled or possessed. No dark spirits dwell inside her. Her easy laughter brings to mind the sound of the bulbul birds that hide in the green groves of mango trees. Only a slight divergence of the eyes suggests that she sees what others do not.

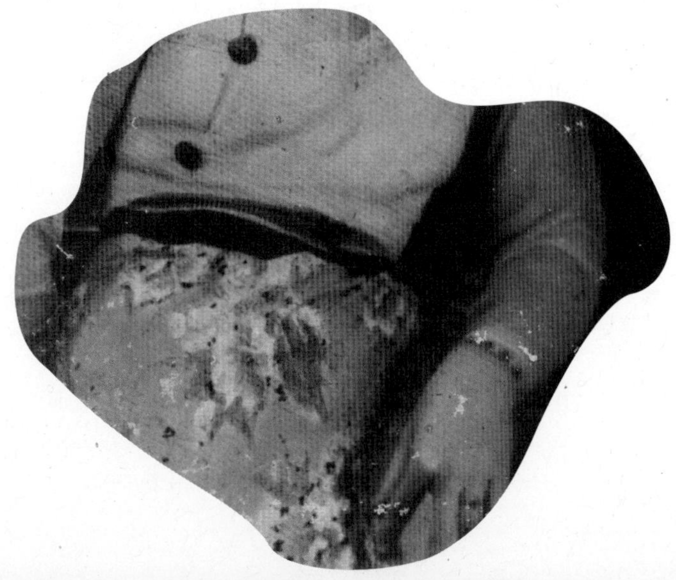

But death changes the lives of those who remain behind, even those with second sight, even those living in the space between a clock's hands. On the streets below the great pagoda the Burmese people rally together to ask: what is the price of freedom? The question is answered with bullets and bombs, and suddenly every face is streaked with tears. No one is safe. Su is both six and 23 when she learns too late of her father's arrest and, before she can reach him, his 'suicide' in prison.

At first she denies his death. She senses his presence in the next room, catches sight of his silhouette at the market. At home she pours two cups of tea, in faith as much as from habit. But then, like a dying fire, the warmth fades. She feels no shiver on her forearm. If fate is written on our palms or in the stars, she wonders, how can his death not have been predicted? How could her gift have deserted her? How can it be that she cannot – will never again – hear his voice? In her grief Su finds the simplest decisions evade her: when to unroll her sleeping mat, whether to eat *bein moun* or curry and rice for her evening meal. She can barely lift her feet to climb the stairway. The palmist begins to doubt.

Two weeks later a young man stands before her, asking for guidance. He is a second year biology student named Thu Maung and he wants to know about lucky dates. He has finely shaped eyes and a bold presence, and touches her arm to emphasise a point. Su dislikes the stranger's lack of modesty but in other ways he reminds her of her father, and in her grief she is drawn to him.

'1931 will be a challenging year,' she tells him, leaning forward to take his hand. 'But 1932 will be different. In that year all will be favourable. 1933 will also be positive and your life smooth as you reach for a higher position.'

Su studies his palm, following heart and lifelines, tracing them to the meeting point, calculating the angle. She relies both on her intuition and on the craft of prophecy, on observation and the

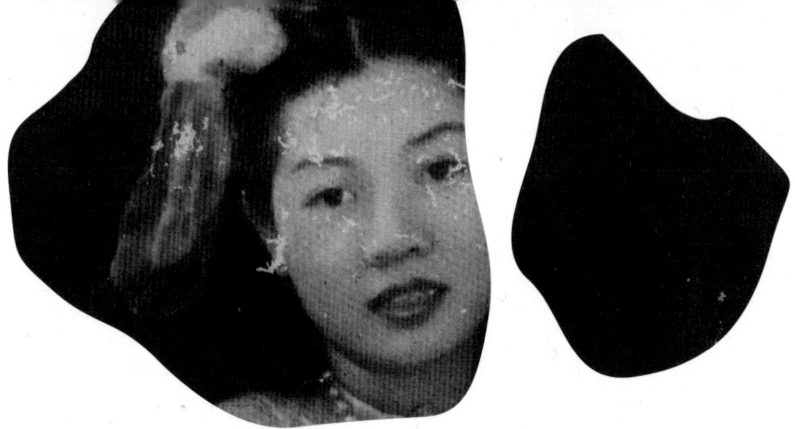

empirical link between character and consequence.

'Wednesday girls are good for you,' she assures him. 'You are prone to lung infections. Your lucky number is 9.'

Thu Maung makes notes in a school notebook, then casts her a flinty glance. He asks to see her again. Su senses danger, yet still wants him to return. She had felt a different tremor.

On his second visit Thu Maung tells her that he is training to be a doctor but that his marks have been poor. 'There are worse things than suffering and death,' he says, hungry for a narrative. 'It is worse to lose your self-respect.'

Su knows from the tone of his voice that he will fail his examinations, that he hungers for admiration. Despite her unease she spins him a story, couching her predictions in talk of success. He is encouraged by her, posing the expected questions, receiving predictable responses.

'You will not die in an accident,' she adds beneath the hissing lamp. 'An accident cannot happen to you because you have vital work to do.'

Thu Maung leaves her double the usual fee.

In Asia the future is more important than the past, prophecy more vital than history. People pay for the promise of better times, of good health and wealth, of a Burma liberated from the British.

'This is our country, not theirs,' Thu Maung says on their third meeting, his tone intimate yet adamant. 'When will the Englishwoman next come to you?'

Su pushes him away with a sudden gesture. Fate is not unavoidable, she knows. Misfortune can be averted by acquiring merit, or by bringing about events similar in strength to the predicated calamity. In a dream she sees Thu Maung walk alone across sun-baked stones, covered ankle-deep in ash. The ash is cold but not dry. With every step a vile red gore rises up his legs, staining his trousers. Trousers. Su sees that the man will wear not a traditional *longyi* but rather a soldier's uniform.

Usually the Englishwoman comes to Su in the quiet of the late afternoon, before Thursday bridge at the British Club. For two weeks Su waits for her, knowing what will come to pass, convinced that she can change fate. On the second Thursday in March the tailored and padded young mother mounts the Eastern Stairway. As predicted, her husband is not with her. She sits before Su and holds out her hand.

Around Su everything seems to give off heat – the paving stones, the yellow *padauk* flowers, the woman's trusting face, and Thu Maung as he steps out from the shadows. His accomplice's first blow knocks the woman unconscious. A burlap hood is over her head almost before she hits the ground. Thu Maung himself straps her arms behind her back. A car waits at the bottom of the stairs.

Terror needs to be strategic and pedagogic, to instil both fear and respect. The abduction stirs threats. Su is arrested, beaten, but she can tell the police nothing, or will not tell them. She feels a duty to protect Thu Maung, even though he frightens her, even when one of the Englishwoman's fingers is left at her stand beneath the acetylene lamps.

Thu Maung's demand is for the release of prisoners held without trial since the January riots. There must be no more 'hangings' in

British jails. He knows that the threat to one British life will not drive out the colonists, but frustration stirs his creeping fanaticism. When the authorities do not respond to his demand, another finger is delivered to the District Superintendent.

As the only point of contact, Su is released and watched. She waits at Shwedagon, as she knows she must.

On the fifth night, when the police watch is changed she is spirited away from the pagoda. The car steals down half-lit lanes, between rickety teashops and shuttered food stalls. Along the roadside grimy kitchen boys hardly look up from their sleeping mats. Blank-eyed rickshaw drivers doze on in palm-thatched shanties. Feral dogs continue to dig in refuse heaps. In her seat Su tells herself that Thu Maung needs her as she needs him, that they depend upon each other.

He awaits her in a low-lying shack in Insein Township. The Englishwoman is nowhere to be seen. Thu Maung steps out of the darkness, his face glowing, and shows Su his hand.

'What do you see, Ma Su?' he demands.

'I see the sun radiant above you. I see that July is your fortuitous month. In July your plans will be advanced with great success.'

'Radiant sun,' says Thu Maung, repeating her words as rats scamper behind the bamboo walls.

Su tailors her narrative to steer more than to anchor, and unmoors herself in the process. She knows that greed and superstition will overwhelm Thu Maung, that he will never be a doctor or save a life. Yet between her tears she tells him, 'You want to make people well, to make them safe.'

'The people will be safe and happy if the leaders are happy. There will be a battle and all will have to fight. It is the only way to open a new path.'

'You must be responsible.'

'It is our responsibility to resist those who run over us as they run over the whole world', he says. 'Yet,' he admits after a pause, 'I never know whom to trust. Tell me, what man can I trust?'

'Trust?' Su says, as if the breath were stolen from her body. She looks back, looks forward, unsettled in the whirl of the present. Before her Thu Maung is at once a boy, a soldier, and a murderer rotting away under house arrest at the end of his life.

'Life has only one purpose: to be and to renew itself,' she tells him.

'Then you misunderstand me,' he hisses, arrogant once more, leaning forward like a conspirator in the dark. 'Must I spell it out to you who claims to see tomorrow? Trust no one, or nothing but destiny...'

Man needs to perceive meaning. He sees significance in a stopped clock, imagines faces in clouds, clings to the prophecies of the fey. Nothing is so alien to the human mind as the idea of the random.

Su spirals around the temple, as the world turns. Jasmine and incense twist into the air. She is a child again, then a teenager looking for signs, finally a young woman in buttoned blouse and coloured beads, reaching to take her lost father's hand.

In life the only real failure is not to open one's eyes. As Su spins through her days, she does not feel the ash whirling around her feet. She does not see the fire springing and snapping up the stairway. At the eastern gate an acetylene lamp has fallen, its flames leaping up the old, sacred timbers. Su doesn't hear the screams, doesn't notice the worshippers running, sees only time stretching, racing out from the centre. The flames lick across the ancient stones, curl around the Temple of the Kakusandha Buddha, loop over the Wish Fulfilling Place. The moon's planetary post is lost in the smoke. Let all beings be peaceful. Let all beings be safe. Let us be born again, she thinks, again and again.

Su walks and circles, and in the moment before she dies she hears her father's voice, calling to her, calling, 'Su Su, *Tha Mee*. Come to me, my beloved daughter. Come and join me again...'

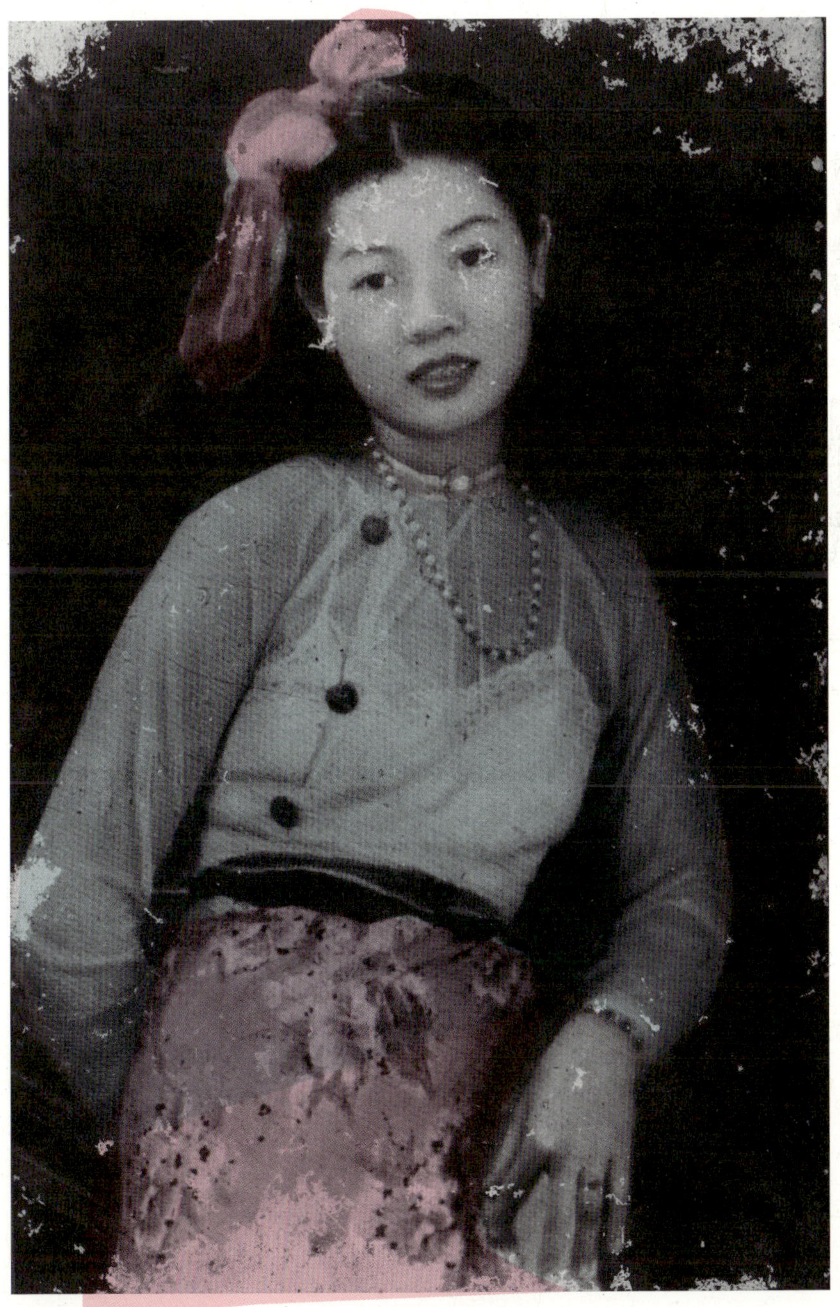

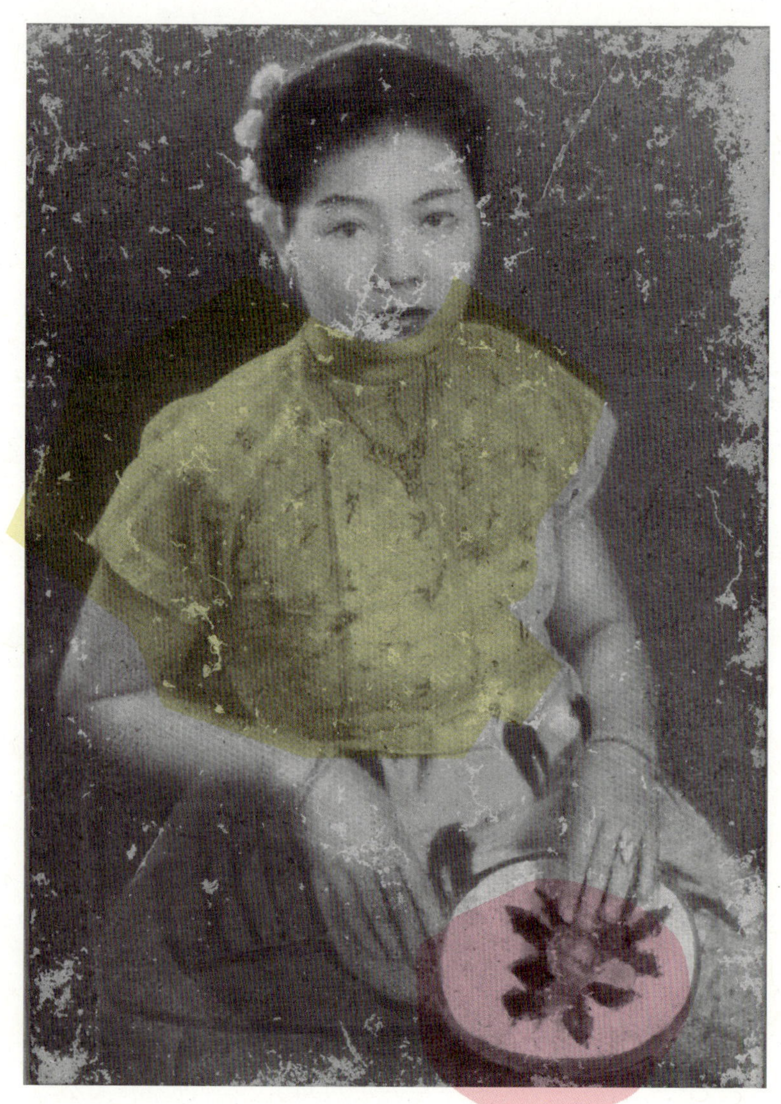

I am in Rangoon. I am buying the portrait of Su from G.M. Ahuja, Burma's oldest photographer. On steamy Merchant Street I climb a crumbling tenement staircase to his first-floor apartment. Its barred windows are thrown open to catch any breath of air, letting in the shriek of sirens and cicadas. Washing drips off a line strung above a desk. Musty graduation photographs rot behind filthy glass. The broken-tiled darkroom-toilet has been drenched by the morning's monsoon rains.

Through a crack in the wall I see a raven drop from a palm tree to pick at the rubbish adrift in a fetid alley.

'These are all I have left,' wheezes Ahuja, his winded voice all but drowned by the noise of the street. He gestures at some leaves of curling black-and-white prints. 'All the others are gone.'

I've traced the 89-year-old photographer through a Burmese friend. I'm in the country to write a newspaper travel article, but I can't leave the archive behind. It's become a part of me, or at least I am part of it. I have taken off the afternoon to meet Ahuja. I find him now laid out in the middle of his studio, on his deathbed. I perch on its edge and lean forward to catch his faint voice. At the foot of the bed hover his niece and her teenage daughter. They know I want his last prints.

'In old time photography was very hard, very costly,' he tells me in pidgin English. 'In past days I worked all night in darkroom developing glass plates. We had seven workers. Seven! And so many customers.'

His father R.A. Ahuja had founded the studio in 1916 when Rangoon was an imperial capital. G.M. had worked alongside him in both the lab and the studio, starting out with a plate camera with an aperture but no shutter. To take a photograph he simply slipped off the lens cap.

'During world war, I left for India by foot. The Japanese were on their way and they would have beaten me because I had photographed everything with my outdoor camera. I'd sent pictures and news from Burma to other countries. So I walked away to India, like so many others. There were so many people on the road, so many dead.'

'Are any left?' I ask.

'People gone,' he murmurs. 'Photographs gone.'

In 1945 G.M. Ahuja returned to Rangoon and reopened the studio to photograph brides, graduates and – after the 1962 military coup when men like Thu Maung came to power – soldiers. Year after year he took graduation class portraits at the Defence Services Academy and the Burmese Naval Institute. Together he and his father documented almost a century of the country's history until Cyclone Nargis, the 2008 storm that killed 150,000 people across Burma, swamped their archive. His niece then threw out most of the remaining negatives.

'She was destroying the photos already,' croaks G.M., trying to lift himself, stabbing a bony finger towards the woman. 'She threw

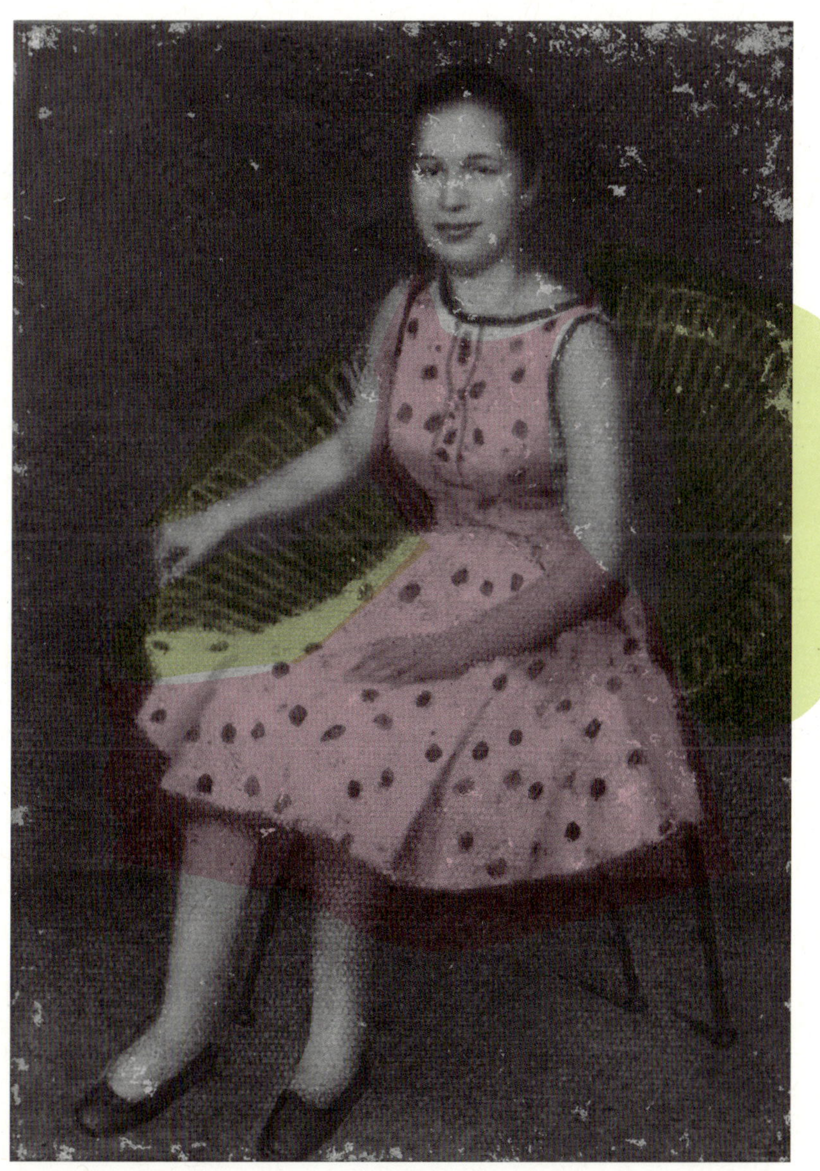

them away. So many photos. So many thousands of people photos,' he goes on, his voice rising into a hoarse shout.

He then falls quiet as he shifts position in the bed. The sheet slips off him and I catch sight of raw, red bedsores. Arthritis and a heart condition have sapped his strength. I turn away and pick up one of the surviving prints. It is Su the fortune-teller. I feel the emulsion peel off in the humid Rangoon heat.

'I've lived a very simple life,' says G.M. in a sudden, unexpected declaration. I bend back towards him to catch the wheezed words. 'Every morning I took a bath. Every morning I prayed and did my duties. I brushed my teeth and opened my studio shop at eight o'clock. Every morning there were always customers waiting at the door - workers standing in the shade, poor people crouching by the road. I took photographs for their marriages, of their babies. I took photographs of their identity papers before there were copiers. I helped them too when they were sick. Five children I have helped, and saved, paying to send them to hospital, paying the doctors to put a needle in, to stop the TB when their parents ran out of medicine. I paid for chicken soup and other expenses. My aim was always this one - to help the poor and needy. Never to drink. Never to smoke. Never to go after the girls. My life has been very simple.'

He whispers in Hindi to his niece, calling her to his side. She who has all but completed the destruction of his life's work tries to make him comfortable. Leathery skin clings to the grey bones of his face. His eyebrows, pronounced by sunken sockets, seem raised in furious incomprehension. He can no longer walk.

'I am old, but in my whole life I never speak the lie. Every day I speak only truth. But now I am sad inside my heart. I don't know why.'

Outside on Merchant Street, families sit cross-legged on broad armchairs of woven rattan, eating crispies and peanuts. Girls yawn under parasols in the back of ancient pick-up trucks. Cyclists wheel around buses, carrying yard-high stacks of government newspapers. Children dart out between the passing cars to gather the star-flowers that fall from a *kha yay ban* tree.

Did I pay the niece a hundred dollars for the photographs, or a thousand? Did I leave the studio with them to fly back to London, or wake up with them on my lap on a sofa bed in Holland Park? I cannot say for sure. But G.M. Ahuja – the oldest and last analogue photographer in Burma – did die the following week.

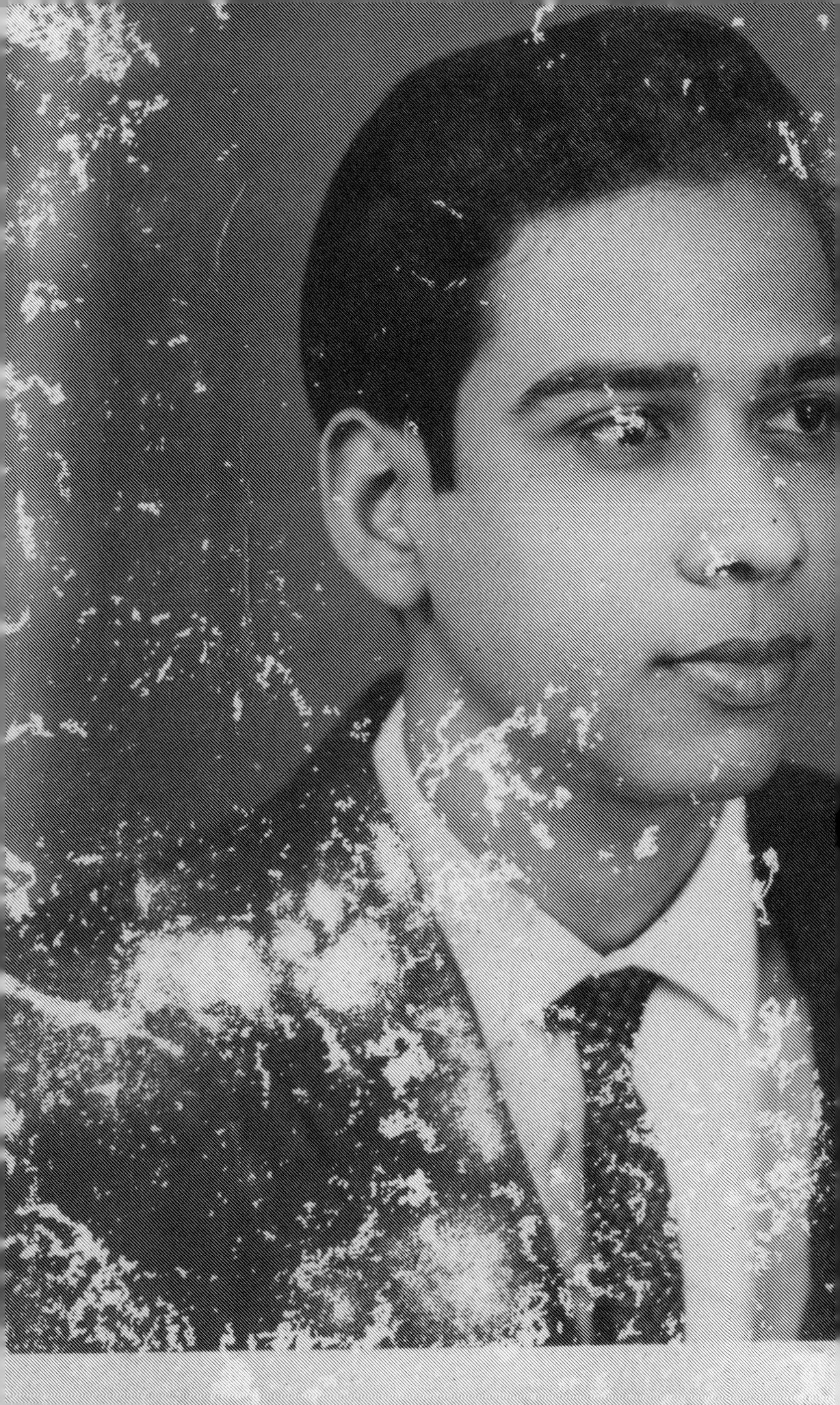

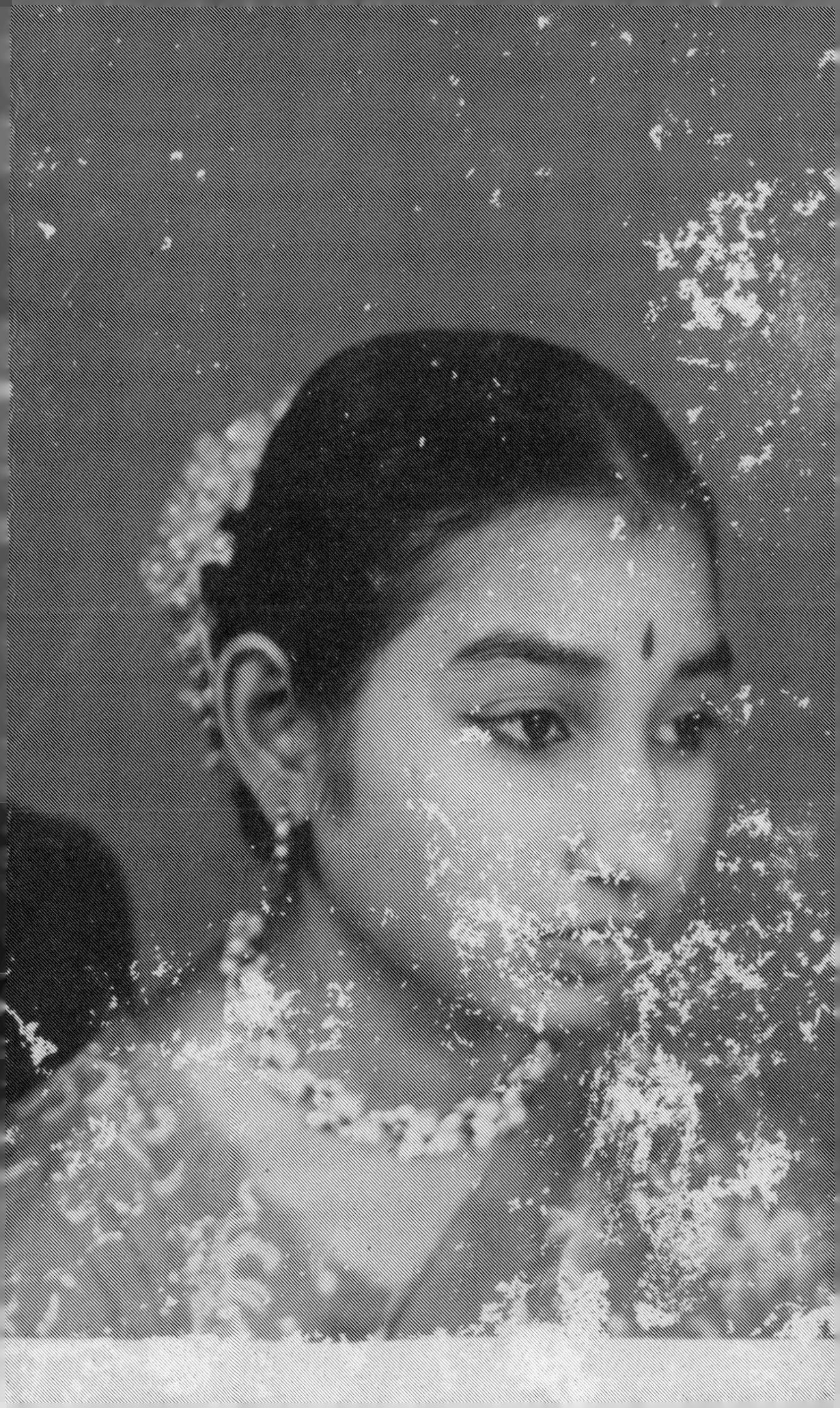

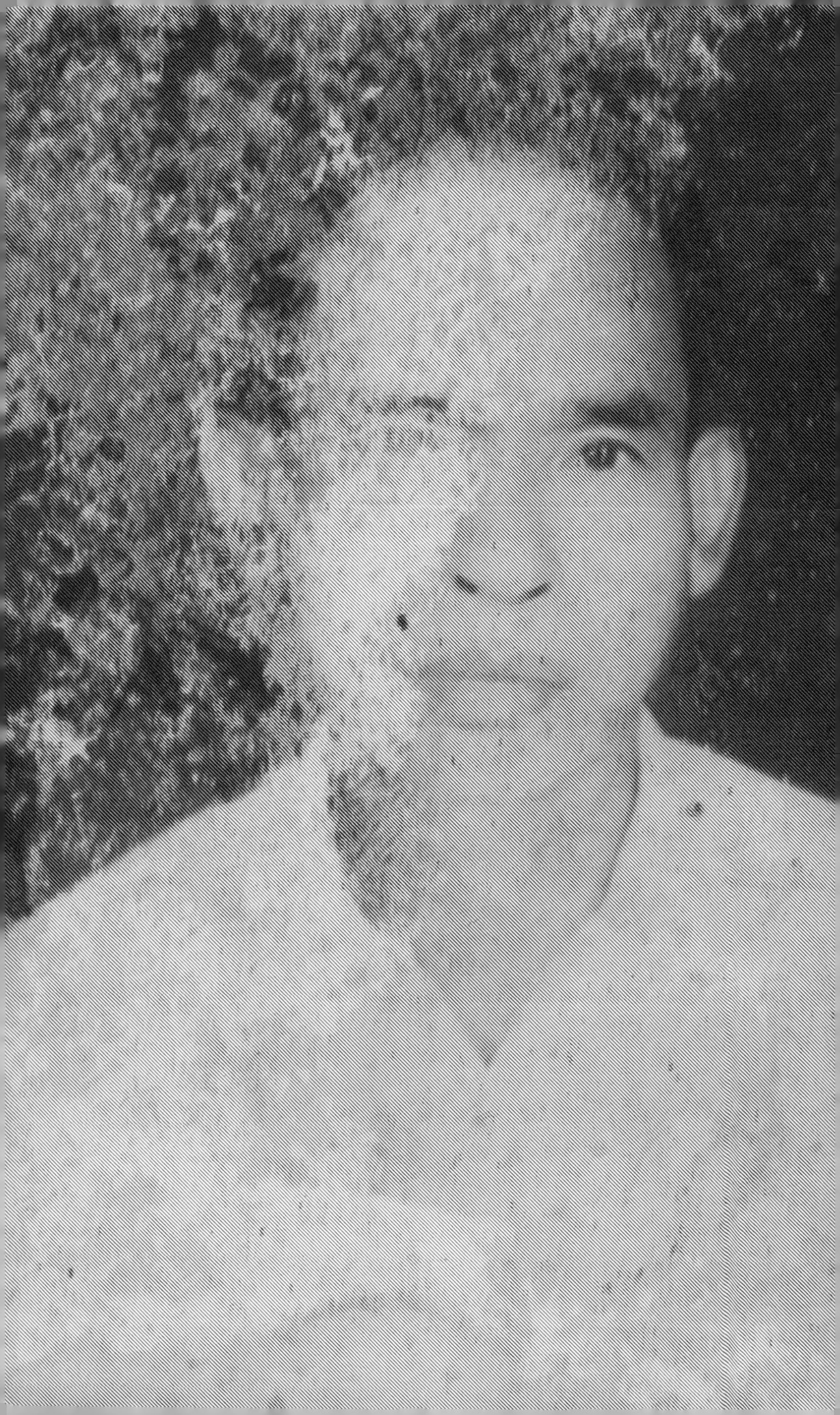

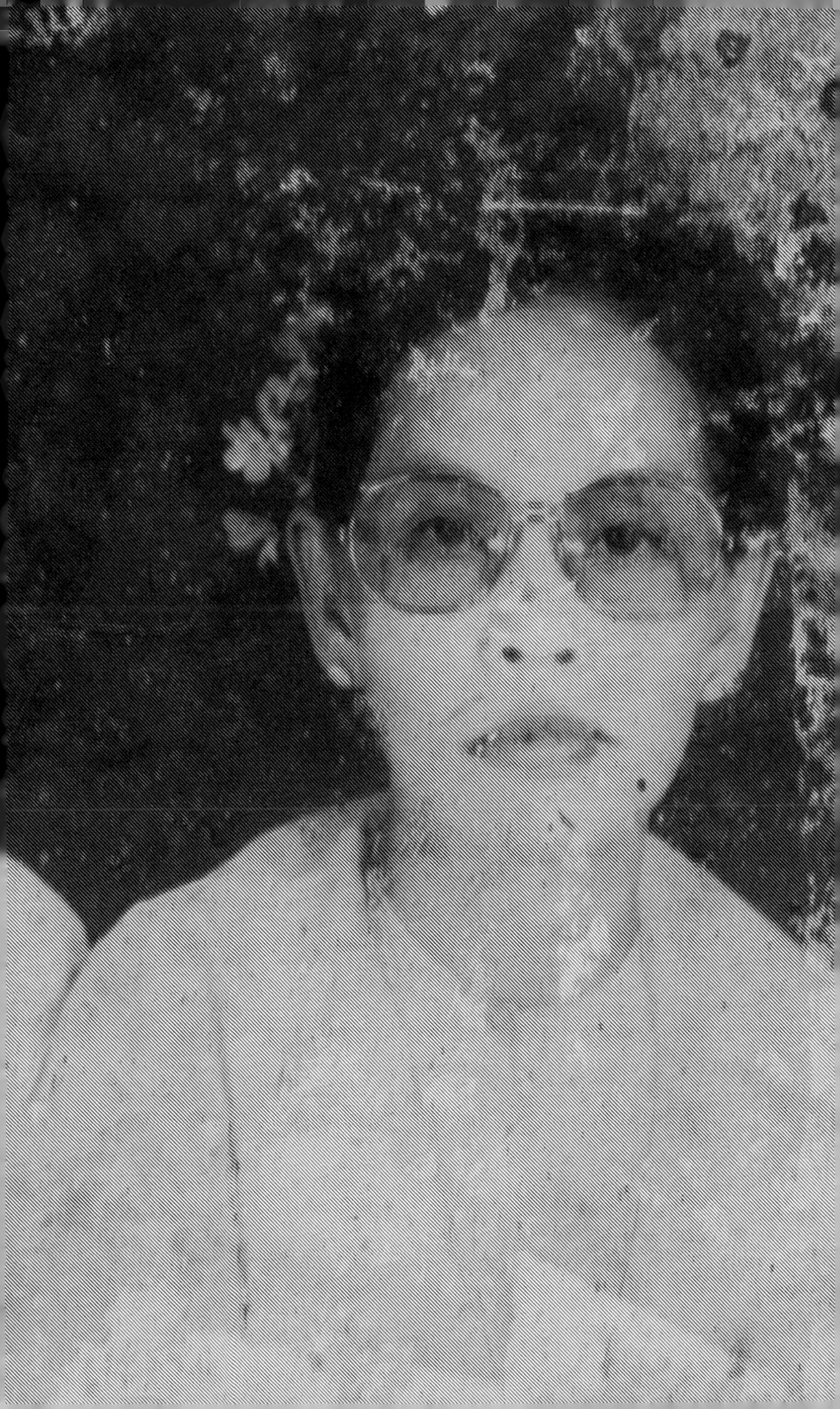

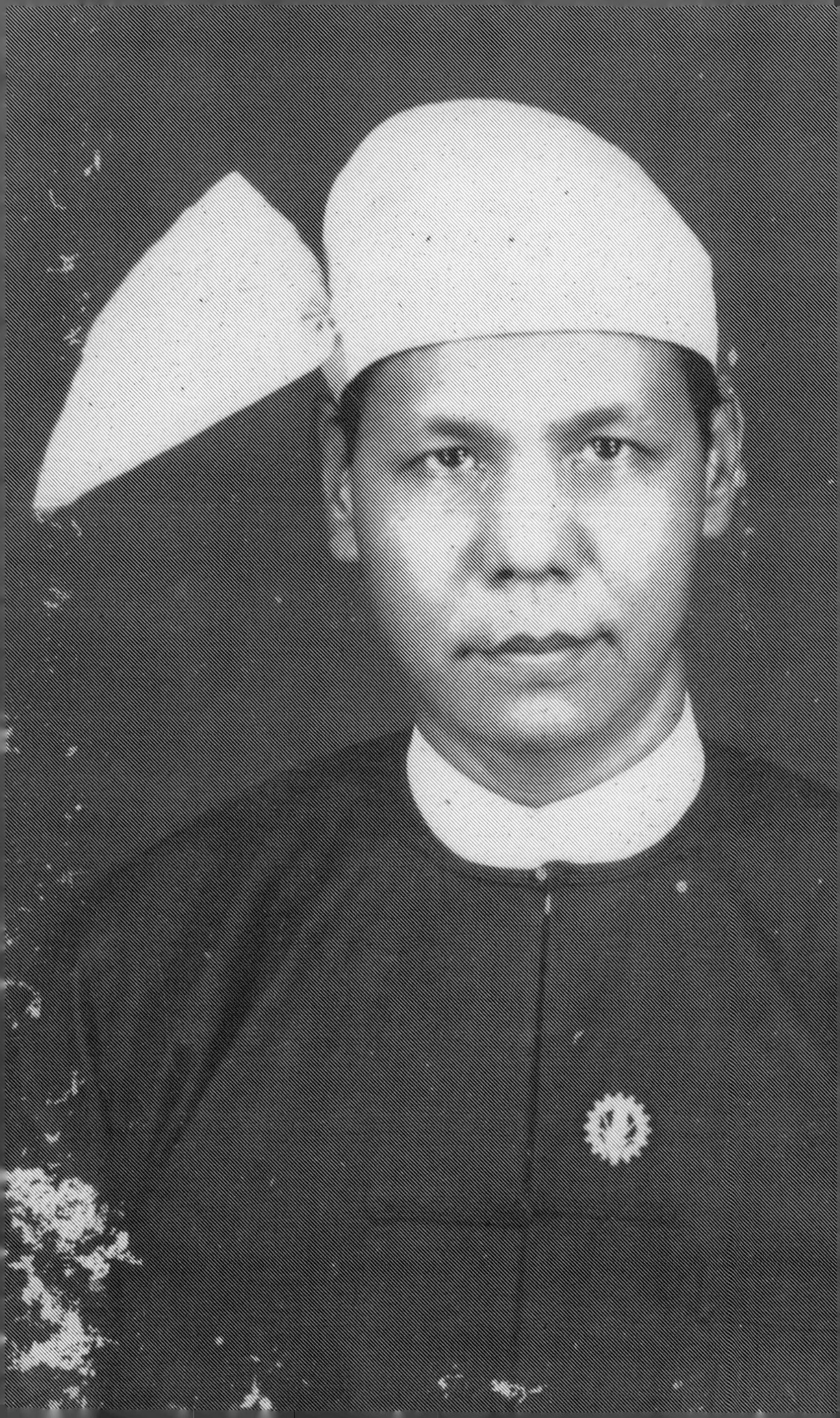

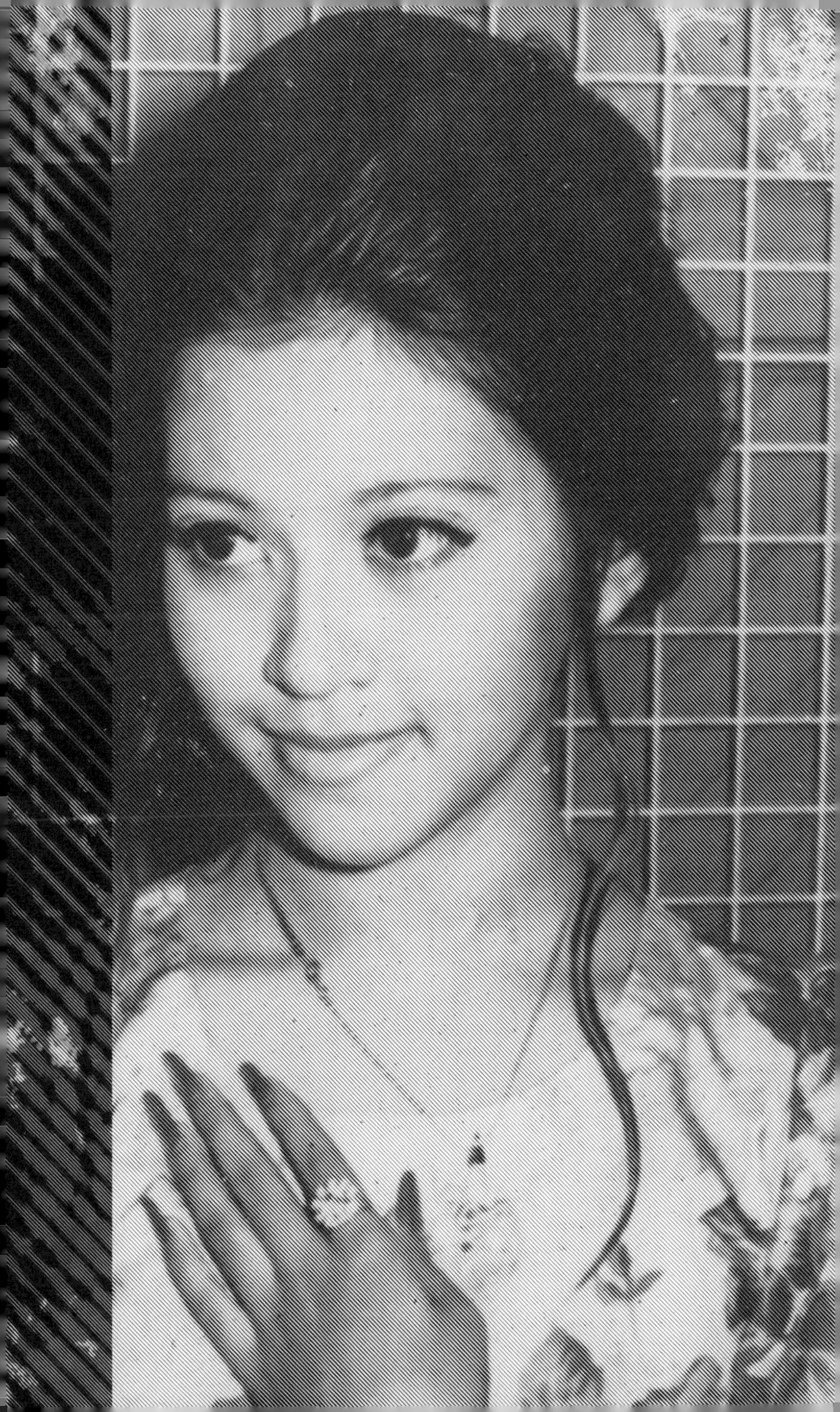

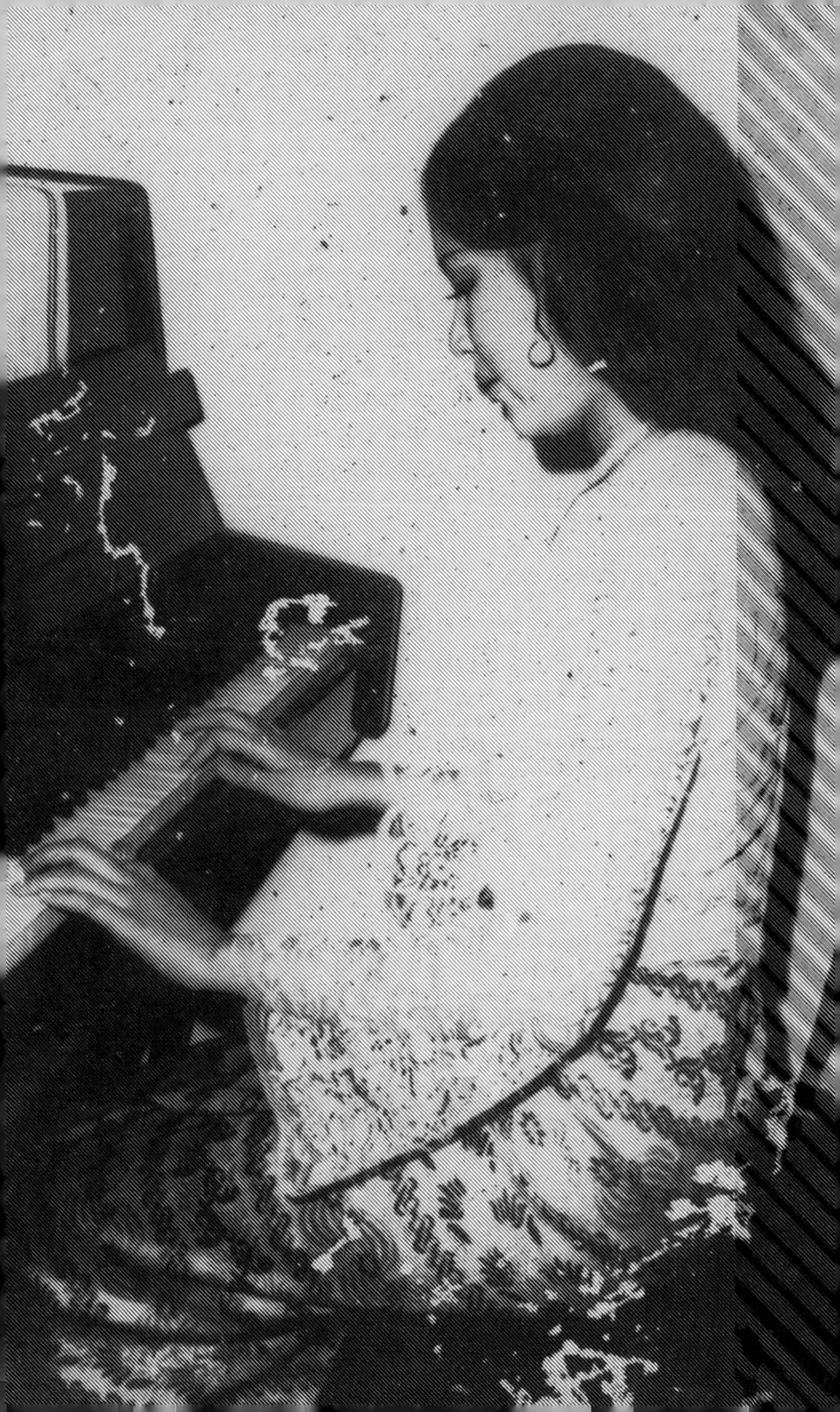

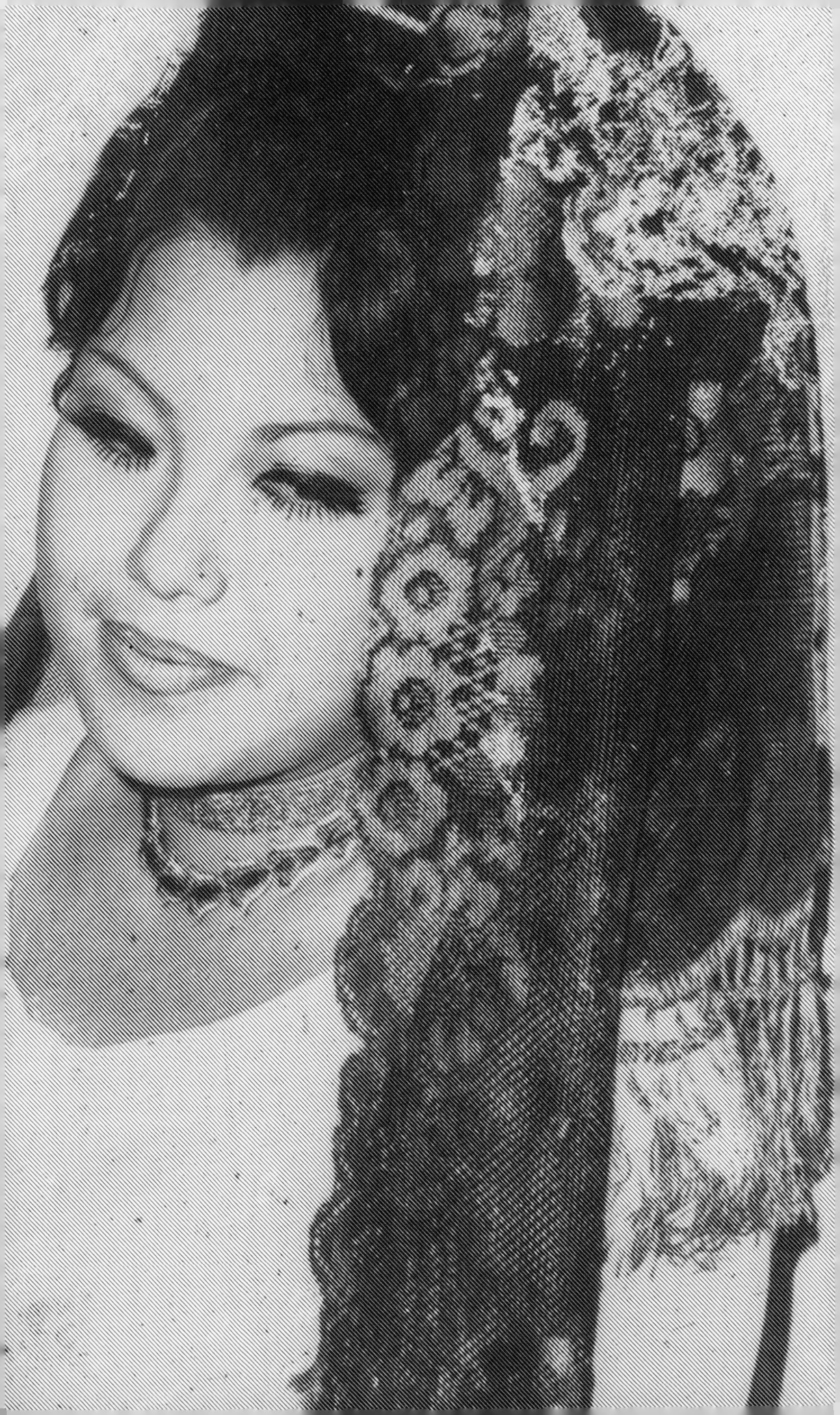

A Sense of Duty

Latvia-USSR border

31.12.1926

Vasili Ilych stamps the snow off his boots, stamps again to be sure that he is heard, then pushes open the passage door. Tania isn't alone in the front room. She and her sisters sit around the table playing cards, their fingers fluttering in the lamplight like anxious birds. Five of clubs. Six of hearts. Vasili Ilych stares at the women. Once he had stirred nervousness in people, made them shudder, watched their eyes dart away in fear. Now no one gives him the chance. His wife does not even look at him.

On the floor the samovar hums by the brick oven. Next to it the tray is cluttered with the tea things: the jam, the sweets, the chocolates, but no vodka. Of course, there is no vodka.

Theirs is the finest house in the village – double-fronted brick with an iron roof, and two windows looking on to the street – but it is not good enough for Tania. Nothing is good enough for her, Vasili Ilych thinks with bitterness, at least not since those nights in Moscow.

'Jack of spades,' says Tania to her sisters, laying a card on the table, not lifting her eyes from her hand.

Outside the wind howls and snow squeezes through the gaps around the shaking door. Vasili Ilych shrugs his greatcoat onto a chair. Next to it he drapes his holster and the knife sheath. As the steam rises from the stiff, frozen wool, he sees that her icon has been restored to its former place. Old habits die hard, but die they must. Without a word he unhooks it from the wall and throws it in the oven.

Vasili Ilych had been forged by the Revolution. To survive its fires he had joined the Party. When his ambition and zeal became apparent, he was moulded like a crude chunk of pig iron into the Cheka, the Extraordinary Commission to Combat Counter-Revolution and Sabotage. At the Butyrka and Lubyanka prisons the iron was beaten into a sickle-sharp blade. Vasili Ilych slashed and stabbed whatever he was told to, knowing that without obedience there could be no society, that loyalty was to be measured in the blood of traitors. Revolution was not made with silk gloves. The bourgeoisie must be purged of their venal ways and petty dreams. All power to the Soviets!

Some prisoners were shot, others tortured until they were no longer recognisable – not as class enemies, not even as human. In his savage trade Vasili Ilych preferred the swift, silent certainty of the knife, flashing in the dark cells as it did its heroic work. Survivors were sent to the Solovki Special Purpose Camp or the gulags in Siberia.

No one asked questions.

In Russia's new world of equals, Vasili Ilych simply followed orders – when tightening blindfolds, when pissing in a kneeling whore's face, when the people's enemies lay naked on his iron bed with electrodes on their fingers or balls. Like so many others, he believed that he was part of a great collective endeavour, and so felt freed from the burden of self.

At home, Tania struggled with his rising temper and lust, his drunkenness and sudden, unpredictable cruelty. Once in a Moscow park he tempted a sparrow into his hand then snapped shut his fist, crushing the bird, laughing even as its beak tore his palm. He wasn't the man she'd married, Tania told herself. She tried to manage him by locking away the vodka, along with his other pleasures, reserving them for Saints' Days and the May holiday. But to no avail.

Vasili Ilych was convinced that everywhere and always, the state was in peril. To protect it he had to perform the duties expected of him, without mercy. He brought innovative methods from the provinces to Lubyanka. He saw to it that priests were cut and crucified, that naked aristos were dunked in water then staked in winter courtyards until they became living ice statues. He even placed rats in an iron tube and pressed it against a prisoner's stomach. When the tube was heated, the terrified vermin were driven to gnaw through the man's body in an effort to escape. To prove his worth both to himself and to the revolution, Vasili Ilych had to kill.

Then quite suddenly, and without warning, his blade went soft.

One night after another he failed as a man. In their mean Moscow bedroom, in his fury he roared at Tania, forcing her to take him in her mouth, bullying her into attempting acts that repulsed her. He cried louder and louder, waking the neighbours, blaming her for every disappointment. He called her frigid, ugly, a hag. But there was no denying that the failure was his alone.

Later, in the darkness of tormented half-sleep he would hear the sound not of Tania's weeping, or the blood pounding in his ears, but the laugh of a single, defiant prisoner. He would press his hands against his ears, trying to block out the echo of that laugh.

'You don't know how I suffer,' he would wail, clinging to Tania like a child.

When Vasili Ilych was reassigned to a frontier detachment on the new border with Latvia, Tania damned him for it. She knew that it was not a promotion. She'd become accustomed to the privileges that came with his work in Moscow, whatever the cost. Like his superiors, she understood that he was feeble. Unlike them, she knew his real weakness. She called him inept, impotent, a boiled turnip. He beat her for it, on her buttocks and the soles of her feet where the bruises would not show, then tried again to take her by force. After he failed, she never again met his eyes.

'I need a man whose knife isn't blunt,' she told her sisters over cards, opening a box of Red October chocolates.

After Moscow, she'd found her comfort in food, any food that was available in that world of scarcity. 'Everyone is hoarding these days,' she explained. 'I might as well hoard on my body, for all it's worth.'

In the evenings when husband and wife were alone, Tania ate fast and loud, as if to swallow the words she dared not utter, as if to make herself both silent and repulsive. At the supper table she chewed with her mouth open, letting the soup or pork juices drip from the lips that Vasili Ilych had once longed to kiss. Conversations snagged on barbed words. Their nights were bitter, and bruised.

The last dawn of 1926 breaks with an icy wind reeling over the fields, blurring earth and sky. Vasili Ilych's border post stands on the edge of nowhere, in a broad clearing at the place where rail line and manure-stained road emerge from the pinewoods. As he inspects a local farmer's papers, the snow squeaks under the leather soles of his boots.

The Moscow train isn't due for an hour, so he takes shelter inside the guardhouse, a small cabin built of rounded logs, and dispatches the two guards to patrol the line to sober them up. Alone in the small room, he watches the smoke from the stove curl upwards through the vent in the gabled roof. One day, he muses, when Communism has triumphed and all national boundaries have vanished, I will be remembered as a tireless fighter at the forefront of international revolution. One of the true comrades. One who will never surrender!

Never lose! Never die!

Uplifted by his thoughts, Vasili Ilych's mind drifts to a New Year's supper of roasted grouse, or pigeon stuffed with currants and a five kopeck roll. To make the meat tender, a teaspoon of vinegar must be poured down the bird's throat three hours before slaughter. Snipe can be kept until January if brought in fresh from the fields, plucked and wrapped in cabbage leaves, baked in dough and sealed in a barrel. Yet all the while, he knows there'll be no special meal at home this evening. Tania will be too busy playing *Vint*, or weeping over the ashes of her icon, or whispering to her sisters about him or about starvation in the Urals, about peasants killing and eating their children.

Lies. Lies.

Suddenly he has the taste for a drink.

In winter few motor vehicles risk the journey to his isolated border post, given the state of the roads. So it surprises him to see through the mud-splattered window a car emerge from between the pines. He notes its good repair and its Leningrad plates. He sees how low it rides on its axles. Above all he spots the woman in the passenger seat. He empties another glass. The vodka feels cool and clean on his tongue.

Outside, the willows moan in the wind as Corporal Kotov begins the search. All the couple's effects have to be examined – suitcases unpacked, boxes unsealed, letters read. New Year's gifts fall onto the snow, and Vasili Ilych casually orders that they be unwrapped. The smoked ham will do for supper, he thinks. The driver surrenders items as ordered, submitting himself for the body search, showing respect, but the woman doesn't leave her seat. Vasili Ilych knows her sort. They are called bourgeois, fellow-travellers. He recognises the airs and graces, and to shake her up he orders her into the guardhouse for inspection.

She is slender, as slender as Tania had once been. He tells her to remove her sheepskin coat, and watches her as he goes through its pockets. The coat and her handbag contain nothing of value: cigarettes, compact, needle and thread. She has no Party card.

'Take off your boots,' he orders.

As she obeys he sees her turn and bend and thinks, the hut is warm enough, why not? He steps forward to trap her against the desk, groping for her breasts. She struggles against him, squealing in alarm. He strikes her in sudden fury, spinning her round and slamming her head down hard onto the desktop. He kicks her legs apart. He unbuttons himself. But he hadn't hit her hard enough. She twists out of his grasp, yelling, 'Get off! Get off!'

He unsheathes his knife as she grabs her coat.

'So cut me, Comrade,' she jeers and – unsteady, with forehead bleeding – weaves barefoot out of the cabin, across the snow to the car.

Comrade. The word had stopped him – that, and now the sound of the approaching Moscow train.

She and her lily-livered partner got lucky, Vasili Ilych mutters to himself, pulling at his trousers. Although maybe I couldn't have taken her, maybe Tania's right, even in my anger I don't have the balls.

It had been easier at the Lubyanka.

He stands at the door, waves his pistol in the air and bellows at Kotov, 'Get them out of here. Out!'

The red flags on the locomotive are frozen stiff by the driving snow. Steam engulfs the frontier arch as the train sighs to a stop. Beyond the arch and its slogan 'Proletarians of all lands unite!' a clutch of Latvians appear, wrapped up against the cold in hats and caps and snow-dusted greatcoats. Jacobson, head of Latvian frontiersmen, places a table and stool beside the rails on their side of the border. Vasili Ilych – still livid – notices a cine-camera mounted on a tripod.

Soviet police guards file from the train to flank the third-class carriage. An OGPU officer steps through the thin line, all but pushing aside Vasili Ilych, further inflaming his anger. There is to be a

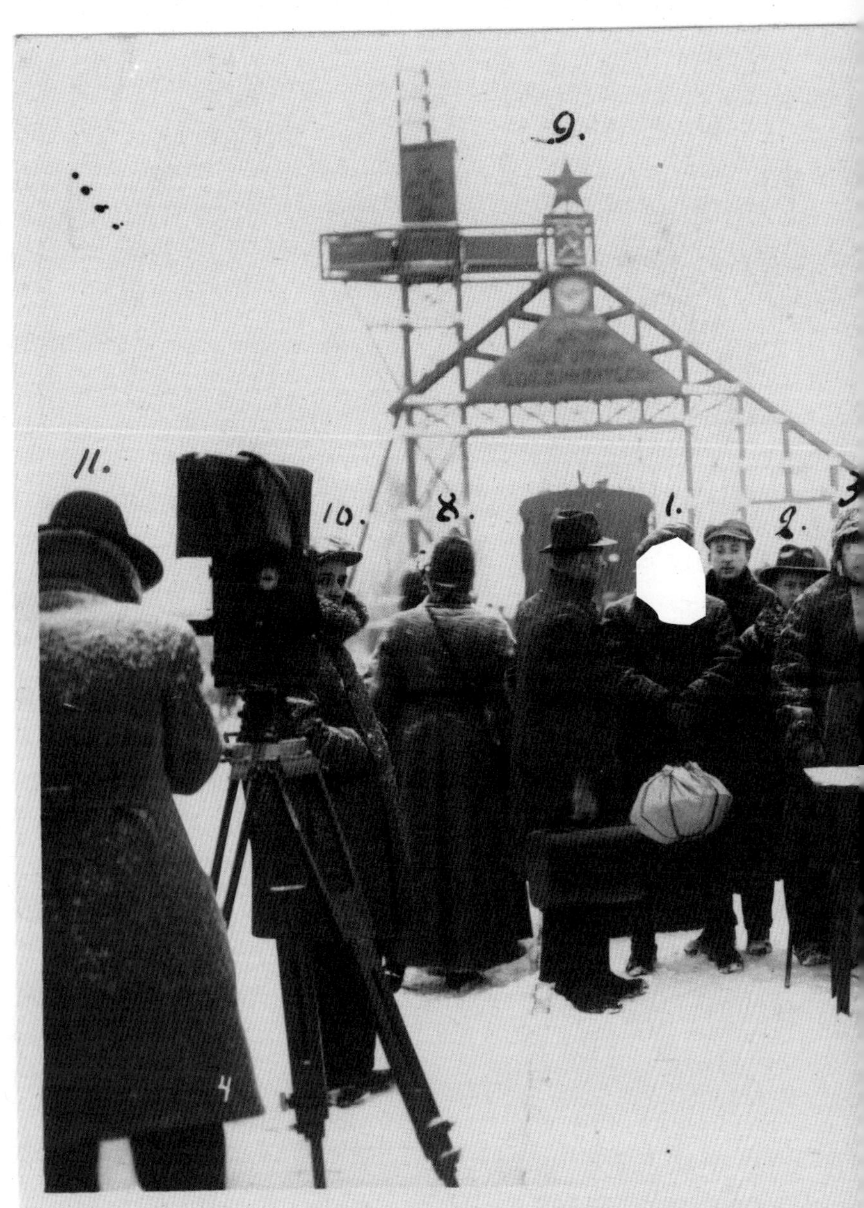
9.
11.
10.
8.
1.
2.
3
4

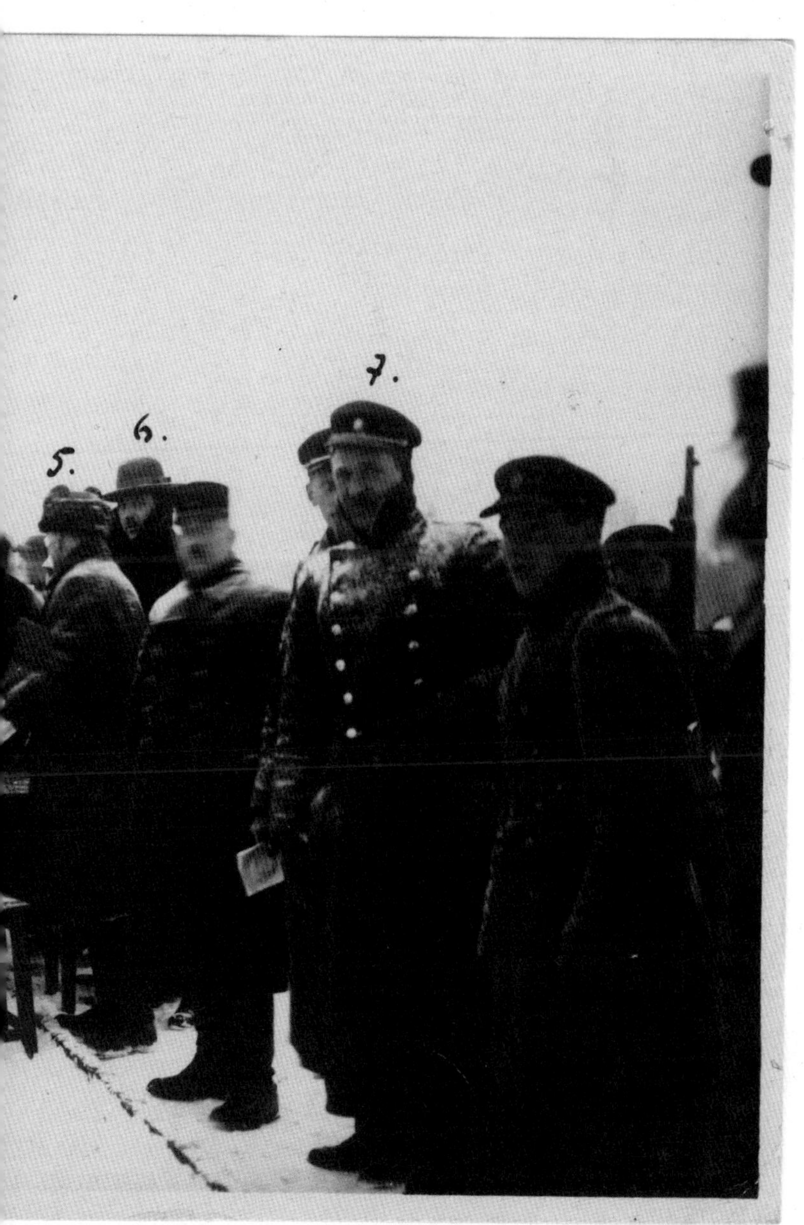
5.
6.
7.

prisoner exchange, the officer tells him. Thirty-four loyal Bolshevik agents captured by Latvia are to be swapped for thirty-four agitators, traitors and provocateurs, men and women of whom the Soviet Union will be pleased to be rid. The frontier detachment is required to facilitate the action and nothing more. Vasili Ilych manages to scan the order papers, and recognises a prisoner's name.

Brunovsky.

Vladimir Brunovsky had been a colleague of Lenin and Trotsky. In 1919 in Moscow, Lenin himself had asked Brunovsky to victual the Third Army on the Eastern Front. But soon after, amidst rumours of treason and espionage, Brunovsky had lost his revolutionary fervour and applied to immigrate to Latvia. The official word was that he'd been unwilling to accept the orders of the Government without reference to his principles, thus proving himself to be an enemy of the people. In the Party newspaper *Rodina*, Brunovsky had even published an open letter about the failures of 'my poor, miserable, discredited country'. The betrayal resulted in his immediate arrest and imprisonment at Lubyanka.

Vasili Ilych remembered Brunovsky. Five years ago he'd been locked into Cell 10 on Death Corridor, next to the Archbishop of Finland. Like other inmates, he had been forbidden to talk. Exercise was limited to ten minutes a day. No bed clothes were issued, only a mattress stuffed with wood shavings and straw. When Vasili Ilych had entered Cell 10 for the first time, Brunovsky had failed to rise to his feet as required by the regulations. Instead he had lain on his bunk in his rags, without shoes or respect.

'Are you ill?' Vasili Ilych had asked the prisoner.

'No.'

'So stand up at once.'

'You are a butcher. I won't stand for butchers.'

Vasili Ilych had hit him then, hit him in the face with his knuckles, and then drawn his knife. Its blade had caught the light from the high

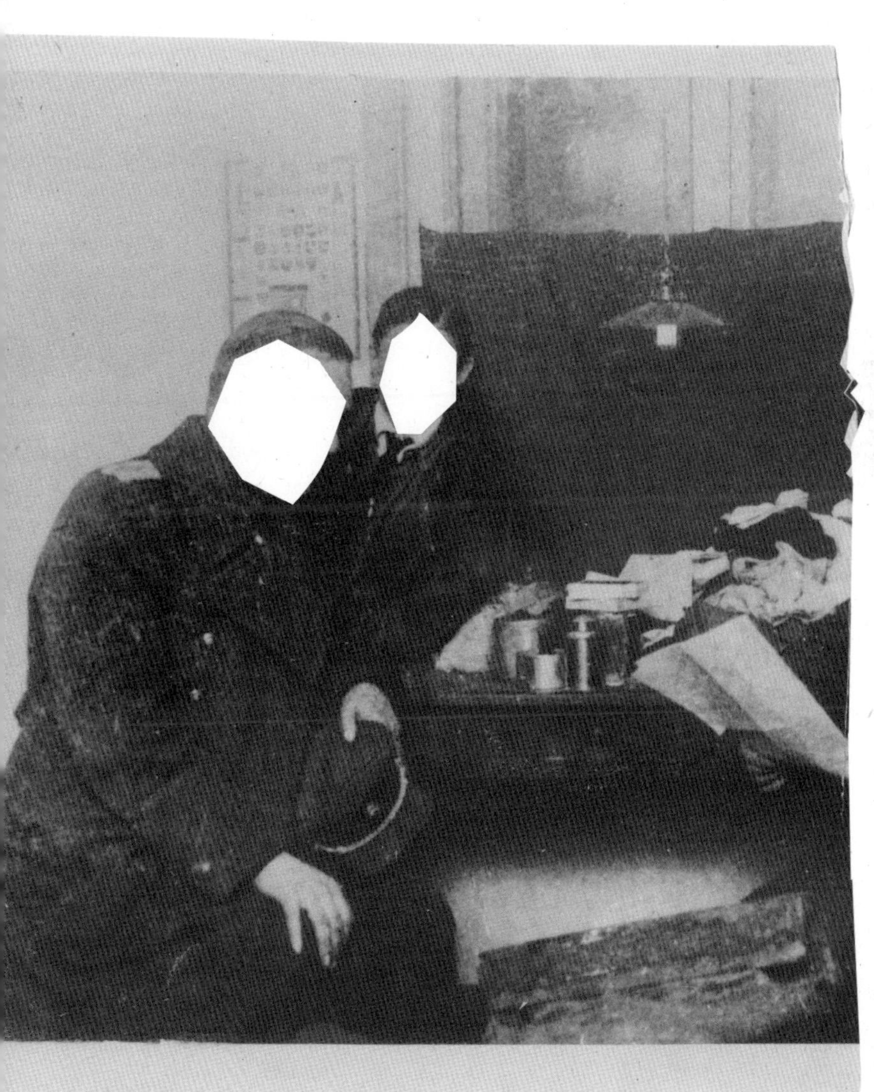

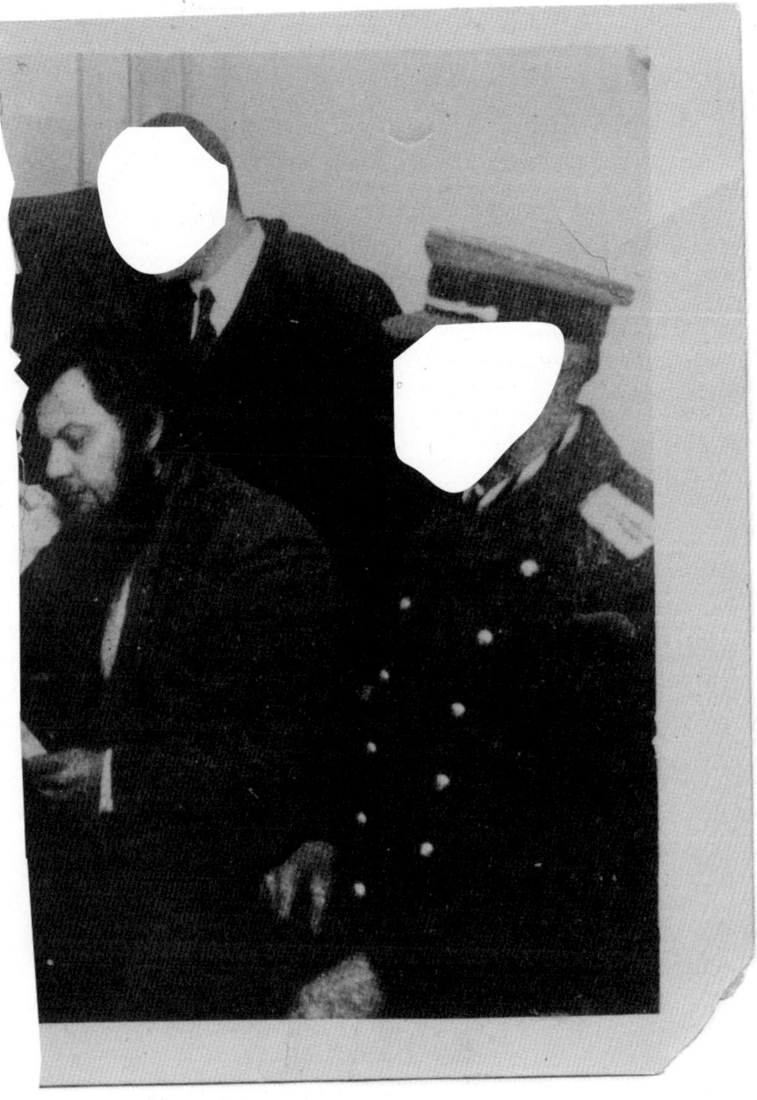

cell window. But Brunovsky hadn't lowered his eyes, hadn't stepped back, didn't whimper as did the others. He had just kept on staring, staring, and from that moment – in that first moment of doubt – Vasili Ilych had hated him, this man who reduced him to nothing with a look, and a laugh.

Now at the Zilupe border post, Brunovsky steps off the train and limps the last few metres towards the frontier, on the verge of escaping Revolutionary justice. At first he looks like an old man: stooped, weary, and with a pitiful bundle of possessions. Good riddance, defeatist dog!

But then Vasili Ilych sees his eyes.

Beneath the arch Brunovsky stops at the table and reaches out a bony hand to steady himself. A representative from the Latvian Ministry for Foreign Affairs rises to greet him formally. Two journalists press forward to snap photographs. The cine-cameraman pulls up his collar then pans to a close shot. Beyond the small crowd is the car with the Leningrad plates, the woman glaring back at Vasili Ilych.

A man is the sum of his actions, of what he has done and will do with his life. Brunovsky's body may have been broken, but his eyes were unchanged – those eyes that had shone with defiance, those eyes that Vasili Ilych should have plucked out five years ago.

Without hesitation Vasili Ilych – in broadcloth *budenovka* helmet – moves directly beside Brunovsky, coming to point blank range. Maybe the Cheka is playing a long game, he thinks, waiting until Brunovsky is forgotten and can be liquidated on the quiet. Or maybe they too are simply weak. Whatever their plan, every loyal Russian understands his duty and destiny.

Vasili Ilych isn't a coward, no matter what Tania says. In a world of equals he will prove himself to be one better. He looks into Brunovsky's eyes and in a moment of resolution reaches for his knife. But the sheath is empty. He had dropped the blade during the scuffle in the guardhouse. Doubt flashes across his face. He sees the prisoner laugh one last time.

Then Vasili Ilych remembers his pistol, unbuckles his holster and feels for the trigger.

On my travel writing journeys to Moscow, Berlin, Rangoon and beyond, I have always found the time to buy photographs and photo albums for myself. Call it a cross between a hobby and an obsession; it makes me feel like a kind of rescue worker, almost as if I - in common with the mysterious curator - could actually save the lives captured in the photographs. I suppose that's why it felt natural to add them - as well as my own pictures - to the collection.

It started after Burma, or at least with G.M. Ahuja's death, when I found myself filing away snapshots of his dilapidated studio to put his life and work in context for future researchers and storytellers. I did the same after a trip to North Korea, just out of a sense of thoroughness. But then, on a quiet Sunday - and I admit feeling something like a character in a John le Carré spy thriller - I filled a folder with images of Cold War Berlin and slotted it into a new home on the shelves. I'd started visiting - and photographing - the divided city in the 1970s when the first sight of the Wall had shaken me to the core. I hadn't understood how the men and women who'd built the Wall had grown blind to their human experience, clouding it with dogma. I'd longed to understand the motivation of people like Vasili Ilych, how they'd come to act as they did, and at the same time I needed to ask myself a question. How would I have behaved under the Communists, or Nazis? Would I have stood up for principles, or allied myself with the majority and followed orders? It was a key moment for me, part of the reason I became a writer, and the start of the journey that had led to the archive.

After the Berlin photos, I'm afraid things did begin to get a little out of hand. I tucked away travel photographs from other trips, to Afghanistan, Nepal and Crete. I created files about canoeing across Canada and following the hippie trail to India. Next I brought in all the snapshots of my childhood. I even took my father's photographs - he had served in both world wars and witnessed the surrender of the German Fleet at Scapa Flow - to add to the collection. I couldn't stop myself. All my life in pictures, and the lives of other people who had crossed my path, seemed to flow onto the shelves as if in a conscious desire to find a timeless, everlasting home.

But I didn't go so far as to Photoshop myself into the crowd gathered around Vladimir Brunovsky at the Latvian border. Or to retouch the *Dr Strangelove* crew shots. Or to doctor the picture of the burning pilot, even though I felt it was me who had held the camera in 1941, that I had slid into the dying pilot's body, that I had been there all the time, and never there.

As I filed away the last of my life's photographs and chose the last stories to write, I began to wonder if I had somehow ceased to exist, outside of the archive I mean. I recalled the yogic notion that humans don't breathe air, but rather the air breathes humans. Perhaps I'd only imagined that I had plucked lives down from the shelves, fleshed out the invisible, slept on an upstairs couch in west London. Had I really merged War Ministry casualty lists with a rabbit hunter's diaries? Maybe I was already dead. I even started to doubt that I had met G.M. Ahuja on his deathbed, or that there had ever been a Czech woman on the number 9 bus, until I opened the Akron album to look for a tendril of wild red hair.

Her photograph is on my desk. His portrait is beside my bed. I look at the picture of you, as you once were, and will always remember you.

Record of Game Felled

Poitou, France

11.04.1911–11.11.1918

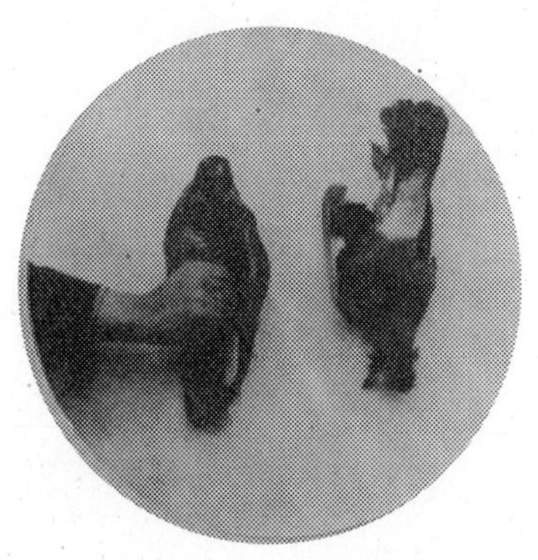

11.04.1911

Marcel shoots his first duck! A beauty. He was in a hide on the bank of the Charente. It flew out over the water. Marcel – who is 15 years old – bagged it through a gap in the dyke. Our ever-trusty Diane retrieved it from the river.

14.04.1911

Marcel took his first curlew, plus two corncrakes that he picked off as they took flight. He also shot a weasel. I downed a snipe and a magpie.

27.08.1911

Marcel and I left home at 10:00 with our panniers laden with lunch. The summer air was scalding. We dropped our bicycles beside the Carcouet and walked up towards la Terrière. There was no game because of the heat. Then in the shade of a great elm, beside the St Laurent à la Perrière road, Diane flushed a young hare out of the brambles. In a flash Marcel rolled over, grabbed the shotgun and laid it low. He saved us from returning home empty-handed.

Our hunt – *la Société de chasse de gallais* – was founded in 1904 by Messrs Beucher, Gibbert, Cornet and myself, Charles Chiquet. Our usual beat is the farmland of Mr Chambourdon (around 150 hectares) and much of the three-hundred acre pine forest belonging to Mr Chevrellière. Our gamekeeper is Charles Thébaut. Our gundogs are Diane, Trompette, Rigolette, Fuyra, Finette and Lucrèce.

06.09.1911 Fouras

A full day away from home on the coast at Les Palles. In the morning Marcel and I ventured out on a fishing smack, breakfasting on the water and then putting a bounty of fish into the basket. In the afternoon we had more wonderful hunting, which ended only when we ran out of cartridges.

Charles Chiquet:

1 northern shoveller duck
2 curlews
5 ruddy ducks
7 sandpipers
2 plovers

Marcel Chiquet:

1 curlew
11 terns
1 ruddy duck
3 red knots (*Bécasseau maubèche*)
8 sandpipers
2 plovers

Total bag: 43 birds

10.04.1912

Belle-île-en-mer. Another seaside shoot off Sauzon in Brittany. One of the sailors attached bait to the end of a line and dragged it behind the dinghy. The gulls couldn't resist the temptation.

Charles Chiquet: 5 kittiwake gulls (*Rissa tridactyla*)
Marcel Chiquet: 7 kittiwake gulls

Later in the evening Marcel brought down a young silver gull (*Chroicocephalus novaehollandiae*). Great sport.

25.09.1913 Gallais

At the very moment I fired at a bolting rabbit, our old gundog Diane bounded into the line of fire. The full blast of lead hit her in the cranium. She died instantly.

11.06.1914 Forêt de St Sauvant

Marcel bagged two buzzards from his hiding place at the foot of their tree. The cock had perched on a nearby branch while the female flew toward the nest. She was carrying rabbit for the chicks. Marcel later grabbed two of them from the nest. Earlier in June he had passed his *Baccalauréat* with Honours.

14.06.1914 Forêt de St Sauvant

Drove to gamekeeper's house. Marcel shot a magpie. The president of our hunt, our fine friend Beucher, appointed me club manager and elevated Marcel to full member status.

26.07.1914 Fouras

From under the plane trees Marcel brought down a laughing gull (*Larus atricilla*). Very unusual in these waters. Also two sandpipers.

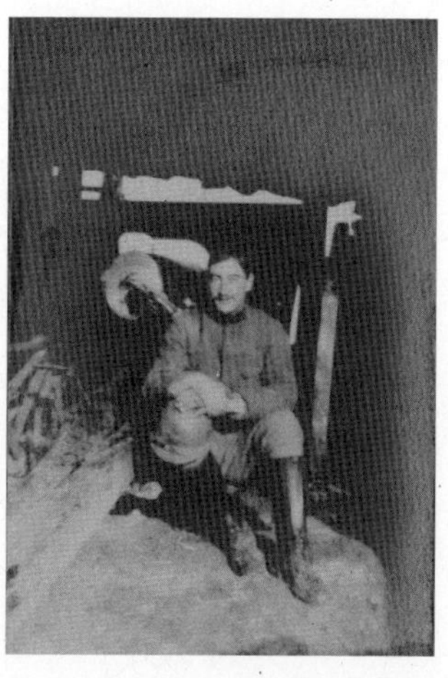

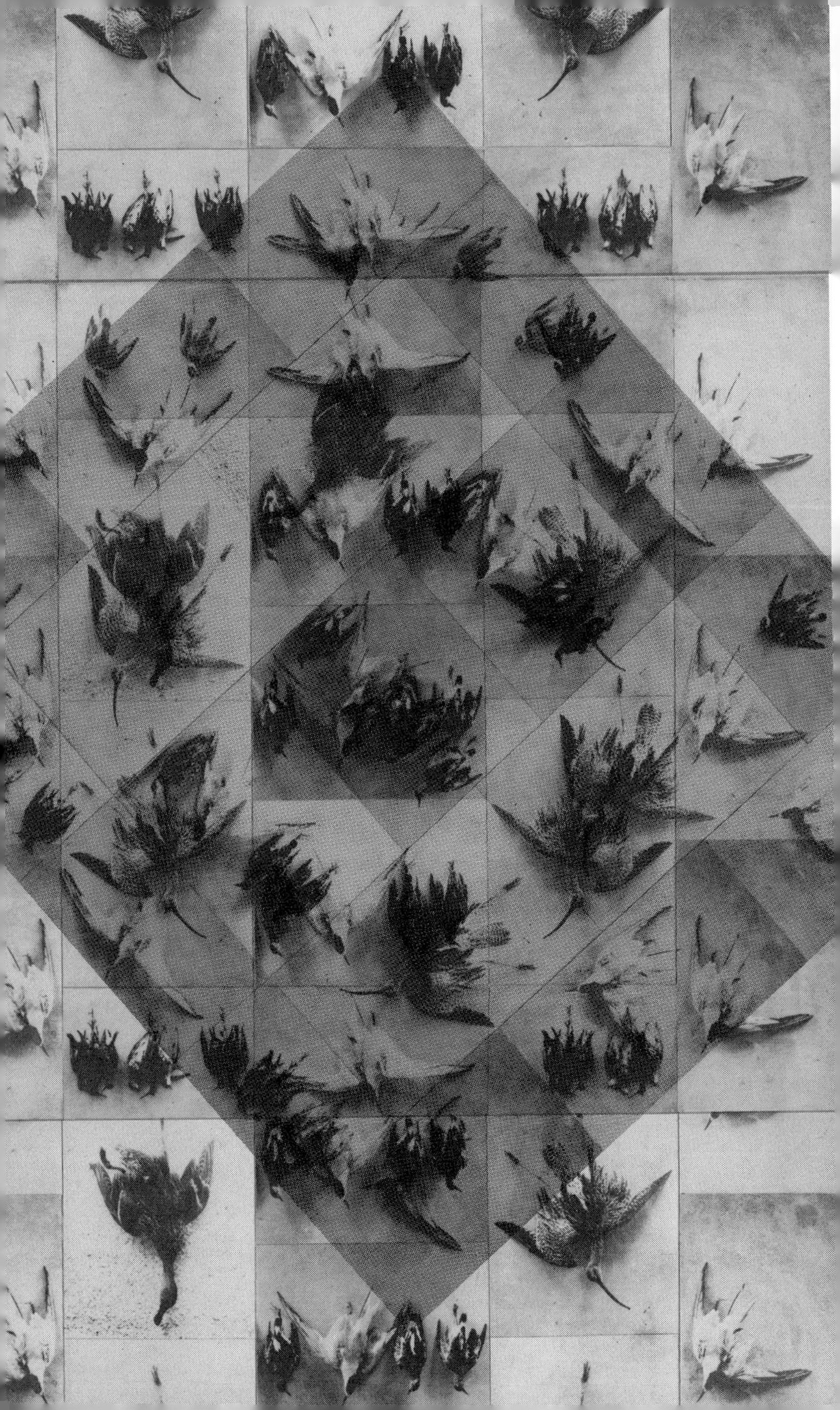

27.07.1914 Fouras

Marcel shot another laughing gull. Remarkable.

01.08.1914

Mobilisation.

04.08.1914

War declared.

03.12.1914 Jallais

No open hunting season in Poitou due to the hostilities. Without guns, we caught rabbits with hounds and ferrets and gave them to the hospitals. The ferrets are fed on bread and milk, but never before the hunt or they drop off to sleep. Our gamekeeper Thébaut was mobilised in December.

27.10.1914	3 rabbits
02.11.1914	1 rabbit
05.11.1914	6 rabbits
08.11.1914	12 rabbits
12.11.1914	11 rabbits
17.11.1914	6 rabbits
19.11.1914	8 rabbits
22.11.1914	12 rabbits
29.11.1914	10 rabbits
03.12.1914	5 rabbits
Total bag:	74 heads

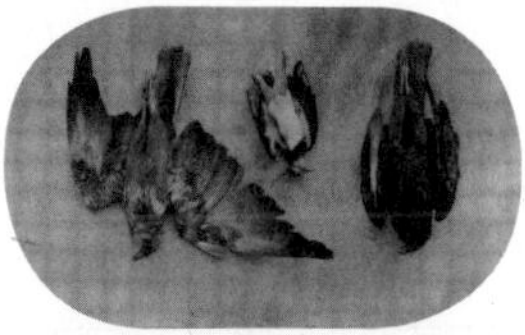

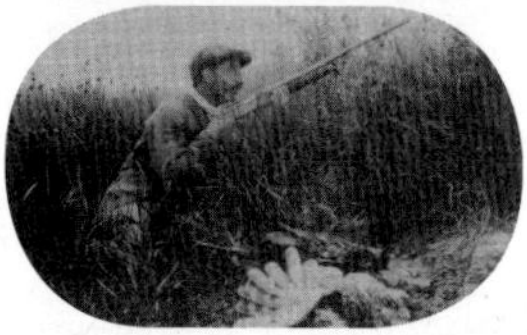

31.12.1914

Total bag for the year (for our two guns):

---

421 heads.

Game:

1 hare

4 squirrels

159 rabbits (with dogs and ferrets)

Game birds:

3 pheasants

2 woodcocks

1 pigeon

1 turtle dove

Marsh:

1 mandarin duck

1 snipe

17 woodcocks

4 gulls

Raptors:

5 buzzards

1 harpaye marsh harrier

3 kestrels

Miscellaneous:

12 crows

4 magpies

1 jay

2 owls

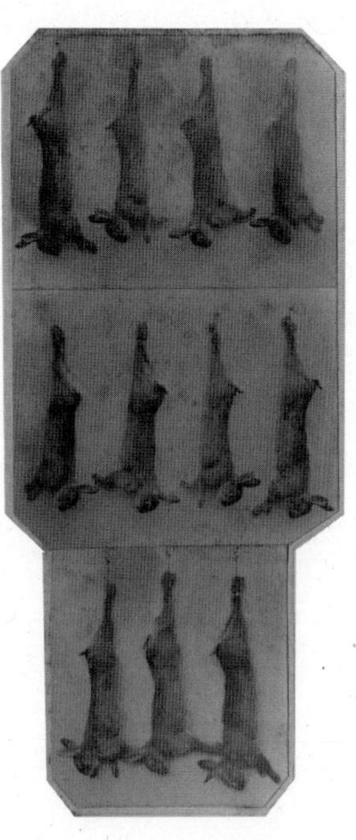

01.01.1915

January was vile with heavy rain and wild winds. On our first outing of the year we crossed the Charente by ferry and bypassed Saint-Agnant en route to Marennes and the wetlands. We hunted for about an hour. Many of the birds fell too far away to be brought in by the dogs. Later in the month the weather improved and we hunted from the car, shooting lapwings with a pistol. Marcel potted one in three birds using a 6mm ball. Poaching can be both great fun and great sport.

01.02.1915

Marcel killed a cock at the edge of the Gallent-Roy road. Picked up by Rigolette.

31.12.1915

Again in 1915 there was no open season. Only rabbits could be taken until the end of March. Marcel was called up on 10.01, but because of a clerical error he didn't report to barracks until 28.02. He left for the Front on 23.11 with the 20th Artillery. I hunted some 25 times without him. Poaching has destroyed so much game. Some of the rabbits we caught with dogs and ferrets had a broken brass wire noose around their necks.

Year's total bag:

---

210 heads (1 hare, 203 rabbits, 1 woodcock, 3 lapwings, 1 buzzard and a barn owl).

La chasse 1916

War continues. Heroic France throws its 20-year-olds into combat. Marcel was on the Somme, at Verdun, in Belgium firing at the rapacious ill-doers who are our enemies. In Poitiers permission was given to hunt any game that destroyed crops. At the Front Marcel captured an ermine.

25.03.1917 Fouras

Marcel on leave 24.03–04.04. Private motor travel now forbidden,

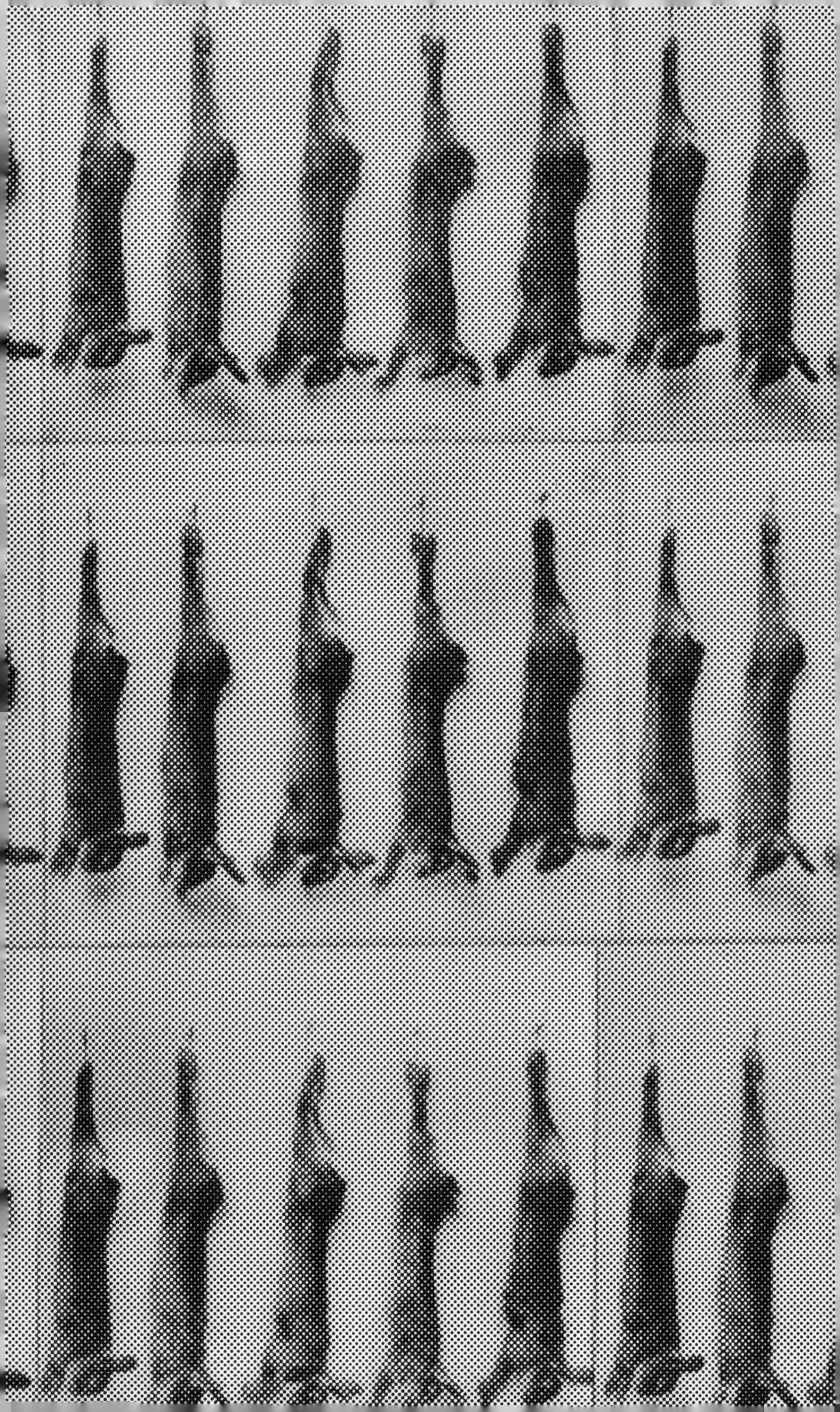

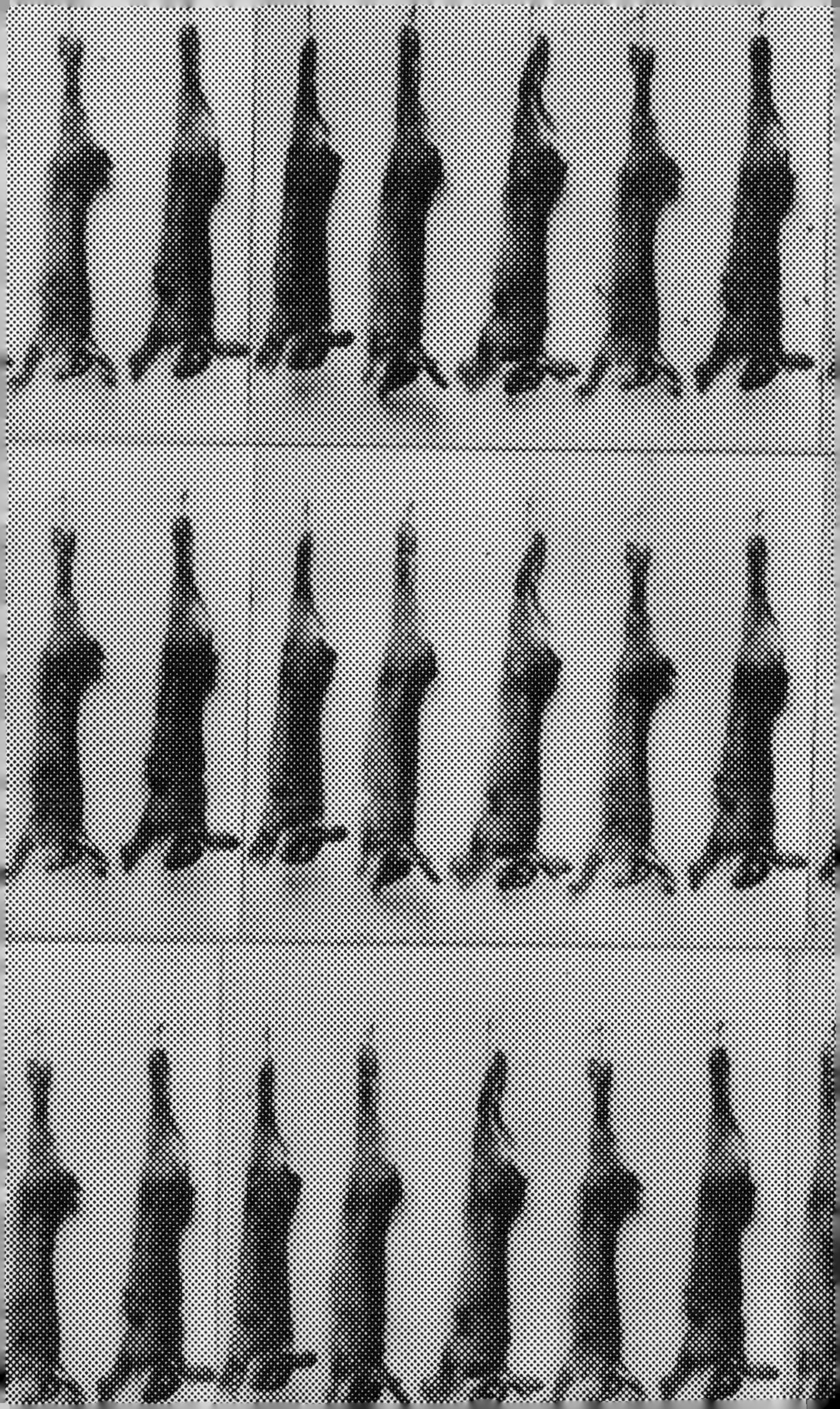

hence we travelled by train and then by bicycle to Carcouet. From his lookout, Marcel spotted a spring of teal nestling in a corner of the marsh. Under cover we stole to within 20 metres of them and then, as they started and took flight, bagged three of them with only four shots.

28.03.1917 Fouras.

On a foray into the marsh, in a corner of a ditch, Marcel killed a heron. We'd left our bicycles at Griffon. From behind the dyke he'd spotted three of the birds fishing in the shallows beside the canal. We were able to get within 50 metres of them. Marcel used 12g *chevrotine* buckshot.

29.10.1918

Vermin, especially foxes, have ravaged the henhouses. The rabbits that were so numerous before the war have now all but disappeared. Foxes eat them whole, badgers leave the head. Marcel was granted only two leaves, one of seven days, and one of 12 days as a reward for bravery. We have given up Mr Seillon's pine forest and leased instead *la chasse de la Foy* from Madame de Clisson.

11.11.1918

The war has been very hard. But even though the game has been decimated, France by contrast has bagged a marvellous quarry. The beaten Germans now beg for mercy. After four years of this frightful nightmare, our Marshall Foch called out: 'Hallelujah!'

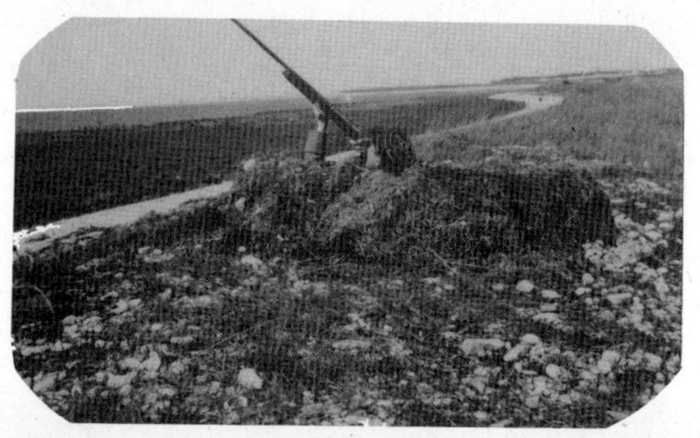

The movement of a canoe is like a reed in the wind. It shivers in a breeze, turns with the current, dips at the slightest shift of weight or weather. The canoeist glides across the surface looking for signs and patterns, buffeted by winds, losing his way. Since the summer days of my Canadian childhood, I have loved to canoe across the dark mirror of northern lakes, paddling with an inside flick of the blade, leaving a trail of twisting whirlpools in my wake. I have loved to travel between worlds and into a sanctuary of deep quiet where man's passing leaves only the faintest trace.

I never met Qiao, Mongo or Vasili Ilych. I've never been to Cameroon or Siberia, never hunted rabbits on the banks of the Charente or watched the sun rise over China from the Zhoushan Archipelago. Yet in a sense these people and places are part of my life. I know them for their century was my century - our ecstatic, ardent, bloody and heartbroken 20th century.

I read somewhere that those who do enough for their time should live for all time. I've done nothing of much importance with my time, nor did most of the men and women in the archive's photographs, but others did, and their deeds became enmeshed in our lives. Hence the importance of the stories in this everyday history does not lie in great acts or daring deeds, but rather in their selection from the vastness of the curator's collection, from time and space, in the creation of meaning.

Here are ten photographs, ten lives; remember them.

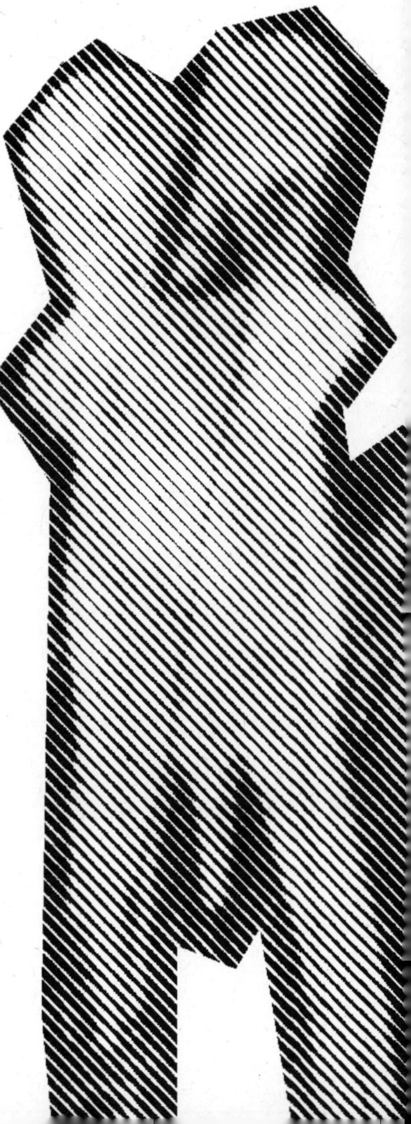

I Am

Siberia 01.01.1900

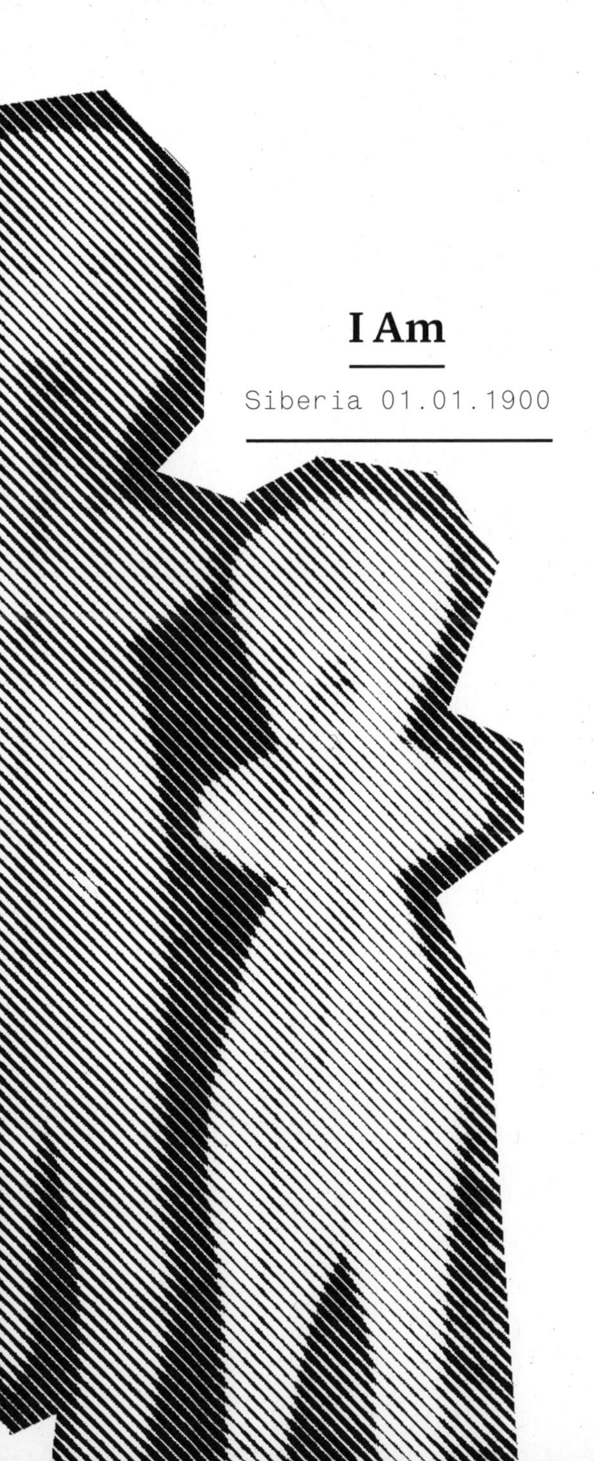

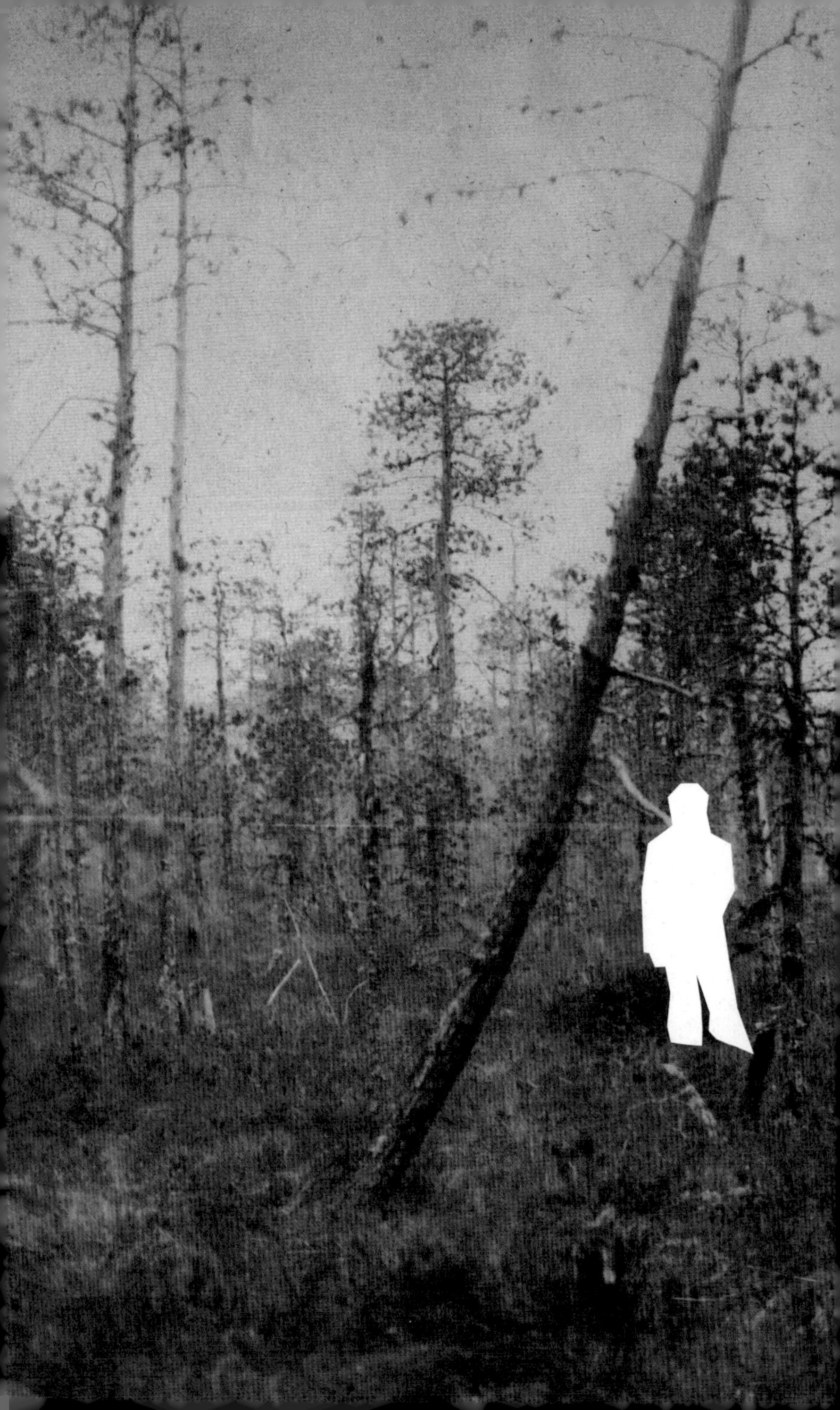

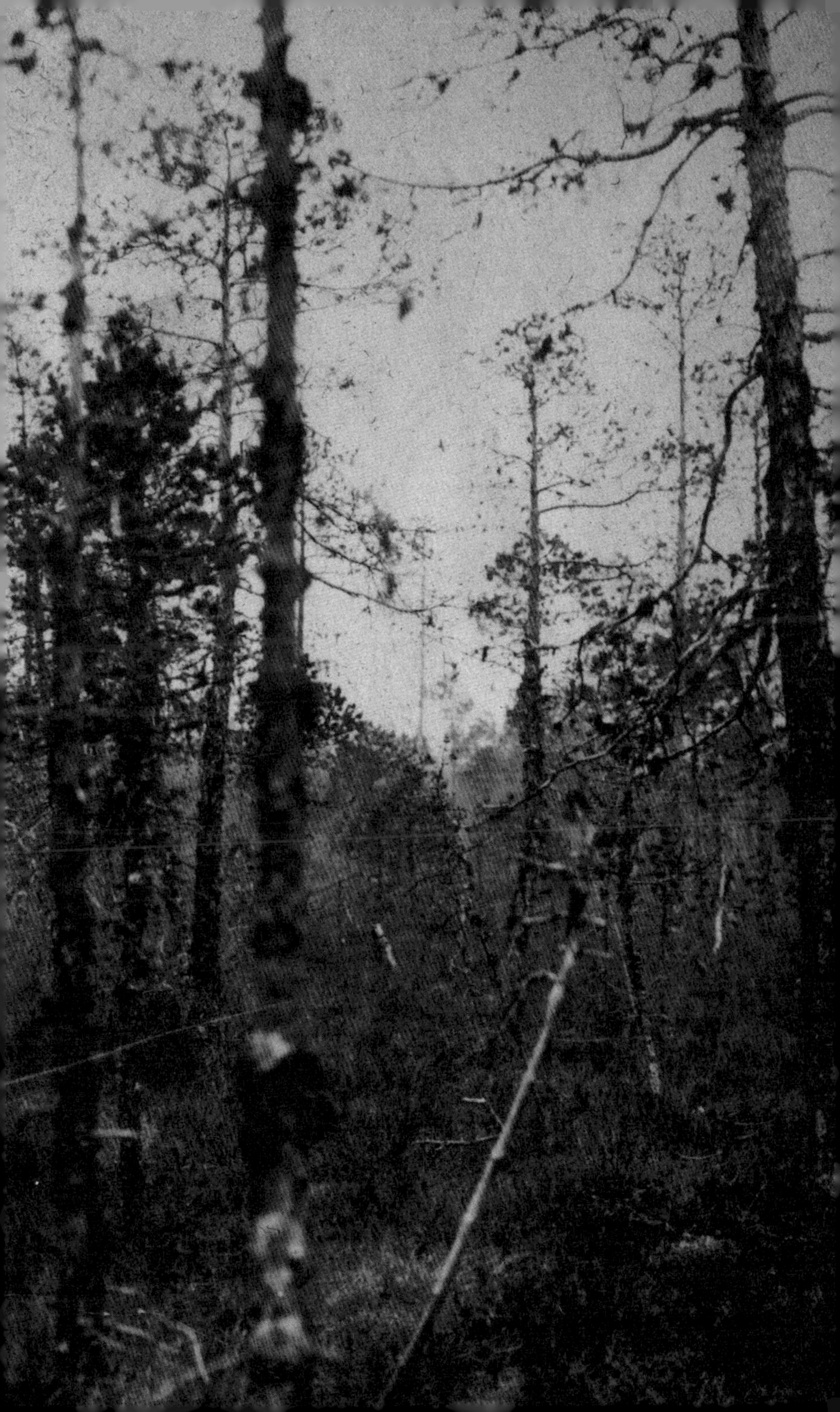

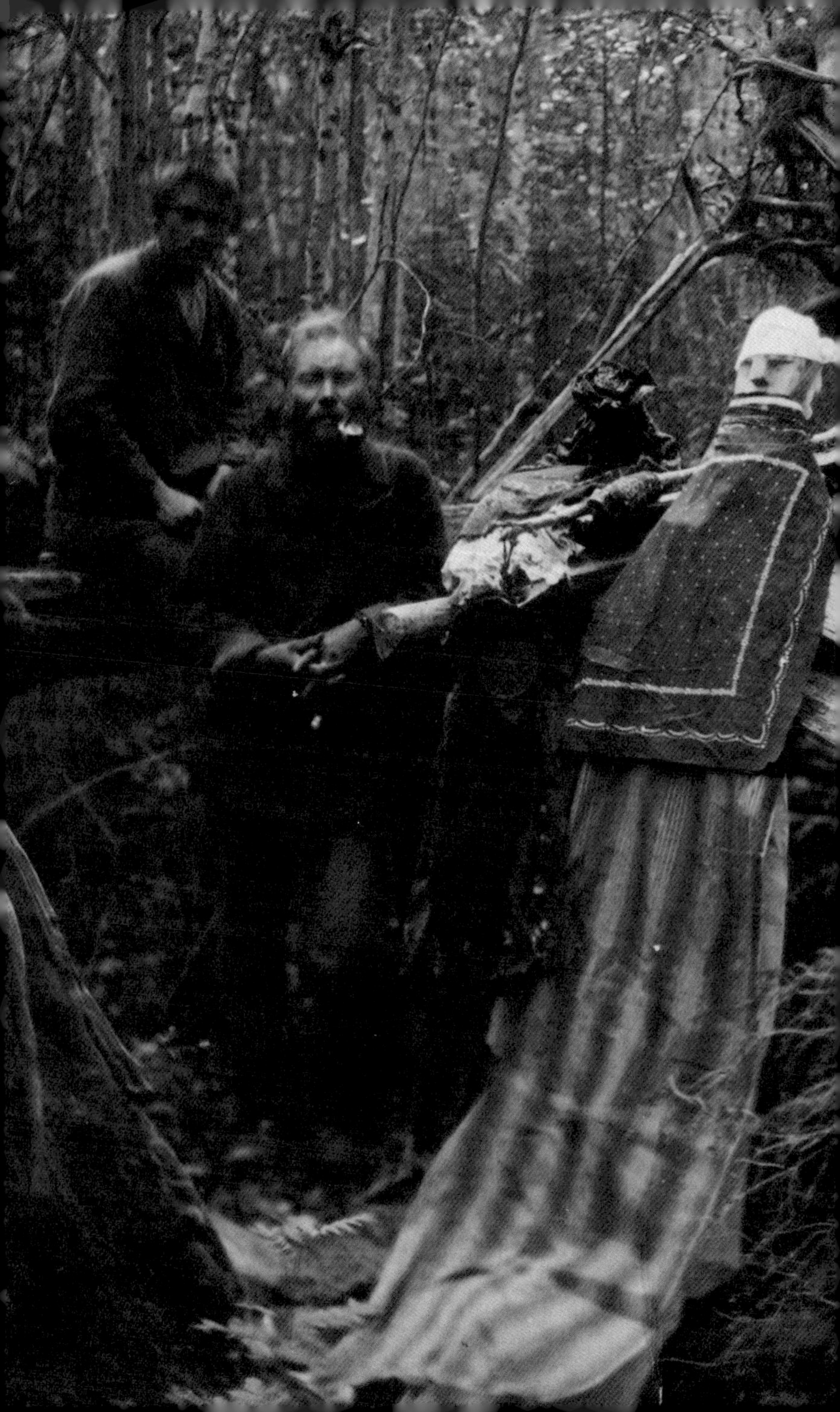

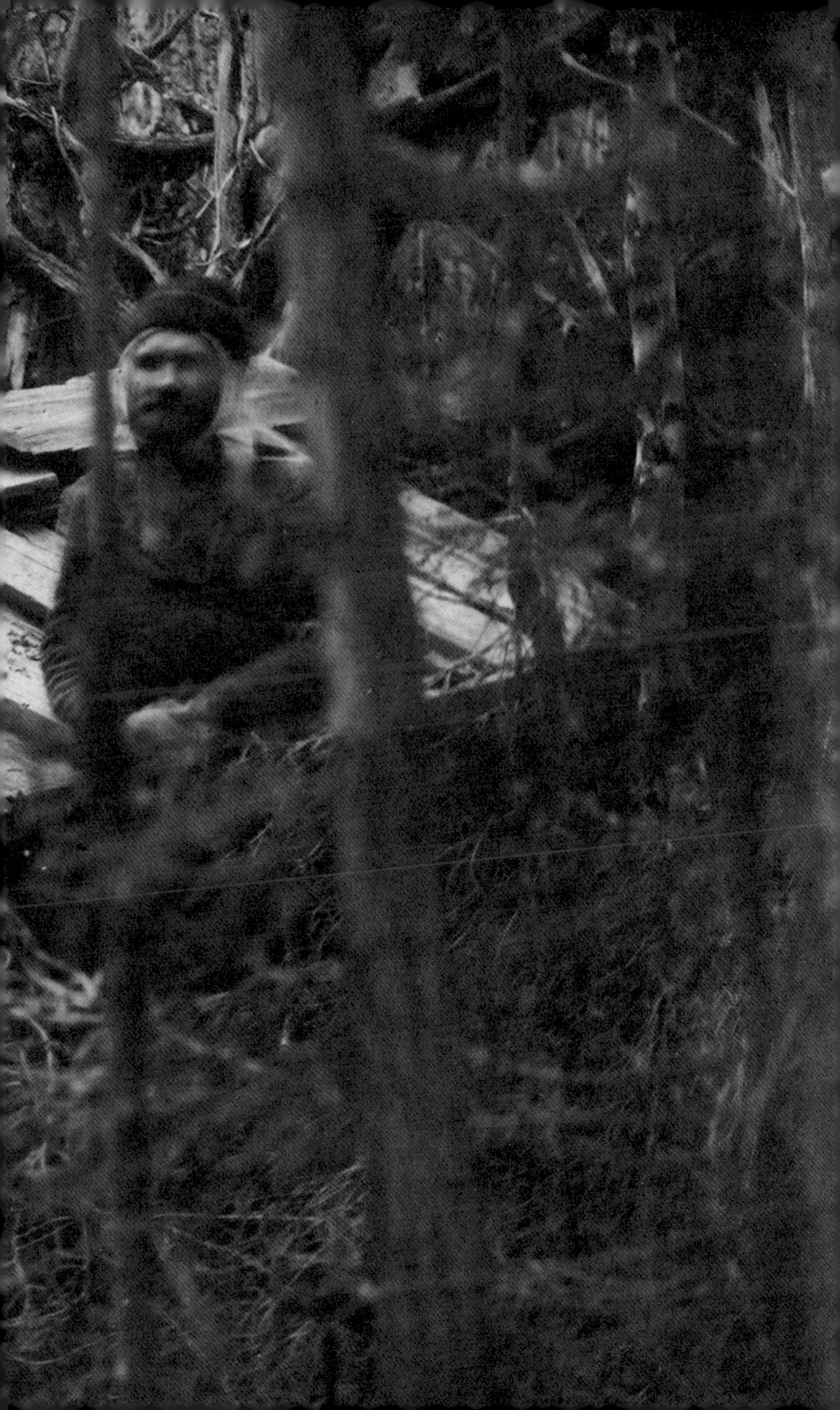

I am.

I am the bluethroat's song.

I am the scarlet mountain ash.

I am the lynx laying tracks across freshly fallen snow. I am the wind erasing them, ever so.

I am bear, elk and owl, cloudberry moor and summer lightning.

I am.

You are

wanderer and priest,

poet and thief.

You stand before me in wonder and exhaustion,

breathless in haughty boots and velvet *shuba*,

looking down your nose, looking through your lens, capturing me at last for your chamber of curios.

Friend, I knew you first as the Khanty and the Karasuk, then the Tagar and the Pazyryk. Once your people sang to me along the old pathways. Once you left me prayers and offerings. In your Second Layer of Heaven you buried your chiefs and princesses in red silk shirts and felt riding boots, for me. You turned their blind black eyes towards the east and ever-rising sun and begged me protect them from time.

But not now. Not now.

I am, ever.

Ever, but for time.

Ever, but for the sun and seasons. And you were part of me, all but the half of me, though no shaman could ever grant your wish. No god has it in his bag of spells. So in the winding Onon valley, in fear and disappointment you turned your back on me. The singing stopped. There came no more pleas to the God of the Sky and me. Instead you built stockades and stole salt and gold. You killed the sables, slaughtered the seals, carved up the land to plant corn and rye. You raised churches, wound clocks, and watched another candle gutter at the end of day.

I was all around you yet you chose to live apart from me. You hacked great roads through the marshes and forests. You drove steel tracks into my cold, indifferent heart. You unearthed iron and ideologies, smelted them and poured them molten into your bloody new century, all in faith of time eternal.

Those who stood in your way, who refused to belie mortality, were destroyed: the Nanai people who held on to their reverence for the spirits of the sun, moon and trees; the Koryak whose secrets had been passed from mother to daughter for a hundred generations; the Yakut horsemen of the steppes who believed the mystic mother Aisyt brings from Heaven the soul of every child.

In the holy cedar groves the old believers fed me reindeer blood and honey, kept me warm in cloth of nettle and hemp. They called me Tonkhi, father, earth mother, holy leader of the ancestors, and you tortured their bodies, burnt their icons and desecrated my sanctuaries.

You marched your own brothers and sisters to death, grinding them to bone in the silver mines, and the gold-pits of Kara. In their canvas tents they built windbreaks out of corpses. In the dying light they scratched their names on the wall of their cells. No one escaped, no one stood tall. All were bent like a million birch saplings weighed down by snow.

Now you fold away your camera:

winded, wheezing, lost.

You call yourself an explorer, a pioneer. You've travelled for months to find me, hunted me down over years. Yet as you catch your breath I see you know not which way to turn. You have become separated from your fellows. You have gone hungry for days and your cries are unanswered. You wept when you stumbled upon your own footprints. Now you reach out a hand to steady yourself against me. You crumple to rest at my feet, and lean your back against me. You fall into fevered sleep to dream that I will save you, that I will give you berries to eat, that my streams will run clean to quench your thirst. But not now. Not now.

In your arrogance you and your people had planned to seize me as if I were time itself. You'd thought that you could pluck me from the holy grove and put me in a glass prison. You'd imagined that you would reduce me to something that could be shaped into a single great narrative – a book of life! But your need for signs and meaning has always crippled you. No book will help you to find a way out of the darkness, and I am not your keeper. By my wounds you will not be healed. I am the immensities not imagined, the infinite possibilities, all the roads not taken. I am not your story.

A sliver moon rises in the sky. The night is cold and dark when hunger gnaws you awake. You are afraid, alone, crying out at nothing, at the nothingness. I do not answer your prayers, of course. I have never answered them, although I have always been here with you. It can be no other way, and I can be no other way. But you have a choice, and you choose to strike flint and stone, to make a spark, to cradle the flame in a bed of moss. In a last, senseless act you pull me down, my wooden images, and set them alight, to warm your rotten, mortal bones. Smoke drifts skyward as goshawks and cedar waxwings stir in the high branches.

Why will you never see the beauty in your moment, in your hands, in summer lightening, even when your fancied angels and Archangels sing in exaltation?

All you have is a picture of me.

I live
    in the wind,
    in the whispering stars,
    in the twisting whirlpools,

in the bluethroat's song on midsummer morning.

You

have defiled the dark-earthed steppe. You have poisoned the reindeer pastures. You have abandoned the places where once you lived with the spirit of the world. Now autumn's birches turn amber against the dark layers of cedar and you will be gone while I remain,

here at the beginning of it all.

Ever, but for time.

Other books by Rory MacLean:

Stalin's Nose
The Oatmeal Ark
Under the Dragon
Next Exit Magic Kingdom
Falling for Icarus
Magic Bus
Missing Lives
Gift of Time
Back in the USSR
Berlin: Imagine a City
Wunderkind
Beneath the Carob Trees

Rory MacLean is the author of more than a dozen books including UK top ten bestsellers *Stalin's Nose* and *Under the Dragon* as well as *Berlin: Imagine a City*, a book of the year and 'the most extraordinary work of history I've ever read' according to the *Washington Post*. He has won awards from the Canada Council and the Arts Council of England. He has written about the missing civilians of the Yugoslav Wars for the ICRC, on divided Cyprus for the UN's Committee on Missing Persons and on North Korea for the British Council. His works, wrote John Fowles, are among those that 'marvellously explain why literature still lives'. A Fellow of the Royal Society of Literature, Rory divides his time between London, Dorset and Berlin.

www.rorymaclean.com

Published in 2017 by
Bone Idle
65 Queen Street West
Toronto, Ontario
M5H 2M8
Canada

ISBN 9780995185517

Edited by Ed Jones

Design and Illustrations
by Melanie Mues
Printed in Spain by SYL

Library and Archives Canada
Cataloguing in Publication
Data available on request.

British Library Cataloguing
in Publication Data available
on request.

Distributed in the UK
and Europe by:
Antenne Books Limited
Studio 55
Hackney Downs Studios
17 Amhurst Terrace
London E8 2BT
United Kingdom
+44 (0)203 582 8257
antennebooks.com

Distributed in North,
Central and South America by:
D.A.P. Distributed
Art Publishers, Inc.
155 Sixth Avenue, 2nd Floor
New York, NY 10013
+1 (0)212 627 1999
artbook.com